THE BACK HOME SERIES

SERIES TITLES

Hound Dog
M.L. Liebler

Powder Plant
Carolyn Dallmann

Mostly Woodcock
Joe McKnight

In the Room at the Top of the World
Ben McCormick

Water Spell
Catherine Broadwall

An Ignorance of Trees
Jim Daniels

Our Bodies Are Mostly Water
Katherine Riegel

You Shoulda Been Here Last Week
Ted J. Rulseh

The Past Ten: An Anthology
Donald Quist, Kali White VanBaale, & Bailey Gaylin Moore (eds.)

Table Talk & Second Thoughts
Michael Martone

Points of Tangency: Essays
Scott Russell Morris

Lessons in Geography
Phillip Sterling

This Season, The Next
Casey Knott

Wildlifer
Neil F. Payne

We Come from Good Stock
Kay Oakes Oring

Squatter
Yolanda DeLoach

The Arc of the Escarpment
Robert Root

Soul of the Outdoors
Dave Greschner

From the Heart: The Story of Matrix
John Harmon

The Long Fields
Anne-Marie Oomen

Kick Out the Bottom
Erik Mortenson & Christopher Kramer

Wrong Tree: Adventures in Wildlife Biology
Jeff Wilson

At the Lake
Jim Landwehr

Body Talk
Takwa Gordon

The In-Between State
Martha Lundin

North Freedom
Carolyn Dallmann

Ohio Apertures
Robert Miltner

PRAISE FOR
Hound Dog

In *Hound Dog*, acclaimed Detroit poet M.L. Liebler offers a compelling account of his journey through America's cultural transformations. With perceptive insight, he chronicles pivotal moments—from discovering Elvis on his grandmother's hi-fi to witnessing The Beatles on Ed Sullivan when "the world truly became colorful for the first time." Detroit remains Liebler's enduring inspiration and the city he champions with unwavering loyalty. Through his thoughtful poetry, teaching, and cultural activism, he has helped preserve Detroit's rich artistic heritage while connecting with figures from Al Kooper to Eminem. This engaging memoir reveals how music, poetry, and social change intertwine in one remarkable life dedicated to building vibrant creative communities that bring together poets, authors, and musicians from across Detroit and beyond.

—DIANE DeCILLIS
author of *When the Heart Needs a Stunt Double*

M.L. Liebler is an unstoppable force of nature, the likes of which neither the world of poetry nor the world of music, has ever seen. He has seamlessly blended the two throughout his long, distinguished career with generosity, good humor, and artistic integrity. And in the process, met and befriended a very eclectic, fascinating group of people, as you'll see in this incredible memoir that is centered in and around Detroit, but spans the entire globe. Reading this book is like sitting down with M.L. and listening to his stories—the informality and warmth, the insight and intelligence, come through in every story. What a treat for us that M.L. has written it all down to share with us!

—JIM DANIELS
author of *An Ignorance of Trees*

M.L. Liebler lives his poetry the way he lives his life: fighting injustice with humor, searing stories, remarkable language, and true compassion. *Hound Dog* has all this and more. I promise you, this memoir, like Liebler's poetry, will refuse to die.

—GRACE CAVALIERI
Maryland's Tenth Poet Laureate

In this poignant memoir, M.L. Liebler invites readers into the tapestry of his life, a journey marked by passion, resilience, and the transformative power of art. Through a series of vivid vignettes, Liebler shares his experiences as a poet, educator, and advocate for the arts, revealing the struggles and triumphs that have shaped his working-class identity. With warmth and candor, he delves into his roots, exploring the influences of his childhood, the friendships that have enriched his path, and the moments that sparked his creative fire. This memoir is not just a reflection of one man's life; it is a celebration of the human spirit, the importance of community, and the unyielding pursuit of one's dreams. Join Liebler as he navigates the complexities of existence in the 1960s and beyond, offering insights that resonate with anyone who has dared to follow their passion.

—MARIA MAZZIOTTI GILLAN
author of *When the Stars Were Still Visible*

Not unlike the work of John Steinbeck, there's a lot of humanity in M.L.'s writing. They're always engaging stories, and walking constantly throughout them are his Grandparents. They are deeply etched in M.L.'s own being, and it's touching to me that they live and breathe in these pages, as he pays homage to them.

—BILL FAY
Singer-songwriter

Liebler's writing is too real for words. He envisions how we wish our world could be and offers us the hope we need to make it so.

—DADA ZILCH
co-editor of *101 Mirages*

*M.L. is the Godfather
of Detroit poetry.
He keeps poets poppin',
Spittin' rhymes with
Dope music hittin' it
at the hot spots
gettin' it.*

—MELBA JOYCE BOYD
　Michigan Poet Laureate

Hound Dog

*A Poet's Memoir
of Rock, Revolution,
and Redemption*

M. L. Liebler

CORNERSTONE PRESS
UNIVERSITY OF WISCONSIN-STEVENS POINT

Cornerstone Press, Stevens Point, Wisconsin 54481
Copyright © 2026 M.L. Liebler
www.uwsp.edu/cornerstone

Printed in the United States of America.

Library of Congress Control Number: 2026930658
ISBN: 978-1-968148-26-3

All rights reserved.

This is a work of nonfiction. All of the events in this book are true to the best of the author's memories. Some names and identifying features have been changed to protect the identity of certain parties. The author in no way represents any company, corporation, or brand, mentioned herein. The views expressed in this book are solely those of the author.

Cornerstone Press titles are produced in courses and internships offered by the Department of English at the University of Wisconsin–Stevens Point.

DIRECTOR & PUBLISHER	EXECUTIVE EDITORS
Dr. Ross K. Tangedal	Jeff Snowbarger, Freesia McKee
EDITORIAL DIRECTOR	SENIOR EDITOR
Brett Hill	Paige Biever

PRESS STAFF
Lilly Kulbeck, Brianna Loving, Christiana Niedzwiecki, Lilli Resop, Grady Roesken, Asher Schroeder, Sam Zajkowski, Allison Lange, Sophie McPherson, Sam Bjork, Madison Schultz, Autumn Vine, Andrew Bryant

for Jeffrey Lloyd Ensroth

ALSO BY M.L. LIEBLER:

Poetry

Beneath My American Face: Five Decades of Poetry
I Want to Be Once
The Moment That Shines (with Maria Mazziotti Gillan)
Wide Awake in Someone Else's Dream
The Fragrant Benediction of Life
A Moment of Understanding: The China Poems
Breaking the Voodoo & Other Poems
Written In Rain: New & Selected Poems
Brooding the Heartlands: Poems of the Midwest
Stripping the Adult Century Bare
Whispers by the Lawn, Volumes 1 & 2
Measuring Darkness
Unfinished Man in the Perfect Mirror
Knit Me A Pair of Your Shoes
The Martyr of Pig

Anthologies

RESPECT: The Poetry of Detroit Music (with Jim Daniels)
Heaven Was Detroit: From Jazz to Hip-Hop and Beyond
Bob Seger's House and Other Stories (with Michael Delp)
Working Words: Punching the Clock and Kicking Out the Jams
Abandon Automobile: Detroit City Poetry (with Melba Joyce Boyd)
Northern Lights: Poetry from Northern Michigan University

CONTENTS

LINER NOTES

Foreword by COUNTRY JOE MCDONALD	xiii
Prologue by ED SANDERS	xv
Preface	xxi

TRACK LISTING

Introduction	1
Elvis	7
The Beatles	19
Bob Dylan & Country Joe McDonald	29
Jimi Hendrix	37
Al Kooper	45
MC5	59
Paul McCartney	69
Neil Young	79
George Harrison	89
John Lennon	97
Hüsker Dü	111
Robbie Robertson	119
Tom Waits	127
The Doors	135
Carl Ra & Sun Ra	149
Captain Beefheart	173
Blair Channels Stevie Wonder	193
Jorma Kaukonen	209
Eminem	217

BONUS TRACKS

Epilogue	227
Glossary	231
Acknowledgments	239

FOREWORD

In an ever-materialistic and self-centered world it is a pleasant surprise to find a man who chooses to not only write poems as an occupation but to strive to include all other poets and points of view. This memoir of a poet tells us much about not just the poet but the land and the people he lives with and in. M.L. Liebler not only attempts to describe and relate his feelings and insights but to draw the audience into his vision and make them aware of who and what they are.

His poetry and this memoir, like his life, is about "community," something we will spend the next century trying to rediscover. This book will help us in our quest.

M.L. best describes his goals in the poem "Allen Ginsberg's Dead." The poem helps us to understand this eternal human occupation, his occupation: the writing of poems; and to see and hear the beauty of his style and mind:

But, isn't that what poetry is all about? Images speaking to the unspeakable

In our dreams as we lie awake in our sleep?

And, now, because I've shared this poem With all of you, we are forever connected All of our bones together

Side by side in the rich graveyard Soil of poetry and life.

M.L.'s attempts to "connect" people through the beauty and insight of his poems give us all that sense of "community" that makes life worth living.

—*Country Joe McDonald*

PROLOGUE

M.L. Liebler, born in 1953, came forth from a surging, super-curious childhood, raised by his Elvis-loving grandparents in a working-class town just outside of Detroit. Elvis was his first turn-on in the world of music, but his grandmother also played the recordings of The Ink Spots, Pearl Bailey, Ella Fitzgerald, and others.

Grandpa was a Union activist who took part in a United Auto Workers Sit-Down Strike at a Dodge plant in 1937.

Youthful M.L. surged through the post-World War II era, the Elvis era and the Vietnam War era, and the technological advances of rock 'n' roll and the process of moving from two track, to four track to eight track to sixteen track to twenty-four track recording and beyond. From Doo-Wop, to Folk Rock, to Detroit Rock, to The Beatles, to Psychedelic, and Acid Rock, Erotic, Revolutionary, Post-Revolutionary. A whole Soul Train of hotly lived Americana.

Born a Protestant, M.L. converted to Catholicism and has been a devout practitioner through much of his life, and, throughout a successful career on the faculty at Wayne State University and as a poet and regional leader in the promotion of poetry.

As M.L. himself recalls it, "Maybe somehow I started to soak up word-creativity through rock 'n' roll music. Then Dylan and John Lennon. I was 10 when The Beatles were on *Ed Sullivan*. Then later The Beatles are singing about Chairman Mao and Vietnam was in the air, and I started getting involved in the anti-war movement in high school."

PROLOGUE • xvii

In 1976, M.L. and Pam were married. They had children, Shane and Shelby. And M.L. somehow balanced a life of exploration of the counterculture he was exposed to in Detroit, and as a Catholic family man devoted to his church, yet still exploring the poetic and countercultural haunts he had discovered in his rock-spirited youth.

M.L. became fascinated with what I've called "Perf-Po," or Performance Poetry— as practiced, for instance by the Beat Master Allen Ginsberg, Vachel Lindsay, and others.

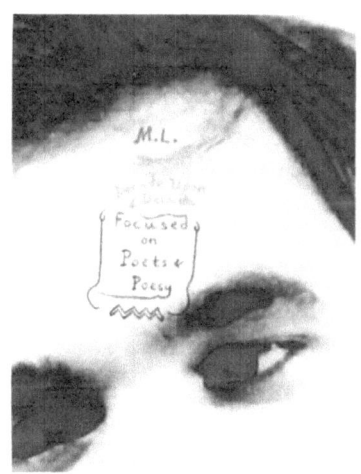

M.L. has evolved into a leading regional Poesy Helper. Over the decades, M.L. has constantly worked tirelessly to help improve the lot of poets and poetry movements— setting up conferences, reading series, and helping fellow poets survive in the often shaky economic realms of the working poet. For M.L. Liebler is a Workers' Worker, in the heights of the Working Class commixture with the Leadership Class.

M.L. became active in the Vietnam Veterans Movement, and has published a number of poetry and literary books. He has toured the world, reading his poetry and studying other poetry scenes. He even once toured a war zone where he was protected by troops.

GRAHR!
M.L. reading w/ Michael McClure!

M.L. Liebler & John Sinclair!! off to a Poetry Reading! Detroit 2023 October — Ed Sanders

And all these years he has been an honored member of the English Department at Wayne State University in Detroit.

In his office at Wayne State U.: Where he has taught for over 40 years

So, hail to M.L. Liebler for his life of service to the promotion of Poesy, its reading and performance, its place in people's lives, and his good willed hope for human betterment.

—*Ed Sanders*

Detroit skyline from a window, near W. Grand Blvd.
© Creative Hina By.Quileen

PREFACE

Oh, my name, it ain't nothin', my age, it means less. The country I come from is called the Midwest.
—Bob Dylan

But I've reason to believe we all will be received in Graceland.
—Paul Simon

"Everything is everything" from the Book of Marvin is more than words in a song by Marvin Gaye; it is a powerful testament to his artistry and the cultural influence of his work on the world and me. The iconic recording of *What's Going On* was made just a few blocks away from where I was born, and it has deeply resonated in my life, especially during my nearly 50 years of teaching at Wayne State University. I was born on the Wayne State University campus at Art Center Hospital, next to the Detroit Historical Museum. The closeness of this music to my personal and professional journey highlights its significance, making it more than simply songs—it's a part of my story and a reflection of America's shared history.

This memoir offers a collection of vignettes, intertwining humorous anecdotes and poignant moments that I hope will resonate with my readers. For years, folks have encouraged me to share my stories in book form, and I'm finally answering that call. While I primarily view myself as a poet rather than a memoirist or fiction writer, I wholeheartedly embraced the idea that, as Marvin once said, "Everything is everything." Join me on this journey through the American story filled with laughter and reflection, and discover all that has shaped my American life.

    I have arranged these short pieces chronologically to guide readers through these experiences. This book transcends a complete autobiography or a traditional memoir—it invites you to explore it as an album featuring various tracks or mini creative nonfiction essays about my life growing up in America throughout the 1950s, 60s, 70s, and beyond. Each piece stands alone yet flows like a song or an oral story, intertwining sub-stories along the way. Think of these stories as songs or conversations that can twist and turn on a dime. While the tales may not always follow a linear path and may diverge at times, they ultimately return to a familiar melody. This memoir is a collection of literary snapshots, each crafted with a beginning, middle, end, and overarching theme. I draw inspiration from my musical heroes for each track. When I mention these figures, it's not merely to name-drop; I am authentically sharing my story and experiences with notable individuals who have had an impact. I've worked and recorded with many of these heroes or interacted with them personally, while others have profoundly influenced vital parts of my life. I aimed to shape this book to the length of a short memoir—one that isn't daunting with a thick spine and hundreds of pages like Pynchon's *Gravity's Rainbow*. My goal is to share scenes from an America that once was, offering younger readers a glimpse into a world that existed before the authoritarian and oligarchic madness took hold of our country in January 2025. I wrote this also to offer Boomers a look back at a different time.

    The assault on our democracy has transformed everything, eroding the America that my grandmother gifted me when she brought me home from Art Center Hospital on the Wayne State campus. My America was an America filled with the sounds of Elvis, Little Richard, Dion, Fats Domino, Ricky Nelson, Howlin' Wolf, Muddy Waters, and my grandmother's favorites, Pearl Bailey and The Ink Spots. This book is a heartfelt journey through those cherished memories, and I hope it resonates with you as deeply as it does with me.

PREFACE • xxiii

My America, a land of innovation, once captivated the world with the advent of television—yet it shrouded itself in silence after the 11 p.m. news. In those simpler times, the day's events were summarized in just 15 minutes as Dick Westerkamp delivered the news with clarity, and Sonny Elliot lightened the mood with his signature humor on Channel 4. His nightly weather reports often featured a quaint Upper Peninsula town named Engadine, which holds a special place in my heart. It was a town I have revisited many times while performing with my library Beatles and *Heaven Was Detroit* shows. Engadine, a symbol of nostalgia, reminds us of the richness of our cultural tapestry, making us appreciate smaller stories that weave into the larger narrative of our history.

America has been a vibrant canvas for several cultural phenomena that I and the world have cherished. From Howdy Doody and Ed Sullivan to Ozzie and Harriet, we've witnessed Beatlemania's birth, the Hells Angels' badassness, and the creation of movements like the Beat Generation, Hippies, and Punks. America gave the world the sacred game of holy baseball and iconic symbols such as Sting Ray bikes and the Anti-War Movement, which reflects a spirit of rebellion and creativity—figures like Walt Whitman, Jack Kerouac, W. E. B. Du Bois, Frederick Douglass, Robert Hayden, Philip Levine, Malcolm X, Rosa Parks, Dudley Randall, Rebecca Harding Davis, Langston Hughes, Gil Scott Heron, The Last Poets, and many others have created a beautiful tapestry of our shared American heritage.

America is the cornerstone of the Civil Rights Movement, giving rise to influential leaders like Martin Luther King and Gloria Steinem while honoring the legacy of trailblazers such as Medgar Evers.

Our nation's rich musical heritage—from the timeless grooves of Motown to the soulful beats of jazz and blues, culminating in the revolutionary sounds of MC5 and on to The White Stripes—continues to inspire and unite people around the globe.

The world has always considered America a beacon of hope and possibility. In my travels from Russia to Europe to Afghanistan, I've witnessed firsthand the aspirations of countless individuals who yearn to embody the American spirit. This longing has ignited a recurring question: "What has happened to America?" This inquiry resonates with the profound desire to reclaim the ideals we once held dear, as people around the globe remain eager to grasp the essence of the American dream.

There was a time when Americans boldly fought for their liberty and creative freedom, leading the charge in innovation. America was a vast country and a vibrant canvas on which we painted our lives and innovations, both triumphs and tribulations. Our history is not a mere tale of love, peace, and bliss. Instead, it is woven with angst, disagreements, and uninhibited artistic expressions, grounded in our constitutional right to voice our ideas and embrace our differences, even as we stumble along the way.

Despite our myriad challenges, America birthed legendary genres from jazz and blues to rock 'n' roll, alongside remarkable inventions like Silly Putty, Hula Hoops, and Spoolies. America proudly gave the world the vaccines for Polio, flu, measles, and COVID. At the same time, our beloved Detroit revolutionized the automobile industry, contributed to the rise of the middle class, and organized millions of workers into unions. It became a land of dreams where ordinary Americans could own a modest home with a garage and backyard—a place where dreams flourished amidst everyday life. Here, regular folks could own boats, cottages up north, and travel trailers, allowing them to savor life's simple joys.

In one of the creative nonfiction workshops I attended while working on this book, the acclaimed best-selling memoirist Harrison Scott Keyes remarked that my stories reminded him of a blend of *A Christmas Story* and *The Wonder Years* on television, infused with a generous dose of Detroit rock 'n' roll. Although I have never seen *The Wonder Years*, I grasped the essence of his point.

Let us remember and rekindle the passion that defines America. Together, we can reignite the spirit that once made our nation a symbol of hope and possibility with democracy for all.

This life has been enriching for a kid born to a single teenage mother with an unknown father, raised by wonderful grandparents in St. Clair Shores, Michigan. I have been fortunate to travel the world numerous times to teach, perform my poetry, and broaden my horizons. Throughout these journeys, I've had the incredible opportunity to meet many of my music and political heroes. I've dedicated nearly 50 years to teaching at an urban university in the heart of my beloved Detroit, with my WSU office just one block from where I was born.

As Randy Newman beautifully put it, "My life is good." At the age of four, Grandma lifted me onto the rock 'n' roll bus, and I have been "on the bus" ever since, as my late friend Ken Kesey would say. It has indeed been "a long, strange trip," for which I am deeply grateful. I've had the privilege to connect with countless cultural icons and heroes during my career, and I have shared many of them here. I reserved some of those tales of rock, revolution, and poetry for another time. Writing this book has been a lengthy endeavor. But now, I must return to nurturing my poetry garden. This book is not an attempt to name-drop but rather a reflection of my fortunate encounters with numerous cultural figures.

So, if readers or listeners are interested in discovering the America I knew, hop "on the bus" with me and explore the world of America and the beauty of Detroit. Detroit was a fantastic place to grow up and live. After extensive travel, I often say, "A bad day in Detroit is better than a good day anywhere else in the world." Detroit, with its working-class values, music, and poetry, is where I come from and where I will remain. Detroit will always be the place for me.

—June 2025

INTRODUCTION

Straight Outta Motown and Right Into Mudville

You ain't nothin' but . . .

None of this was supposed to have happened this way. I was born out of wedlock to a young teenage girl who lived with her parents (my grandparents) in a town that was established in the late 40s and 50s as Roseville. Before that, Detroiters referred to it as the city of "Mudville." I, of course, had no knowledge of this at the time; I hadn't been born yet!

Immediately after World War II, factory workers and other working-class members searched for their own tiny ranch houses, complete with a backyard and a garage. Those traveling from the bustling city of Detroit to this new township often found their cars stuck in deep mud ruts after crossing the city limits and 8 Mile Road. Yet, from that mud and the challenging journey of the working class, my love for early American rock 'n' roll emerged. It flowed straight into my heart and soul from the old blonde wood hi-fi speakers.

My grandparents moved out of Detroit in 1947, taking their teenage daughter with them. This marked the beginning of the American suburbs and the first hints of decline for our once-great city. Back then, Detroit was overcrowded, with individual housing scarce and at a premium.

Additionally, many young Detroiters were weary of living with their parents in the large old houses with four flats on Rohn Street in Detroit's Eastside (where many of my family members lived until 1947). That street has now become another I-94 overpass, a remnant of a bygone neighborhood.

My grandmother's three sisters (Ethel, Mildred, and Hazel) moved out of the old German neighborhood in Detroit in the early 1940s to a place that felt more like paradise than just another small town. It became, and still is, my private paradise to this day—St. Clair Shores. This is the city where I would grow, dream, love, and awaken to the essence of everything good about American life. There were hard times to learn from, but those lessons were valuable and essential. This was a town I was destined to call home. I always regarded it as my "Mayberry." Having been raised on 1950s and early 1960s black-and-white sitcoms, I knew this was the town for me.

The world was truly black and white back then: television, people, life, work—everything! Whether people believe it or not, in the 21st Century, this was our way of life back then: Truman with his Marshall Plan, S.S. with his Kresge (long before K and his Mart), Sears and Roebuck, and of course Roy with his O'Brien's ("beep-beep, get on the right track to Nine Mile & Mack…"). America helped rebuild Europe after the devastation of WWII; the world created NATO, and Eisenhower—a steady leader who implemented America's New Look Policy—built our impressive Interstate Highway system, connecting our country from east to west and from north to south. Ike established the Civil Rights Division at the Department of Justice and even had the foresight to warn Americans about the impending "military-industrial complex." Both Truman (the Democrat) and Eisenhower (the Republican) were conservative presidents from different parties, and in general, many Americans did not have much of a problem with them; at least, most had few issues with them as leaders of what was called "the greatest nation on Earth" and later "The Great Society." I was never sure how I felt about that.

During this time, I sensed the world was changing, much like our TVs transitioned from black and white to color. Then, on a chilly February Sunday evening in 1964, the world truly became colorful for the first time. I will explain how that transformation occurred in the next chapter.

In late 1961, we moved from Roseville to St. Clair Shores. It seemed to me that most residents knew each other across many generations. The corner store owner was familiar with everyone's parents and every kid on our street. Many streets in this town are named after people who once lived here and are now buried in the old 12 Mile Road Catholic Cemetery. I was Lutheran then, but most of my neighbors were Catholic.

This place was special. It had a lake—a huge lake that I couldn't see across! Wow! A real lake with another country on the other side: "O Canada." Who could imagine such a cool thing? I have remained loyal and grateful to this lake my entire life; I still love it today as much as I did back then. I marvel at its beauty, the fresh air that fills my lungs, and its connection to life. I don't even mind the annual invasion of the fish flies every summer; it's a tradition. The other side of our lake was, for me, a distant land. Wow! A damn foreign country on the other side!

Forget the fact that we couldn't see it out there; just knowing it was there was cool to us. Lake St. Clair was miles and miles of blue-green water. I think my life didn't really begin until I was 8 years old, right there on those very shores. I remember walking out on the ice in the winter, pulling my sled filled with all my dreams. Now, I believe this is where I belonged all along, even before I was born.

In those early suburban days in Roseville, from what I was told, an older teenage guy was roaming this area of Mudville, "knocking up" many young girls. One of them was a young girl who became my teenage birth mother. She had been a troubled child throughout her life and caused a great deal of stress for my grandparents. She was moody and did not perform well in school. Today, she would likely be diagnosed with bipolar disorder or possibly even schizophrenia. But back then, our family simply saw her as "moody" and someone who was always "changing her mind." Later, I learned, or imagined, that I heard about this young troublemaker "knocking up neighborhood girls." He likely recognized my birth mother's unstable mental state, so he acted like any jerk who runs around getting neighborhood girls pregnant: he exploited the situation.

My family always viewed my birth mother as just a typical kid with an attitude problem. This attitude brought significant challenges to my beloved grandparents throughout their lives. It wasn't solely her fault or theirs, but I know it affected my grandmother profoundly, possibly leading her to blame herself. During that era, psychological issues were largely unknown, and access to psychologists was limited to wealthy individuals. Mental illness only began to be recognized as a suburban issue in the late 1960s or early 1970s, often managed with Valium prescriptions or outdated shock therapy. My grandparents told me he "knocked up" several girls in the new neighborhood near Gratiot, between 11 Mile Road and Martin Road. I now have several half-brothers and sisters.

At eighteen, she married a man named Leroy and moved out with him; he also worked at the plant. They had another son named Ronald, followed by another son named after our grandfather, Vernon. Vern appeared to be a typical child, but as he grew, he never progressed beyond the age of three, which caused considerable distress for our grandma. He was nonverbal and spent hours alone, often engrossed in anything he could find, including the Sears & Roebuck Catalog, which he read repeatedly. Grandma carried this burden to her grave. Eventually, they had to place him at the outdated Lapeer Home for the Mentally Disabled. I visited twice with them—first to check the place out, which had a sad and isolating atmosphere. Young children and teenagers screamed incessantly in the sterile hallways, shocking me, but it broke my grandmother's heart. Doctors and family advised her that it was best for him to live there. The second visit was when we took Vernon there, and I never saw him again. My grandmother cried endlessly afterward. My oldest half-brother maintained some responsibility for Vernon, but that contact seems to have faded over the years. When they closed Lapeer, he was moved to a group home in Oakland County.

The last time I saw him was in the late 1970s when my brother Ron picked him up after our annual Thanksgiving Day Lions game. At that point, he was a grown man, subdued and quiet, looking much older than I remembered. I sobbed all the way home from that game, unable to articulate my feelings. By then, my grandparents had both passed, leaving me with the weight of their struggles. It felt surreal to see the young boy I once knew, now in his late 20s and likely in his mid-60s by now. My brother Ron, his legal guardian, no longer knows where he is or keeps in touch. This continues to trouble my mind. I liked him, although I often felt embarrassed by him as a child, which I recognize is my burden. I wouldn't mind seeing him now, but no one seems to know his whereabouts.

My birth mother had three more children whom I barely know: Gregory Thomas (now deceased from lung cancer), Paul Richard Thompson, and a sister named Sharon Faust, who became a nurse and lives near Saginaw, although she has fallen under the influence of extreme right-wing political views. We occasionally connect on Facebook, but I prefer limited contact due to her involvement with that cult.

Additionally, my birth mother experienced a stillbirth in 1969 before my half-sister was born, which heightened my grandmother's anxiety as she prepared for the new baby with a crib and cloth diapers secured with safety pins, among other necessities. After the stillborn baby, my grandma sadly discarded everything; she couldn't bear to keep those items in the house. That was heartbreaking as well. My mother later moved to northern Michigan with Greg, Paul, and Sharon, using her inheritance from my grandparents. Unfortunately, she squandered her funds and ended up relying on welfare, supplemented by what I could provide. She wasn't addicted to alcohol or cigarettes; instead, she appeared to be an undiagnosed mentally ill person doing her best.

When she passed away in the mid-90s, we traveled for her funeral. I felt terrible sitting in a funeral home with just her five children and their spouses present. The preacher was a local man hired by the funeral home. Once again, I wept. I told the small group, "I am crying for her, not for me." How heartbreaking it is that when someone passes away, there are no friends, neighbors, or family to witness their farewell? We decided to contribute to a fitting headstone, but I have never revisited her grave in northern Michigan.

M.L. Photo by Diane DeCillis

ELVIS

Rockin' Grandma, Mr. Presley, & Me

Before Elvis, there was nothing.
—John Lennon

Before all the seeming sadness of the past and before my grandparents passed away in June and August (on the exact same day of each month) in 1979, we formed a tightly knit three-person family. We did everything together and that was the only life I knew.

Over the years, I never felt a desire to know who my father was. In fact, people in real life or on TV who dramatize this "search" for their parental lineage have always bored me. My grandparents originally planned to adopt me out to a Jewish family that happened to be childless and close friends with our Jewish family physician. That's how things were back then. The family doctor could help find a home for an unwanted child without any legal issues. In fact, my own story of staying with my grandparents wouldn't hold up today in this "politically correct" legal environment. I selfishly feel relieved that things were as lame as they were back then. I loved my grandparents. It would have been a real disappointment if I had been placed in foster care, a term I had only heard; I had no understanding of what it meant. Recently, my good poet friend and colleague, Dr. Caroline Maun, mused over lunch that I share a similarity with Jesus. Neither of us had a father, but I told her, "Yeah, but Jesus didn't have a cool grandma like I did," as far as I know.

My grandmother introduced me to Elvis when I was four years old. She bought me Elvis's Golden Records from the local Federal Department Store in the new strip mall called The Eastland Center in Roseville. This was during the hip-swirling Ed Sullivan era, featuring the "You Ain't Nothin' but a Hound Dog Cryin' All the Time" Elvis of yesteryear, not the overweight, caped, and rhinestone-belted version who appeared in Las Vegas in 1969. Our little improvised family consisted of me, Grandma (whom I called Ma), and Grandpa (whom I called Grumps). We were all music lovers from the beginning. There was always music in our house: Elvis, The Ink Spots, Pearl Bailey, Lenny Dee on the big Hammond B, The Harmonicats, Ethel Merman, Ella Fitzgerald, and God knows Grandma loved her some Sophie Tucker—who The Beatles once labeled their "favorite group." Funny Beatles. Grandma even resembled Sophie. So there was that. They both showed me love, compassion, and honesty. Our little family unit was built on trust and love—always.

When it came to music, Grandma didn't listen to classical, opera, jazz, or accordion tunes. Nope! Not that woman. In fact, Grandma was quite young. I believe she was just under 40 when I was born, and Grumps was maybe 48 or 49. In hindsight, they were young grandparents but well past the age of raising kids. I'm not sure I could have taken on a newborn baby at that age, but they were extraordinarily good people.

I understood their sacrifice in dedicating their love and time to raising an infant 18 years after their children had grown.

My grandma was a hilarious lady. She was of average height at 5'6", with snow-white, curly hair. Both her and my grandfather's hair turned bright white in their early 20s (as did mine), and I can see my son's hair gradually transitioning to white in his late 20s. Grandma loved joking with short quips and dancing as much as her legs would allow. On the other hand, Grumps was a quiet and humble man with no ego to speak of. He was a true "working-class hero" and a "well- respected man," to borrow phrases from Lennon and the Kinks. He was honest, and I don't remember ever hearing him argue with my grandmother or anyone else. He stood over six feet tall, yet he was truly a "gentle giant." He was quite handy around the house and skilled at building things; I remember he and my uncle built a sturdy wooden dock on a piece of land that both families had purchased to eventually build a cottage on Rush Lake near Pinckney, Michigan. I only saw him step out of character twice. Once, while building the dock, he jumped out of the water nervously, yelling that he had a "bloodsucker on his leg." When he leaped onto the bank, I saw this ugly, rather large bloodsucker stuck to his leg. The last time I saw him out of character was on his deathbed. As he drifted into eternal sleep, he grabbed my hand and shouted my name, "Mike! Mike! Mike!" Through my tears, I replied, "I am here, Grumps." He squeezed my hand and slipped away.

The man I believed would save me from bedtime monsters—scary, imaginary monsters, illnesses like meningitis when I was 4, bullies, and schoolboy blunders—was gone. I lost one of my foundational rocks then; I had just lost my main pillar. My sweet, funny, and incredibly strong-willed grandma had died exactly two months before Grumps. At 24, I was an orphan. Damn! I called them several times a day to check in. I often stopped by for our traditional breakfasts of fried eggs, bacon, and fresh bakery bread with butter. I felt homesick for them every time I went away or returned to school at Oakland University. I could always count on them to save me.

However, that all ended on June 16, and by August 16, 1979, they were all gone.

I always knew my grandparents would pass away before my friends' parents, but it still left me in shock for quite some time.

We were that close as a family. We loved music, singing, Sunday drives (usually downtown), and trips to the cider mill, the spinning water wheel that made well-water taffy in Grosse Ile, and other places. I remember we always stopped on Gratiot near 7 Mile Road (across from the long-gone Monkey Wards store) to grab a *Sunday Detroit Times*, which she read closely, and then clipped coupons from. *The Detroit Times* was Grandma's newspaper of choice. I couldn't have asked for better parents or a better home to grow up in. I created that same environment in our own home for our children less than two years after they passed away. I loved my grandparents, and I know they loved me.

On the history of how my Grandma and Grumps became fans of African American music and Elvis (vanilla R&B)? I'm not entirely sure about the answer, and I never thought to ask. It was just the music we listened to, loved, and danced to all around our old 1950s gray and red swirl, thin carpeting in our working-class bungalow. We never discussed race in our home, and I never heard the now-infamous derogatory N-word spoken there. I don't believe my grandparents were politically correct liberals (that term hadn't been invented yet) or good Christian, churchgoing folks. In fact, they made me go to Sunday School and church, but they never went with me. Going to church just wasn't part of their reality. Back in those days, things were more like Trump and his "deplorables" and Archie Bunker (the first Trump) than they are now.

Perhaps my grandparents' attitude was different because my grandfather was one of the first UAW members to participate in the 1937 Dodge Main Strike. One big union means "everybody." I assume that influenced their thinking. They weren't what Phil Ochs would call "liberals," but they weren't uptight, old, conservative farts either. FDR had done right by their generation.

Ma loved her Ink Spots and Pearl Bailey, and I still listen to them today. She played those albums repeatedly. She adored her music, which in her time would have been known as "race music," and she loved Elvis. I don't think Grandma was "post-racial." She was just a cool, hip, working-class woman who enjoyed what she enjoyed, and I admired her for that. You might find it hard to believe that a person (or both my grandparents) from an early 20th-century background with no formal education and limited worldly experiences could be so open-minded, but they were. If you doubt what I say is true, go find your own damn grandparents and write your own damn boring memoir.

Another significant Elvis experience my grandma gave me occurred when I was 7, in second grade at Pierce Elementary School in Roseville. My grandma and Grumps took me to the Bel Air Drive-In on the Edsel Ford Freeway Service Drive, just south of 8 Mile Road. The freeway was built to help the new suburbanites reach their factory jobs in the city. Back then, the Edsel Ford Freeway ended at the now-famous "8 Mile Road." Cars were forced off the freeway right in front of the Bel Air Drive-In. A drive-in, in those days, was the place to catch first-run films year-round, especially for families. People paid one price for everyone in the car. We would pull up to a stand with a worn-out speaker featuring a single knob for volume. It sounded like listening to my small Sears transistor pocket radio. They had an equally old heater for winter viewings. Later, in our early teen years, we heard stories of older high school kids piling people into their cars, with several hiding in the trunk. Once inside, everyone would pop out and sit on top of the car, which offered the best seats.

Later, when we were in high school, we often went to the Gratiot Drive-In, which was very close to St. Clair Shores and became famous in a 1955 photo titled "Drive-In" by photographer and filmmaker Robert Frank, whom I became familiar with through my friendship with Edie Parker Kerouac. Through Edie, I later was introduced to several members of the Beat Generation when she introduced me to my heroes like Ed Sanders, Allen Ginsberg, William Burroughs, Michael McClure, Diane di Prima, Amiri Baraka, Ed Dorn, Timothy Leary, Herbert Huncke, and many others. This was unbelievable to me as a working-class kid. Robert Frank was very famous for his 1958 book, *The Americans*. I guessed he was traveling through Detroit on his American photo tour when he spotted the Gratiot Drive-In from a freeway on a humid summer evening. We heard he slipped under the back fence to take the shot. Later, my childhood friend, Greg Hallock, would slip under the same fence to get a similar shot.

On our way to see my first drive-in movie, Elvis's *G.I. Blues*, my grandparents turned off the Ford Service Drive and drove up the familiar long gravel driveway toward the drive-in ticket booth. Grumps plopped his money down at the window, and suddenly it was Elvis time! "Here we come, El. I'm here!" It was a chilly fall weekend night in 1960. This would be my very first Elvis movie on the big screen. Elvis made this film right after finishing his tour of duty in the

U.S. Army. Not only was I getting good at curling my lip like Elvis by this age, but I also wanted to serve in the Army like my hero, G.I. El. What was I thinking? A few years later, my grandma would oppose the Vietnam War, telling me that I wouldn't be serving. Grandma was smart and cool before her time.

Then, there he was! I finally saw my hero, Elvis, on a giant outdoor screen in vivid color (television was only black and white back then). On that chilly autumn night, I was nearly brought to tears with excitement. There was so much that appealed to me in that *G.I. Blues* film. The music was fantastic, Elvis looked fabulous in his U.S. Army uniform, and there was even a German puppet show in the movie where Elvis sang "I Don't Have a Wooden Heart." That cleverness and irony were not lost on me. I have always loved puppets ever since I saw them in that movie. I remember being a devoted fan of *The Howdy Doody Show*. I watched the show religiously on Saturday mornings (it had moved to Saturdays in 1956 from after-school weekdays). I grew very fond of puppets and clowns, especially Clarabelle, the mute clown who finally spoke in the last show at the very end of the series in September 1960.

Because of my love for clowns, I also fell in love with the circus. Every year, my uncle took me to the Shrine Circus at the State Fair Coliseum. As a Detroit police officer, he was fortunate enough to have traffic duty at the annual event, which significantly nurtured my passion for the circus arts. We often went two or three times a year for both matinees and some evening shows. I loved it.

One year, things got downright strange, scary, and weird. In late January 1962, while the famous Wallenda family performed their widely acclaimed high-wire act without a net, two of the renowned Flying Wallendas fell to their deaths in front of 7,000 spectators at the State Fair Colosseum, located at 8 Mile Road and Woodward. We were not there the night of that bizarre tragedy, but we attended the very next night when one of the Wallendas seemed to slip while walking up to the high wire. The audience cringed and gasped in unison. These were the golden days of the circus when Clyde Beatty was the famous lion tamer who had been nicked a few times and bore the scars to prove it.

It was also the era of the great clown Emmett Kelly, the saddest, funniest clown I had ever seen. The sadness affected me. Even though I was young, I realized this guy was a sad sack. I loved the hilarious clowns packed into that tiny "clown" car. In hindsight, it must have been a foreign car because back then, American cars were more like boats in size. The clown car, which has recently become more of a political joke for the Republican Party, always reminded me of the Marx Brothers, the Three Stooges, and Charlie Chaplin, who are just as much a part of the "Def Comedy Jam" today as they were in the early 20th century.

I love circuses so much that I go whenever and wherever I can. I take my children and grandchildren whenever possible, and I've even gone solo to experience a classic "old school" circus under an authentic tent in Munich, as well as in St. Petersburg and Novosibirsk. I've seen circuses under the Big Top and in buildings designed for year-round performances in Russia. If circuses become politically correct again, I will be there.

Circuses also remind me of my favorite TV show from back then, *Circus Boy*, which starred a young Micky Dolenz (later known for *The Monkees* TV show). The series depicted a traveling circus in the late 1800s, which moved from town to town using horses and wagons. I own the complete series on bootleg DVDs.

In the end, I loved Elvis, clowns, circuses, puppets, black-and-white television, and both my grandparents. I would say my life was pretty damn good. I suppose I had the occasional flare- ups. My wife recently found my first-grade report card. It noted in the comments section that "Michael is generally an enjoyable, easy-going boy and a well-liked child, but when angered, his fists will soon be flying." Hmmm. I thought I was a peaceful soul born to be a hippie. Maybe not so much?

Speaking of being a hippie, our neighbor once saw me riding my bike down the street when I was about 14 or 15, making my transition into hippiedom. I was on my "knock-off" Schwinn Sting Ray, with a fringe hippie bag on my shoulder that I had bought at the Plum Pit Head Shop on Gratiot and 10 Mile Road. The Plum Pit is still there and still open today. Anyway, that neighbor lady, whose name was Bunny (my grandma always thought that name was silly for an older woman), came to my grandmother in tears one afternoon, telling her that she saw me riding my bike with "a purse." Grandma was horrified and briefly crazed. When I came home that afternoon, Grandma wanted to know if it was true that I "now carried a purse." I truly didn't get the point at the time. "A purse?" Much later, the insinuation dawned on me: Grandma thought I might be gay. Nope, wrong guy, Grandma—just a hippie!

Another time, when I was 18, a guy came to that same neighbor's house asking questions about me. They asked Bunny a lot of questions. Grandma said it was likely a Sears agent because they investigated their employees before hiring them, or so Grandma thought. At that time, I had applied for a job at Sears & Roebuck in the first mall in Michigan, in Roseville. As a young teen, I was quite politically active, drawn to SDS (Students for a Democratic Society), and I had become a strong proponent and user of the holy marijuana. Later, I suspected they were the FBI or the much-talked-about grand jury on drugs investigating hippies in St. Clair Shores. However, if Grandma thought it was Sears, I was satisfied with that.

Grandma and Grandpa have been gone for over 43 years, but I think of them all the time. They often appear in my dreams, and the lessons they taught me are still ones I try to apply to my life today. They were incredible people, and I was extremely fortunate to have been cared for by them. I can't wait to see them again. I have so much more to share about the days we spent listening to and reliving the old songs during our Sunday drives around Belle Isle or Downtown Detroit. I bought Ma Willie Nelson's newest album, *Stardust*, just before she passed. It was the first time I'd seen Grandma happy in years, and it turned out to be the last Sunday we'd spend together. I can still remember that day vividly. It was a good day, but it was Grandma's last Mother's Day. She passed away less than a month later, and Grandpa followed her into the great beyond exactly two months after that. Goodbye, sweet people who nurtured and cared for me and kept me from adoption. We shared many laughs and a few tears, but it was a joy being part of our own little "Gang of Three."

When Ma passed away, I was on a weekend camping trip in Frankenmuth, Michigan. I knew she was sick, but she had always recovered. However, this weekend in mid-June would be a different experience—an experience I had dreaded since I was a young child. While camping, around 2:30 a.m., I was jolted awake by a horrible, empty feeling. It felt as though something had left me. I tried to shrug it off, but I knew that was no good. It was like a gnawing sensation in the pit of my stomach.

I finally fell back asleep, only to be awoken around 6:00 a.m. by a ranger walking through the park, calling my name. "Mike Liebler! Is there a Mike Liebler here?"

I thought I was dreaming. I poked my head out of the trailer and replied, "That's me." He instructed me to call my grandpa immediately. At that moment, I realized that the sadness I had felt lying awake that night was the same sadness and fear of losing her that I had experienced as a young child and throughout my early adulthood. My beloved Ma was gone.

When I called Grumps from a pay phone, he told me, "Ma's gone." I couldn't breathe; it felt like the wind had been knocked out of me. I dropped the pay phone in shock. *What? How? When?* He said she passed away around 2:30 a.m. I just couldn't grasp it. Ma's gone?

Pam and I jumped in the car. She drove us home while I sat there in shock. Soon after we got back, preparations for the funeral began. I knew I would never see her in this world again. How could I move on? I called her and Grumps at least two or three times a day just to check in and say hello. Sometimes, I would stop by for breakfast because Grumps made the best meals: fried eggs, bacon, coffee, and good French bread layered with butter and dunked in hot coffee. That was the breakfast I loved and always cherished.

My Grumps struggled through two months without his beloved wife of 50 years. I could tell he was heartbroken. Shortly after Ma's death, it was discovered that Grumps had an aneurysm ready to burst in the vein extending from his stomach to his upper thigh. He was taken to the doctor, where it was determined that he was strong enough to undergo the surgery due to his excellent health at 76 years old. The doctor noted that his insides resembled those of a much younger man. The operation was a tremendous success, but two days later, Grumps developed pneumonia from lying in a hospital bed.

On August 16th at around 2:00 a.m., I received an urgent call from the hospital asking me to come down. My grandfather was fading fast. Stunned and still grieving Ma's death, Pam and I raced to Bon Secours Hospital on Cadieux and Jefferson in Grosse Pointe, where Grumps was breathing heavily and seemed out of it. However, he was calling my name—"Mike, Mike, Mike."

I replied, "Grumps, I'm right here!" He kept calling for me. I took his hand and reassured him, "I'm here, Grumps. Right here!"

We stepped out of the room, and minutes later, the doctor entered the Intensive Care waiting room and said, "Mike, your grandfather has passed away." Holy shit! I was now an orphan. Losing them both was a deep pain in my heart. I felt empty, alone, and broken.

"They're dead!" I loved them both so much that I felt utterly devastated. I had Pam, and I was grateful, but no more Ma and Grumps to visit? No more daily calls to our small ranch house on Lincoln Street. This marked the beginning of a long, lonely time for me. I often self- medicated with beer for comfort. I was finishing my master's degree, which provided minimal distraction from my pain. But losing them drove me deeper into a rabbit hole of anxiety and panic. I felt truly lost, and I needed to be found.

After Grumps passed, I remembered a quote I heard after John F. Kennedy was assassinated. Someone told Pierre Salinger, "We will never laugh again." Salinger replied, "Oh, we will laugh again, but we will never be young again." That quote has stayed with me all these years and reflects how I felt for many months after my grandparents' deaths: "I will never be young again."

The issue of death often haunted me. The first Elvis film I saw, *Love Me Tender*, was in black and white on television with my grandma, and it made death feel real to me. I remember how I felt after watching Elvis in *Love Me Tender* on late-night TV. I couldn't sleep, wondering how my life would change someday without my grandparents. Elvis's death in the film made me overthink this dreadful thought, and once I began dwelling on it, I couldn't move past it. It lingered at the back of my mind until they both passed away in 1979. They were my rock, my foundation, and my salvation. Back then, my young mind would work overtime in bed, and I would get sick to my stomach thinking about death. Sometimes, I would run out of my room to the living room just to have Grandma hold and soothe me. I don't know if I ever told her what my fear was. Those frightening nights often led to thoughts of my death. I began to picture myself in a casket, having dirt thrown on me until I was six feet under. It was a scene I remembered from a Saturday matinee movie titled *Premature Burial*. That was pretty scary stuff for a 6-year-old, and honestly, it's still scary now. I was never a fan of dying then, and I'm not now. I was only in kindergarten at the time of *Love Me Tender*, but Elvis dying at the end of that movie really troubled me. From a young age, I always knew that my Grandma and Grandpa would pass away long before my friends' parents, simply because they were older. As I expected, they did. I was just 24 when they both passed away two months apart, in the summer of 1979. I remember feeling grateful for having had them for 24 wonderful years. I would have loved for them to see me graduate college, become a teacher at Wayne State University, meet our two children, know our incredible grandchildren, and witness the publication of my poetry books. I guess it just wasn't meant to be. They were great people whom I loved living and growing up with.

As a young boy, I believed my grandparents would rescue me from any danger, any problem, and even from death itself. With them, I felt secure—always secure. I raised my children with that same love and care. I wanted my son and daughter to always know that no matter what happened in their lives, I was there as their safety net, their good counsel, and that I would always be there waiting to sweep them into my arms and protect them from the boogeyman, just as my grandma did for me. After their deaths in 1979, I could never regain that same sense of security.

THE BEATLES

There Are Places I Remember...

...In My Life I Loved Them All.
—The Beatles

1964

In 1964, my life was coming into color like many of our TV sets back then. All hail Magnavox televisions! My third miracle was about to occur after my grandparents adopted me and Elvis. The Beatles on *Ed Sullivan* was my third miracle. I jumped on the bandwagon and never looked back. I feared hurting Grandma's feelings by abandoning Elvis; it was a betrayal. I hated that feeling when it crossed my 10-year-old mind. Four years later, it weighed heavily on me when Grandma was so excited about the Elvis 1968 TV Special. This was a significant event for her, but I didn't share her enthusiasm. By then, I had started dabbling in marijuana and a little LSD, and old Elvis was, well, "old Elvis." Grandma wanted me to come home by 8:00 p.m. that night to watch the special with her. I didn't. That evening, I had taken a hit of psilocybin. As I walked in a little before 9:00 p.m., tripping, I saw Elvis on our color Magnavox television set in a black leather jumpsuit, singing, smiling, and laughing with his bandmates from the past. I hated myself for missing this, and for how much I had changed in just four years, but by then, The Beatles had gone to

India, released the *White Album*, and things had really shifted in my life. Grandma didn't hate The Beatles, but Elvis was her jam. I may have started to tear up, staring through our big living room picture window, curtains wide open—the same living room from my youth where so many wonderful things had happened.

So many joyful times with Ma and Grumps watching Dick Van Dyke, Ed Sullivan, and Captain Jolly while Ma prepared potato pancake dinners and baked cream pies. And here I was, standing outside looking in at one of the happiest moments in Grandma's life. What a fool I was. But this is the kind of mistake I've repeatedly made. Perhaps I developed this behavior as a coping mechanism for being born out of wedlock without a father. I could never, and in some ways still struggle to, allow myself to be drawn into a make-believe world. I remained detached from certain things until I met my wife over 50 years ago at 15. That changed much of my perspective on life. She amazed me with her kindness and her steady view of a world gone mad, and she continues to astonish me to this day. As McCartney sang, "Maybe I'm amazed at the way I really need you."

Grandma introduced me to rock 'n' roll at a young age, and I've always enjoyed "good" music. However, as the early 60s began and after Elvis was drafted, I believed adults in society took this as a sign to trade that swiveling hip punk music for something tamer. Milquetoast artists like Fabian, Pat Boone, Bobby Rydell, Paul & Paula, Frankie Avalon, and Annette Funicello (may she rest in peace) were all squares in my eyes and in Grandma's too. That music felt lame, tame, and a doggone shame. I couldn't connect with it after being "All Shook Up" and "Jailhouse Rock."

At this part in my story, I really liked (and still do) Dion's 45 rpm "Ruby Baby" from late 1963. It was the first 45 single I ever bought with my allowance money. I'm not sure why I received my allowance, but shaking a few rugs for Dion's "Ruby Baby" was definitely worth it. I played that record to death on the little crummy record player my grandma bought me, using a sewing needle to play the vinyl. This would easily be considered a mortal sin and heresy in today's hipster vinyl culture. I would sit in our built-on "sunroom" for hours, playing music from my small collection over and over on that thing. After Elvis was drafted, I thought rock was dead, and it turned mediocre. So, as mentioned, I genuinely prayed for God to send new music. I first sensed a new dawn in late December 1963.

For the record, I do not dislike the Four Seasons or Lou Christie; I chose them as symbolic representatives of the high-pitched pre-Beatles squeaky vocal style of that era. I have come to appreciate the Four Seasons after the Broadway play and film about them (*Jersey Boys*), and I've since discovered that Lou Christie contributed to the Sgt. Pepper/Tommy spirit with his unique story-style album, *Paint America Love*. It actually isn't that bad, considering Jan & Dean attempted a Sgt. Pepper psychedelic album back in the day that still sounds like "The Little Old Lady of Pasadena." Oh, rock 'n' roll fate!

I turned my memories of those times into a performance piece by incorporating 28 Beatles songs along with a captivating film montage projected behind us during the story reading. Since 2014, we have performed this show at numerous libraries. The first "Beatles Forever" performance featured me, my dear friend Steve King, Charlie Palazzola, and Eddie Baranek from The Sights. Later, we welcomed drummer Lou DeCillis and the 12-year-old musical prodigy, Max Beardsley. The final addition to our show was our radio producer friend Bob Koski, who created a visual film montage to play behind us, aligning the film scenes with the story. We maintained this lineup for quite some time, but eventually, Charlie and Eddie chose to retire and focus on their solo albums. HA! Nevertheless, people continued to enjoy the show (we played some libraries two to three times), so we welcomed the wonderful Rick Beardsley (Max's dad) and Beatles fan and talented guitarist and singer Brian Dean to the team. What follows is the story of The Beatles "In My Life."

Beatles Forever

The phone rang, jolting *me* awake! I slowly turned my head and glanced at the clock. Through the darkness, I could see a red number five glowing in the corner of the room. It had an eerie light. I rolled my head back into the pillow, closed my eyes, and quickly drifted into a misty, milky dream.

It was 1963, and I was ten years old. All I cared about back then was making my lip curl more like Elvis's, which I practiced endlessly in front of the bathroom mirror. I spent a lot of time posing in the mirror like Al Kaline at the plate or smiling like Elvis with a curled lip.

Even the briefest meditation on those years transports me to a time that was so different from today. When I think back, I realize how much has changed. I'm not certain why it changed, but connecting the dots, I can see how it did. It was a time when people in most homes in Detroit and the surrounding suburbs were just beginning to think that it might be a good idea to lock their doors at night or when they left their homes. A time when folks still shopped at independent stores like Connie's on Mack for children's clothes or bought their groceries at Pete's Village Market, with his now-nostalgic sign "Home Deliveries Available." Now, you can't even find Pete's damned grandson to grab you something from Aisle 3. Damn it!

This was also before Macomb County opened Michigan's first enclosed mall. Back then, the idea of a "mall" felt like something straight out of *The Jetsons*. It was a time when people in our neighborhood couldn't even fathom something as farfetched as our local paperboy delivering historical, sorrowful news. A headline that read: "Michigan's First Boy Killed in Vietnam." Yeah— during those days, our dream was simply to get a job on the line at Chrysler. We aimed to earn the big union bucks just like our fathers. We believed it was important to make enough money to keep the grand old American dream (or illusion) alive. Of course, even that notion seems absurd and hard to grasp in this new world order we all inhabit. Nevertheless, the world was about to erupt with a bang, followed by waves of protests that would forever alter our future.

This was when my half-brother could be heard constantly singing Lou Christie's silly songs around the house. That was one part of those times that drove me nuts! I couldn't stand Lou Christie's shrieking voice. It seemed to cut right through to my heart and soul every time I heard it. It still, to this very day, makes what's left of my hair curl every time I think about it. I mean, if I ever hear "Lightning striking again and again and again" AGAIN! I am going straight for my brother's skinny-ass throat, and if he isn't available, I'm going after his father's skinny-ass throat (we had different fathers) for taking part in helping to create that kid's screechy voice. And in my insanity, or should I say my temperamental fantasy, I might strangle our mother for birthin' the boy with the skinny-ass throat. God, I hated that music so much that I remember running into the church bathroom while attending Sunday School and praying to God to send the world some new music. I remember thinking that the church bathroom was the closest place I could get to God to ask him a question that I was sure that the Pastor would never condone—condone outright anyway! I found myself doing a lot of that back then ... asking for new music, not running into the bathroom!

Well, I guess I was a gullible kid, always ready to take a person at their word. So when Pastor Schem once announced during a Sunday School lesson that "The Lord giveth and the Lord taketh away," I truly believed that it would account for everything, from a red, sore, sunburned neck to new music. It never seemed effective with those sunburns, but I remained highly optimistic.

Anyway, my brother kept up with the Lou Christie stuff, and I focused on my praying. The times were ripe for something positive to happen, especially after our popular president, John F. Kennedy, had just been assassinated. The morale was not what you would call "high," at least not in my neighborhood. Despite this, I was young, and my world was still alive with possibilities. It was still normal to have something as simple as two parents. I had boundless energy and loved so many things (except for Lou Christie). I remember that back then, it was okay to watch a lot of TV. Of course, there were only five channels—unlike the 190 we have today. And no one ever thought you'd have to pay to watch TV!

It also used to be cool to start smoking at 11 or 12. God, I only had a year or two to wait. Do you remember Captain Jolly? Now that was a fine character for kids to look up to—an old, bearded, toothless sailor. I mean, what do kids have to look up to nowadays?

SpongeBob? Xbox? Instagram and selfies? WTF? And what the hell is a sponge wearing square pants (or even pants) for? Well, maybe that isn't so bad!

This was also an era when it was popular to play baseball all day in vacant lots, and a time when the Licavoleis, those tough guys over on Lake Boulevard, didn't stand a chance of ever being cool or playing baseball with us.

And hey, what about the Schwinn Sting Ray bikes? Do you remember them? Now that was the bike of the future: long white banana seat, high-rise handlebars, and a sissy bar in the back. Wow, what a bike! On that kind of bike, you could do a wheelie. Imagine—a damn wheelie right there in front of my grandparents. It always scared the heck out of them—good for a laugh with the guys. Kids don't do wheelies anymore—they play Pokémon or text while walking into the street!

But in 1963, something began to change and stir. When I reflect on those days, I still believe that God was answering my bathroom prayers. I remember driving to my uncle's house with my grandparents and brother for a Christmas celebration. Anyway, my half-brother and I were sitting in the backseat of our Dodge Polara. My brother asked our grandparents to turn on the radio, a custom by then due to his innate love for bad music. So, we drove down Gratiot Avenue, and my brother started singing his cacophony of noise again. This time, it was a terrible song called "Walk Like a Man." I thought to myself, *Who is this Frankie Valli guy? He sounds like Lou Christie but worse.* Then I yelled at the top of my lungs, "What's with these shrieking singers all of a sudden? They sound like someone is squeezing their nuts." As you might expect, my grandma reached back and backhanded me for my "vulgar language," but that didn't stop me from jumping up and reaching into the front seat to change the radio station. At that moment, a fight broke out in the backseat of the Polara, which, by today's standards, was roomy, but not spacious enough for the two of us. My grandmother turned around and yelled, "Cut it out right now before I belt the both of you a good one." I told her I hated that music, and she replied that it wasn't so bad; in fact, she and Grandpa thought it was kind of nice. I mumbled under my breath as my brother shot me a big shit-eating grin. But as we drove on, the station I punched stayed on, and nobody seemed to notice. Then it happened! Jesus had answered my prayers. The radio blasted out "I Wanna Hold Your Hand." I thought, *What a great way to celebrate Christmas. A miracle right there in my grandfather's car. And whoever said a miracle can't happen in a Dodge?*

When my brother finally stopped shrieking with his high-pitched voice, I knew a genuine miracle had occurred. Suddenly, I felt alive, and it felt good. Like everyone else, I immediately wanted more songs—millions more. I thought this had to be the first time we had truly heard "real music." Yeah-Yeah-Yeah!!! That was when the countdown began. It was the end of December, and the word was that The Beatles would appear on *The Ed Sullivan Show* sometime in the early part of the new year. Sullivan always had a really big "shoe," but this one was destined to be a landmark. History notes that now. But why not Sullivan? After all, he brought us Señor Winces, Topo Gigio, Dancing Bears, and Broadway's Davy Jones from *Oliver* (later of The Monkees)—didn't he?

Well, the date was finally released: February 9, 1964, I couldn't wait; the world couldn't wait. Even my brother had given up on the Lou Christie and Frankie Valli nonsense. As we switched from the Four Seasons to the Fab Four, our world transformed. A newspaper once observed that The Beatles changed "the way we dressed—the way we styled our hair—and the way we loved."

Finally, it came. Sunday night—8:00 p.m. Ready, set, go. I can still see Ed Sullivan on our black-and-white TV as he delivered those now-famous words that set my world in motion: "Now, yesterday, and today our theater has been packed with newspapermen and photographers from all over the nation, and these veterans agree with me that never has this city witnessed the excitement stirred by these youngsters from Liverpool, who call themselves 'The Beatles.' Now, you're going to be entertained by them right now and again in the second half of our show. Ladies and gentlemen, The Beatles!" Girls in the audience screamed! I screamed! I swear I heard the neighbor girl screaming through the closed windows! My hair grew. My patience grew. My world breathed in deep. ALIVE!

When Monday morning arrived, I had my hair so watered down to keep my bangs flat on my forehead that I caught a really bad cold. My grandma blamed The Beatles. I thanked God! We must have acted out the scenes from *A Hard Day's Night* a thousand times during afternoon recess in grammar school. We had our own make-believe group with paper guitars and the whole bit. A guy named George played George, another friend named Jeff was Paul, and a real guy named Earl Ringle—who rhymes with "shingle"—played Ringo because his name was the closest match we could find. I played John (I could only play John).

I remember running around the playground playing "Eight Arms to Hold" (the original title of the film known as *Help!*) We even gave girls our milk money to chase us around, just like the real Beatles—well, almost! Through one thousand lunches, we would laugh and be witty, just like the Fab Four, or so we thought. We practiced what we thought were witty one-liners on each other; we dreamt about making enough money on our paper routes to buy "Authentic Beatle Wigs," and we paid girls in our class to scream whenever they saw us gathered on the playground. Through countless warnings, we stayed out on the playground singing Beatles songs from a monthly publication called *The Beatles Song Book*. Beatle songs and Beatle cards were all that mattered then. Tardy bells ringing—phone bells ringing—always bells ringing, crashing our fantasies and ending our dreams.

Damn bells, I thought to myself as I rolled out of my pillow once more. The phone was ringing incessantly. I angrily grabbed the receiver from the hook. It was my brother. He didn't hesitate for a second. In a trembling, nervous voice, he said, "They shot John Lennon last night." I was speechless. I should have realized something was wrong; his voice sounded just like it did the night he called to tell me our mother had died. I jumped up in bed. My heart was pounding wildly in my chest. I felt hot and sick. I thought to myself, *No!* A long silence hung over the phone. I didn't know what to say to him. He continued, "Well, I heard it this morning while I was shaving, and I wanted to tell you before you heard it on the radio or on TV. After all those years, I didn't want some stranger telling you something like this." Dazed, I let the phone drop to my chin. "I'll call you later today, and we'll talk," he said. I sensed a sensitivity from him that I had never felt before. I hung up the phone and dragged myself out of bed. Still half-asleep and very stunned, I made my way to the living room and opened the doors of the record cabinet. I turned the receiver on low for any late-breaking news. Then I began pulling out Beatles albums and tossing them onto the carpet. I felt lost. For the first time, I sensed that "it" was over. Shit, John Lennon was dead! I couldn't believe it.

The years rushed back, hard against my somber mood. The answered prayers in the Sunday School bathroom; Sundays (three in a row) with my grandparents watching *The Ed Sullivan Show*, the recesses of *A Hard Day's Night*, singing Beatle songs and being tardy; Beatle cards—Beatle hopes—Beatle dreams.

Gone! I was crushed. My youth had suddenly slipped away, and it hurt. The pain burned deep into my soul. Even before I ventured out that day, I knew the world would be dragging itself around. It was a Tuesday, and the world was a drag. "And then somebody spoke, and I went into a dream."

Photo of M.L. Liebler and Country Joe McDonald by Rebecca Cook

BOB DYLAN
&
COUNTRY JOE McDONALD

A Hard Rain's a-Gonna Fall on Decoration Day

1965/2000

After The Beatles "invaded America" to hold our hands, my world changed radically and significantly. I felt alive again with music, hope, and curiosity. It was like a sudden return to my early pre-kindergarten years when I first discovered Elvis. There were many good times, plenty of great music, and even movies during this period. The Beatles released a film in the summer of 1964—just five months after that iconic Ed Sullivan appearance. They showed the film nearly around the clock to accommodate audiences; I believe they rotated kids and parents in and out every ninety minutes or so. My grandma drove by the Woods Theater on Mack to get me a ticket. I forget which show we attended, but it seems we attended a weeknight screening. The audiences screamed their bloody heads off as if they were at a live Beatles concert—these movie tickets were as rare as hen's teeth, but Grandma stood in line to snag me one. Some might find this strange, and it was, but in the 21st century, in the year 2000, I walked into the Film Forum in Greenwich Village to see an anniversary screening of *A Hard Day's Night*. It was sold out and packed, with young kids and some parents still screaming their heads off throughout the whole movie, like thirty-five years earlier. I couldn't hear a thing. So, I have actually never heard The Beatles in person or on a screen in a theater, but I was happy to be alive in times like these. It was a blast, and I felt truly blessed.

The Beatles (and my world) changed at Christmas in 1965, specifically on December 11, with the release of *Rubber Soul*. That album set my life on a whole new path. On that same day, the first boy from St. Clair Shores was killed in Vietnam—Dennis Carroll Manning. He was the neighbor kid, the tall, lanky, good-looking guy we'd seen walking past our house on his way to high school. He was the older brother of my friend from the neighborhood. Dennis was the mythologically perfect 1950s boy who never had a major fight behind the bowling alley and never got drunk. He was the local hero and the son of a Marine, so he enlisted for Vietnam War duty right after graduating from Lake Shore High School. Little did he, his family, or the rest of us on Lincoln Street know that the tall, slender kid from three doors down would no longer exist less than six months after his family celebrated his graduation. In 1965, I didn't understand much about Vietnam; I only knew it was somewhere in Asia, and I realized that our neighborhood had a local teen who wouldn't be coming back alive from that place.

Interestingly, 35 years later, while hosting a weeklong tribute to the Vietnam Generation at Wayne State, I invited the well-known Vietnam veteran fiction writer Wayne Karlin. During the car ride from the airport, I learned that his first mission in Vietnam involved helicoptering to Que Son to clean up the human carnage left by the war's first major battle in the Quang Nam province of South Vietnam in December 1965. Wayne mentioned that Dennis Manning was likely one of the many black bags he zipped up and loaded onto a helicopter. As it turns out, Wayne may have been the last American to lay eyes on our beloved neighbor boy from Lincoln Street, as I wrote in my poem, "Decoration Day."

*And this business of murder
Bruises each rising sun
Above every American town.
Towns that were never
More than small dots
On small maps, routing death To innocent lives that
Will be forever lost In the rapid fire
Of the jungle night.*

And the poem concludes with these lines about his mother's broken heart that I have never been able to let go of:

*They took you,
Laid you out,
Neatly uniformed,
Placed you in the funeral Home of the Far East.
The whole thing planned, Planned to the smallest detail,*

Except for your mother's broken heart.

Just days after this horrible news spread along Lincoln Street, *Rubber Soul* was released just in time for Christmas in 1965. This album was radically different—from the stretched photo cover to the introspective songs. It featured a sitar and an organ for "Michelle." It also had a song that would likely prompt a lawsuit these days in our "politically correct" and "cancel culture" world. The song was "Run for Your Life, Little Girl." It was a song about murder, sex, and violence, and they thought Lennon was pushing the envelope in the summer of 1966 with his claim that "The Beatles were bigger than Christ." If only they knew what was to come.

However, we should have sensed what The Beatles might release if Bob Dylan had been their controversial prophet and guru. In July 1965, "Like a Rolling Stone" started getting significant airplay on AM radio. We all enjoyed it, but it wasn't until later that people recognized a notable connection between Dylan and The Beatles; we didn't have Twitter and Facebook to spread news quickly back then. Many of us still used "party lines" on our home phones. Two rings for us, three short rings for the neighbor next door, and so on. It was the working-class phone system in those days.

For obvious reasons—his voice and intelligent lyrics—Dylan didn't appeal to everyone. But that summer, a 45 rpm single featuring a twangy voice and an unusual-looking kid from another Midwest town (probably not unlike St. Clair Shores) made me see life differently. Bob Dylan?

Who was this guy who wrote songs that felt like poems? A musician after my own heart. He crafted songs that demanded repeated listening. What? *It's only 1965*, I thought, *for God's sake, this is completely different!*

Regardless, after "Like a Rolling Stone" broke on the radio, the world slowly began to transform into color and come alive in unimaginable ways compared to the 1950s. With the neighbor boy gone by early December 1965, the Dylan lyrics, "How does it feel to be on your own…" felt like a fitting song/poem that truly resonated with me as I started to immerse myself in understanding what this "V-I-E-T-N-A-M" was all about.

What profoundly affected me and has stayed with me ever since is how I witnessed the neighbor boy's mother descend into a deep depression, from which she never recovered. She passed away a couple of years later due to what the neighbors called "a broken heart." This shattered my heart. I loved my grandmother, who raised me, and I couldn't bear the thought of losing her. The notion that death could stem from a broken heart unsettled me deeply and influenced the direction and focus of my life's work.

And that's exactly what Dylan's poems and music did for me. After I first heard "Like a Rolling Stone," which oddly featured a musician on organ who would later become a close friend, Al Kooper, I quickly dove deep into the Dylan catalog. I listened to *Freewheelin'*, *Another Side of Bob Dylan*, *The Times They Are a-Changin'*, and *Bringing It All Back Home* over and over again. Each listen revealed new insights and meanings in my life. Bob sang about "Masters of War," "The Times They Are a-Changin'," "When the Ship Comes In," and the masterpiece that remains at the core of my understanding to this day, "A Hard Rain's a-Gonna Fall." These albums were my real-life textbooks. I have seen Dylan perform almost every time he's played in Detroit. I don't know him, and I've never met him. I'm not sure I want to meet this "Bob" in person. What if he's not the guy I've been hanging out with on vinyl since my early teen years?

Later in life, through his longtime friend Al Kooper, I edited a book of working-class poems, stories, and nonfiction for Coffee House Press and wanted Dylan to be featured, so I asked Al if he could connect me with the right person. He did! The gatekeeper to the Dylan kingdom is a great guy named Jeff Rosen. One day, Jeff called me directly on my Wayne State phone, back when professors still had desk phones. When he introduced himself, I was in shock. He said, "Bob said you could use any of his lyrics that you want, free of charge!" I was in double shock. Jeff then asked, "So which ones do you want?" Initially, I only wanted Bob's spoken word piece "Notes to Woody," as Nora Guthrie, Woody's daughter, had given me carte blanche to Woody's catalog. Jeff asked if I was sure that was all I wanted.

I quickly started thinking on my feet. "How about 'Union Town' from *Infidels* and 'The Lonesome Death of Hattie Carroll?'" I suggested nervously.

He replied, "Got it! Anything else?" Not wanting to be greedy, I thanked him profusely. Within a day or two, the licenses were in my Wayne State mailbox. They arrived faster than 99% of the poets in the book.

I have kept in touch with Jeff occasionally to check in and see how things are going. I feel less intimidated by Bob now. He is a genuine poet who believes that poetry belongs to the people. Maybe I could meet him now? I don't know. It's probably better to love and remember than to risk disappointment. Once, while sitting in a hotel room in Detroit with Kooper, I asked him if he and Dylan could have a conversation like the one we were having. He said, "Yes, but it takes 30 years." Nobody has that kind of time when "it's a hard rain a-gonna fall." It took me almost 30 years to truly grasp the images and ideas in "Hard Rain." I often told people that one cannot fully understand life in this world unless they understand and feel the lyrics of this Dylan song in their soul's blood. It is as deep a river as anyone could ever cross, but on the other side lies awareness and light. It all makes sense, or at least it did to me. I understood this world much better, and it might have taken an additional 30 years for me to gain the insights I received from this song written in 1962:

> *And what did you hear, my blue-eyed son?*
> *What did you hear, my darling young one*
> *I heard thunder that roared out a warning*
> *Heard the roar of a wave that could drown the whole world*
> *Heard one hundred drummers whose hands were a blazin'*
> *Heard ten thousand whisperin' and nobody listenin'*
> *Heard one person starve, many people laughin'*
> *Heard the song of a poet who died in the gutter*
> *Heard the sound of a clown who cried in the alley*
>
> *And it's a hard and it's a hard and it's a hard hard hard hard*
> *And it's a hard rain's a gonna fall.*

Later, I wrote a widely published poem titled "Decoration Day" and, decades later, recorded it with my anti-war music hero, Country Joe McDonald. In 2000, we produced a full-length CD featuring our acoustic poetry, music, and comedy. The project began with "Decoration Day," which we performed live on a late-night music program on WDET Public Radio in Detroit. The host was my fellow music enthusiast and good friend, Willy Wilson, who often invited me and my visiting guests to join him on Friday or Saturday nights. After a gig at a nearby venue, we arrived at the station around 11:00 p.m. We chatted, and Joe pulled out his Martin guitar, playing a tune or two from his repertoire. Then, we dove into my poem, accompanied by Joe's music. The phone lit up with positive comments and feedback. That first version felt so natural and tight that we started working on the entire CD the next day. Inspired and eager, we recorded the entire project in my basement in just about one sitting. Joe took it back to Berkeley to have his producer and friend Bill Belmont at Fantasy Records mix and master it. Joe named it "Crossing Borders" for obvious reasons. Before long, it was released on Joe and Bill's well-known indie label, Rag Baby Records.

Our unique version of that poem changed my life in many ways during the early summer of 2002 at the unveiling of the San Francisco Vietnam Memorial, a project spearheaded years earlier by Country Joe and Mayor Willie Brown. Country Joe and I performed the poem live in front of thousands near the Embarcadero in downtown San Francisco by the docks. A young Nancy Pelosi spoke after us, referencing lines from my poem. Though she wasn't as nationally famous as she would later become, she was starting to make her mark, and her name was recognized by a news junkie like me. However, after the ceremony, two older ladies approached me by the stage. I noticed them walking across the great lawn. They identified themselves as Gold Star Mothers, just like Dennis Manning's mom, and one of them said to me, "Thank you for that beautiful poem. Your poem expressed everything that has been in my heart for the past 33 years." Wow!

That truly knocked me out. I was so moved that I remember thinking to myself, "Do I need to write anymore? And if I do, can I ever top this moment?" It was a beautiful, sunny day at the wharves in San Francisco. Mayor Willie Brown, Nancy Pelosi, many veterans, Gold Star Mothers, and members of The Arvan (South Vietnamese army) all stood at attention as the monument was unveiled. Then, Mayor Brown introduced us to kick off the program with "Decoration Day." It was an incredible afternoon.

A poet writes in isolation, alone. The words spread across the page, creating miniature paintings. I never considered them anything more than that until that afternoon in San Francisco when everything changed. I remain grateful for my friendships with Joe McDonald and Bill Belmont from The People's Republic of Berkeley, USA. Joe and I performed many shows across the country with great success, and my life was transformed by our experiences from New York City to Colorado, Wyoming, Los Angeles, and finally, the Bay Area.

What began with the mysterious Bob Dylan moved into Country Joe's orbit, where we recorded and performed songs about social justice and peace everywhere that would have us.

Jimi Hendrix in Detroit © Leni Sinclair

JIMI HENDRIX

"Let me stand next to your fire"
while "The Motor City's Burnin."

1967

The year 1967 just felt right. Back then, it seemed as if I'd been born solely to witness and partake in this year. "Purple Haze was in my brain / Lately things don't seem the same." This was the year when my music, my poetry, my politics, my faith in mankind, and my "real" education began to converge. In February of 1967, "Strawberry Fields" started to blossom within me, and I was just beginning to grow my hair and perhaps develop a third eye to better perceive the world. Man, I was vibing on being "experienced?" and "Yes, I are!"

There was no way in hell that this kid weaned on Elvis and nurtured by The Beatles was going to miss this psychedelic train. People, I was ready, and I heard that train a-comin'. Oh man, I heard it loud and clear, and I knew all I had to do was get on board. I did it without hesitation. I was a full-tilt boogie kid from the get-go. Thanks, Grandma!!! The music of 1967 was evolving, just like the album artwork. Albums were now adorned with bright colors, creative distortions, and vivid, lively images. This starkly contrasted with the dull, often black-and-white visuals, such as a photo of Ricky Nelson's head, or those with paint-by-number quality album covers like "Moon River." And by the way, what on earth is a "huckleberry friend" anyway?

I bought The Hendrix Experience's *Are You Experienced* from the local department store. Its vibrant yellow and purple cover was the coolest thing I had ever seen, featuring a full-color photo of a biracial band in ruffled necks, psychedelic-striped pants, and frizzy hair. My body felt ELECTRIC just staring at it—which I did often. I even carried that album back and forth to school to keep it safe and secure, and I used it to troll the squares at my high school. I simply couldn't believe this new music and those images, and oh my God, the wonderfully loud amp feedback shrieking at high decibels, along with the ratted-up frizzy hair. All three Experience members had huge Afros. All three of them! White and Black together!!

WOW! This was just the thing America needed. It had a kind of electricity that would shock my suburban neighborhood. Experienced? I sure as heck was getting there. I was all in with a Black guy and two white British guys playing the freakiest, most electrifying sounds ever known to mankind! It seemed to me to be the most sophisticated and mind-bending music I had ever heard—Whaaat???

Without even realizing it at the time, these guys were making a significant statement during the civil rights era in America. I knew this would drive my white neighbors insane! Who ever heard of such an unusual mix of music, cultures, and personalities? It "blew my mind," a new phrase I picked up in my lexicon during my fourteenth year of life. I was in the ninth grade, and if Elvis changed my life with his twitching lip when I was four years old, and if The Beatles rocked my world with "I Want to Hold Your Hand" and "Tomorrow Never Knows" when I was ten, then these jams launched me into a completely new orbit of existence toward the "Third Stone from the Sun." Holy shit! This was another damn miracle in my life. That's four big miracles, for those keeping score (Elvis, Beatles, Dylan and Jimi).

How many of these miracles can a young person experience in one lifetime, especially before junior high ended? I didn't want to use them all up. However, if I had to use them all, then by the year 1967, it would be worth it. Could I take any more? Would there be any more? There would be many more, and each one lifted me "higher and higher," to quote Sly.

In my view, Jimi was further proof of God's existence; no human could have conceived this electric, psychedelic guitar-playing, frizzy-haired guy. It had to be a pure God thing, in my humble, teenage opinion. I was truly in a "purple haze" heaven! As the late, great *Creem Magazine* rock critic Lester Bangs once wrote, "Detroit was Heaven." And it really was! Unlike my classmates, I was experiencing a wonderful "satori" (a word I came across while listening to Sunday morning talks by Priest-Zen Master Alan Watts on WABX-FM underground radio during my paper route delivering *The Detroit News*). Occasionally, I would even read a bit about Jimi in my local newspaper. What started at age four with Grandma and Elvis, and further evolved with The Beatles at ten, began to nurture my inner "hippie." It truly "blew my mind!" In addition to the evolution of music, many other mind-altering events took place in 1967. The Vietnam War was escalating, and the draft would soon be instituted, ensuring that no male teenager could escape the horrors of that conflict. Motown was just beginning to explore the wah-wah pedal, creating some minimalist psychedelia in the Marvelettes' fantastic single (perhaps the first Motown single I ever purchased), "My Baby Must Be a Magician." I loved that guitar lick and the strange, slightly eerie vibrato sound. It wasn't Hendrix, but I could sense it was about to become part of a new musical repertoire in the changing tide for my beloved Motown Records.

A funky white kid from Detroit named Dennis Coffey was brought into Motown's Studio A, also known to hipsters as "The Snake Pit." His wah-wah sound forever changed the future of Motown. WOW! A simple electric guitar pedal that you push up and down creates a whole new universe of music, thanks to Hendrix. Who knew it would be such a groundbreaking innovation on the unconventional and different "soul" song entitled "Cloud Nine" by those "Temptin'" Temptations? I remember a major rumor circulating around town that Jimi Hendrix sneaked into "The Snake Pit" on West Grand Blvd and laid down the sweetest guitar sounds ever heard on that hallowed ground of American rock and soul. It was "Cloud Nine," which soon became a "Ball of Confusion," a "Love Child" by The Supremes, and later, a very "Superstitious" Little Stevie Wonder—all grown up. Even these titles resonated with our blossoming hippie selves.

Alas, years later, the world would find out it wasn't Jimi Hendrix but Dennis Coffey. A white kid from a hip Detroit public school, Dennis played new psychedelic riffs to launch his professional career. The "wah-wah" eventually propelled Dennis to his own number-one Motown hit, "Scorpio," a few years later. Dennis even made an appearance on *Soul Train* while that tune was climbing the charts. Later, Dennis would go on to perform with everyone from Ringo to Sinatra.

In 1970, Coffey and his business partner Mike Theodore discovered Sixto Rodriguez, known as the "Sugarman," in a dive bar near Wayne State. Today, the world knows Sugarman's story thanks to the Academy Award-winning documentary, *Sugar Man*. When Dennis first met Rodriguez, he was a shy young man who played guitar and sang while facing the wall in a club in Detroit's Cass Corridor. Years later, these two once-young Detroit kids would often visit my Motown class at Wayne State University to discuss everything Detroit. My students cherished their visits, and frequently, their parents would bring records to have signed.

In the spring of 1967, when I was 13 and soon to be 14, I attended my first rock concert. My grandparents took me and three of my junior high friends to Ford Auditorium to see The Blues Magoos perform at what would soon be called a "rock concert."

Another stranger-than-fiction moment happened many years later when I befriended Michael Esposito, the lead guitarist of The Blues Magoos, who was then working as a bicycle repairman in Woodstock, New York. Starting in the early 1990s, I frequently visited Woodstock to spend time with my mentor and friend Ed Sanders and to participate in readings with other poets and musicians from the area. I was quickly embraced by their small but vibrant arts scene in upstate New York, and I still stay close to those folks in Woodstock to this day. It was fantastic to meet Mike, the first "rock star" I had ever seen live, in such a calm and relaxed setting as a bicycle shop, but I digress....

So, the summer of 1967 began, and all of us suburban kids suddenly learned that in San Francisco they had just buried "Hippie," and then we heard they were calling it "The Death of Hippie." What the hell? For us in Detroit, with Plum Street, the Fifth Estate, John Sinclair, Incense, and the Grande Ballroom, Detroit was just coming into its own. The future had finally arrived in Detroit, and suddenly, those West Coast hipster freaks were killing the damn "hippie" and burying the son of a gun. Damn it—we were just warming up to the whole movement in suburban Detroit. Seriously? What? It's over? Already? Really?

Our good childhood friend, who shall remain nameless in case the statute of limitations for stealing a store blind of their records hasn't run out, began pilfering new albums from our local S. S. Kresge's at the shopping center. These were albums by bands with such wild names as The Grateful Dead, Moby Grape, Country Joe and the "friggin" Fish (What?? Are you kidding me??). There were two Boston groups named Beacon Street Union and Ultimate Spinach. Sonofabitch! That was one way to make vegetables cool again. This was long before veganism, organic food, vegetarianism, etc. existed. We thought that album was a way for our new generation of "heads" and "freaks" to get our necessary dose of veggies and other things that came in "doses." All Hail His Purpleness—Owsley!

Anyway, our friend—who was a cross between a greaser and a freak—sold us these stolen albums at the beach on Lake St. Clair for $1.00 for sealed albums or as low as 50 cents or a quarter (depending on how much sand from the beach got between the records and their white sleeves). We were just opening the Hippie Door, so little did we know that this "Death of Hippie," slightly before it embodied flesh in Detroit, was soon to become a metaphor for our city itself. Our city, once vibrant and considered "The Paris of the Midwest," rich with factory jobs, art, culture, and great music, began to unravel and would soon be buried beneath itself and the looming shadow of post-industrialization in America. To add insult to injury, Jimi himself would be gone in just three short years. Just as I was starting my senior year of high school, while pulling into the school parking lot on that chilly September day in 1970, the underground radio announced that Jimi Hendrix had just been found dead of an overdose in London. For us in Detroit, the hippie wave came like a slow wind from the West Coast on a turbulent ride across the American plains, sweeping through the Midwest to us, and by that fall of 1970, it was starting to fall apart. Jimi died at 27 on September 18, 1970, and by October 4, 1970, less than a month after Hendrix, our beloved Kozmic Bluester Janis Joplin also died at 27. The "27 Club" was in full swing, progressing with Jim Morrison's passing on July 3, 1971, and in 1994, just as I arrived in New York for a reading, Kurt Cobain blew his brains out at the age of 27. Wow! It makes me glad now that I didn't heed The Who's lyrical wish to "Hope I die before I get old."

What began subtly in Detroit in the fall of 1966 with the opening of the Grande Ballroom transitioned into the early summer of 1967 with Plum Street, the arrival of MC5 at John Sinclair's doorstep at The Detroit Artists Workshop, the Belle Isle Love-In, and the radical Wayne State newspapers, *The Fifth Estate* and *The South End* (prior to this period, the Wayne State paper was known as *The Daily Collegiate*). This eventually erupted into flames during the hot summer of July 1967. It marked a major rebellion and uprising that John Lee Hooker, and later MC5, sang about in "The Motor City's Burnin'"—"Oh it started on 12th and Claremont / it made the pigs in the street freak out!"

O sacred metaphorical hippie, Jimi, John Lee Hooker Blues, MC5 Jam Kickers, burning buildings and stores in Detroit, murders at the Alger's Motel—people buried that old, young hippie as we have many times throughout our own history, but Detroit has been resurrected and rebuilt countless times. Death has no hold on this tired, hardened, vibrant American city. All Hail the Motor City! All Hail rock 'n' roll! Survivors rise in freedom!!!

M.L. and Al Kooper in Copenhagen, 2006

AL KOOPER

How I Went from Bobby Rusch and His Pet Monkey to Al Kooper

"Child Is Father to the Man"

1968

Al Kooper entered my life with a monkey and a rush. Bobby Rusch introduced me to the musical legend I hadn't known when I first heard "Like a Rolling Stone" as a teenager.

My adventure and youth took off in the kitchen at Bobby's house on Furton Street in St. Clair Shores. Bobby was the son of a tough, old-school police officer and a waitress mother who excelled at archery. The two of them, along with sister Suzy, were quite skilled in their sport.

Bobby seemed to live in a "broken home" before that was a common term. At that time, parents stayed together for the sake of the children—HA! Neither of his parents were home much, which is why we spent so much time at Bobby's place. I met Bobby at my Lutheran church, which my grandparents insisted I attend. They never went themselves but made sure I went to Sunday School from fifth to eighth grade to get confirmed. I hadn't been baptized, so I needed that, too. Back then, it seemed like everyone on my street was Catholic. In my small world, my grandma raised me to believe that Catholics and Lutherans were like mixing oil and water. She frequently said during my formative years,

"Lutherans marry Lutherans, and Catholics marry Catholics"— coming from my grandma, who never attended church. Bobby and I were Lutherans by the unfortunate luck of the draw. Being Lutheran amidst the neighborhood Catholics felt as strange as being a Jehovah's Witness in Afghanistan. I had a friend who was part of that Jehovah's Witness group, again through unfortunate luck of being born into it. I only remember that he didn't celebrate birthdays or Christmas and couldn't play baseball with us on Saturdays. "What the hell was that all about?" I often wondered. Oh boy! Bobby and I were confirmed at Redeemer Lutheran Church on the corner of my street. Back then, Catholics seemed like saints to us. Along with Bobby, a few other kids were also Lutheran. We had two Lutheran prom queens at Lake Shore High School (as rare as having Protestants in the Irish Republican Army). We also had a friend at church, Jim Carrol, who was a great baseball player, but even at the age of 13, that kid seemed better suited for prison. Of course, I met him through Bobby Rusch.

Bobby's parents sent him to a Lutheran school in Roseville because he was "too hard to handle." Another kid I met through our church was from a family that resembled a hip version of the Donna Reed family on TV. This was Billy Ignich from the Ignich Family on Visnaw Street. Billy was a drummer and a fellow music lover just like me and Bobby. He was even in a "garage band" before we even knew what a "garage band" was. I discovered the first Mothers of Invention *Freak Out* album in his parents' collection, and I was thrilled by this find, which likely left a lasting impression (in a good way) with songs like "Suzy Cream Cheese" and "Help! I'm a Rock." To this day, I still enjoy the song "Help! I'm a Rock." In fact, I introduced my own children to the *Freak Out* album while driving them to elementary school. They adored the quirky vocals and strange lyrics and music. Their favorites quickly became "Hungry Freaks Daddy," "You're Probably Wondering Why I Am Here," and "Any Way the Wind Blows."

So, we all went to Bobby's almost every day after school. We experimented with his parents' liquor cabinet, and one time, after a few swallows, we noticed two large display swords mounted on the wall above the fireplace. We yanked them down and started having sword fights. In general, we acted like wild children from a book we read called *The Lord of the Flies*. We were a rock 'n' roll crew with just a little sip of booze (that no adults ever knew about) and acted completely unleashed and chaotic. This was us when there were no parents around.

Things got even crazier when one day we walked in and found that Bobby had a pet monkey. *What the hell, Bobby?* we thought. He had somehow acquired a screaming Vietnamese spider monkey that was perched on top of the refrigerator. "What the hell is that, Bobby?" He replied nonchalantly, "Oh, that thing? That's a Vietnamese spider monkey." "What??" we all exclaimed, almost simultaneously. "Bobby? You act like this is as normal as having a cat or a dog. Bobby, this isn't normal!! Bobby, that's just plain weird!" But looking back, everything about those times felt strange: Vietnam, the Chicago Police Riot, bell-bottoms, and more. Having a monkey in captivity somehow seemed to make sense in a bizarre way back then. It was like having a palm tree in Michigan during winter. They always looked great in the summer, but they'd die once winter hit.

"A freakin' monkey!" Holy shit! Only Bobby Rusch could come up with something like this. Bobby Rusch was definitely an "Original." The spider monkey wreaked crazy havoc in Bobby's house. Looking back, it might have symbolized the America we were living in, with Bobby as the poster child for typical, troubled, hippie youth lost in the chaos of the 1960s, but we loved him. Back then, it seemed to me that kids of cops were often the most outrageous and troubled. Just then, that bizarre monkey leaped out of the shadows, clawing and swinging its way around the kitchen before finally settling atop Bobby's mom's cabinets, where he always seemed to relieve himself like a goose. The monkey let out a god-awful screech, and the smell was unbearable. That damn monkey appeared to hate humans. *So much for evolution,* I thought.

Along with having a monkey in the suburbs, Bobby was involved in archery. His dad was a tough St. Clair Shores cop with a chiseled face like Dick Tracy's, while his mother was quite attractive as a red-headed professional archer. We were just reaching the age when mothers like her appeared exceptionally appealing to our uncontrollable boyhood hormones. Perhaps that was a result of living with my grandma and Grumps, who looked just like a typical grandma and grandpa.

One day after school, we went to Bobby's as usual, played with the monkey, ate some homemade cookies his mom had baked, and then Bobby pulled out a new Al Kooper album called *The Live Adventures of Al Kooper and Michael Bloomfield*. WOW! I had never heard anything as cool as that live set before. The cover looked like a Norman Rockwell painting from *The Saturday Evening Post*. I learned many years later from Al that it was an actual Rockwell painting, and he owned the original. Holy crap! Real Americana!

Bobby and I would listen to this record over and over. I remember loving all the tracks, but the ones I really enjoyed were "Green Onions," "Dear Mr. Fantasy," and "Hey Jude." The standout track on the LP for me was the rare Jack Bruce song "Sonny Boy Williamson," also known as "He's Gone." I was captivated by Koop and Bloom performing a Bruce song about a true American blues hero.

One night, while touring Italy with Kooper's band, he surprised and delighted me by pulling out this gem to perform. I felt as if I was transported from a town in the Calabria region back to Bobby's house on Furton Street in my hometown of St. Clair Shores.

Sometimes after school, I would stop by my best friend Jeff's house at Lincoln and Fifth Street, and we would cross Garfield Street and jump over Debbie Anderson's fence toward Furton, heading down toward the lake and Bobby's. Debbie Anderson was a stunning redhead, the all- American girl whom I secretly loved, and I was simply happy to be considered her friend. She had an epileptic brother who, on occasion, would "swallow his tongue." That always freaked me out. Every time I saw an ambulance over there, I imagined swallowing my own tongue. It didn't seem possible. I tried once.

While we didn't want Debbie to see us running after the ambulance that frequently visited her small, wood-framed house, I often rode my Sting Ray knock-off bicycle past her place whenever I heard sirens nearby. I think sweet Debbie felt a little ashamed. It was her personal burden to bear, and I thought it made her vulnerable to jokes, but because she was so sweet and kind to me, I was more than willing to shoulder some of that heavy load. Chivalry was not quite dead back then! In fact, as a side note, while jumping the fence one gray, early autumn day with my trusty Sears leather-cased transistor radio in hand (which I still have to this day in my office), I first heard The Small Faces' "Itchycoo Park." I had never heard anything like it before. Vocals spun through a damn Leslie speaker. Incredible! This was quite an original and unusual sound, but later, I would swoon over hearing Kooper's Super Sessions album every time we played the blues classic "You Don't Love Me Baby," where Kooper does the same thing with his vocals.

What came first, the Faces or the Koop? A tough philosophical question for me back then. When I hear The Small Faces now, I remember everything like it was yesterday, jumping gleefully over Debbie Anderson's fence, hoping to see that redhead looking out her bedroom window. Until Debbie, I had never actually seen a redheaded kid before. I guess one might say Debbie was "my first."

Once we arrived at Bobby's neglected, parentless house—his dad on duty and his mother either shooting arrows or tending bar—we played like crazy kids. We often took the decorative swords off his living room wall to sword fight in the front room with the curtains drawn. We devoured all the family snacks in the kitchen cabinet, and we frequently took tiny sips from Bobby's parents' special liquor stash, which was kept in a fancy cabinet in the front room. It looked like something James Bond might have in his living room. We never had enough to feel very high, but it was the sneaky aspect of the act that excited us.

In the end, Bobby introduced me to archery, a living room with a monkey and booze, through Debbie Anderson's yard, and sword fighting, where he once accidentally stabbed me in the shoulder blade while taking large swigs of parental liquor that day, and eventually to the Al Kooper album.

I could never have imagined back then that one day I would meet and become friends with Al Kooper. Such things don't happen to people like me, coming from a working-class home in suburban Detroit. But lo and behold, it did, and our friendship endures to this day. We even created a poetry and music album together, which he named Poetry Score. We recorded and mixed it around 1999 or 2000. I visited Al at a studio in New York City where he was remixing *Child Is Father to the Man* in Sensurround. He played an extended cut from our album in Sensurround, and it was amazing to hear that along with his new remixes of Blood, Sweat and Tears' first album.

Right after graduation, Bobby Rusch married a cute hippie girl from our high school, but they quickly divorced. I believe this happened once she discovered what a mess old Bobby was. He disappeared soon after high school, but I'd always remembered him and still often think about him. I would wonder where it was that he disappeared to. One day, many years later in the late 1970s, he showed up at my grandparents' house on Lincoln Street looking for me, just as he used to years ago. I think he expected me to be living in the same house and the same room as when we were kids at Sunday School and on the church baseball team, or when he went camping with me and my grandparents. Grandma always had a soft spot for Bobby. She felt sorry for him, having a chiseled-faced policeman for a father and a barmaid for a mother who shot archery. She believed, although she had no proof, that his father was too mean to him and his mom was too absent to raise a good kid. One night, while we were camping with them, Bobby and I snuck off to the woods to drink a pint of cheap Corby's whiskey. Bobby got so drunk that he threw up all night. My grandmother thought it was due to his home life. I think she believed that until the day she died. I knew the truth: Bobby couldn't hold his liquor at the age of 14, but it kept me safe from getting busted, so I let her believe what she wanted. I never drank whiskey again.

When Bobby unexpectedly returned to me, I was already married. My grandma called and said, "You'll never guess who's standing right here right now!" I felt unexcited. My old drug-and-drinking buddy was looking for me. For all intents and purposes, I had gone underground from all my old hippie friends. I had cut my hair, was balding, and had grown a beard. The old Mike was becoming someone named M.L. Liebler. My thoughts about Bobby and my old friends were Biblical: *Let the dead bury the dead.*

Grandma said, "It's Bobby Rusch! He wants to see you." *Oh, great*, I thought. She said, "He really wants to see you." I should pause here and explain something about myself after high school.

In high school, I couldn't smoke enough pot or take enough LSD to feel satisfied. However, when I turned 17, I began experiencing what I thought were acid flashbacks. Many years later, I learned that I was suffering from what became known as "panic attacks" and a "panic disorder." These panic attacks drove me away from drugs, and eventually, I became agoraphobic. I didn't want to see people or go out in public, and I became suspicious and fearful of all my old hippie friends. I avoided answering the door when they showed up. I would hide from them if I saw them in public, and I would never answer the phone. In fact, I still don't answer phones much. I told my grandparents that if anyone showed up, they should tell them, "I am not here." I asked my best friend Jeff, my future wife's cousin, to inform all our old friends that I had moved to Seattle and was working as a journalist. Everyone in high school knew I wrote poetry and wrote biting political commentary, and the rock 'n' roll column for *The Shorian*, our high school newspaper. Still, to this day, people occasionally ask, "What was life like when you lived in Seattle?" I always drew a blank on those questions until I remembered the big lie I had asked folks to tell to shield me from—wait for it—wait for it—PEOPLE. As Lennon once sang, "You wanna save humanity / But it's people that you just can't stand." So, for many years, except around my girlfriend and now wife Pam, I hid from my past and everyone I knew. I wasn't that pothead fun, fun, fun guy anymore. I'm not sure I ever was. Whenever I took LSD back in the day, I usually did it alone to gain further understanding and insights into who I was and what this world was really about. I didn't take it to "get high." I took it to delve deeper into what I later learned from the Maharishi was my "Cosmic Consciousness."

Pull the pin out here—so when Grandma called to say that Bobby wanted to come to my house to see me, I was far from excited. Still, I replied in an exhausted, unenthusiastic, and defeated tone, "Okay—tell him where I live and send him over!"

When Bobby arrived, I nervously greeted him. He told me that he had been busted a few years earlier for transporting thousands of hits of pure LSD across state lines. That part seemed about right. Then he mentioned that he was one of the first criminals offered the chance to learn Transcendental Meditation instead of serving a life sentence. I, myself, had started practicing TM about a year earlier, so I became interested in what Bobby had to say. It seemed to benefit him and his sentencing judge. At the time we met, Bobby was living, meditating, and teaching at Maharishi Mahesh Yogi's University in Fairfield, Iowa. Once again, Bobby and I shared a bond like we had in the past with church, baseball, and Al Kooper. I felt comfortable with Bobby. We had a good visit, but he was gone again, just like at the end of high school.

Decades later, I started searching for Bobby. I even wrote what has become one of my most popular poems, titled "I Ain't Never Gonna See Bobby Rusch Again." I used Bobby as a metaphor for all the people in our lives whom we once knew and loved but lost touch with. Whenever I performed the poem, I would ask if he was in the audience. I'd tell the audience that he had been arrested for transporting large amounts of LSD across state lines.

Once, while rehearsing with The Magic Poetry Band for a show on our local PBS channel, I shared this story with the band and noticed the director standing in front of me, shaking his head and saying, "Yes, yes, I know... I know..." I assumed he meant he knew Bobby Rusch. Excitedly, I asked, "You know Bobby Rusch?" He took off his headset and replied, "What?" He was shaking his head because he was speaking with the control booth. He clarified, "I don't know what you're talking about, M.L. I was saying 'yes' to the control booth."

Damn—it seemed the long search for Bobby would continue. Finally, after God created Facebook, (or was it Al Gore?) I thought, I'm going to find out once and for all what happened to my old friend. I posted about it on Facebook and started hearing from all my old friends. Some said he had overdosed in the 1990s, while others claimed he died somehow, and so on. All these responses seemed like possible scenarios to me. I dug a little deeper and found his sisters on Facebook. One lived in northern Michigan, and the other lived in Las Vegas. This made sense since I had heard Bobby mention that his mother had moved to Vegas. I reached out to both sisters, and they told me that Bobby lives in Vegas. "What??" I wrote back, saying I had heard Bobby Rusch was dead! His sister in Las Vegas replied, "LOL! He lives here in Las Vegas and changed his name to Anuda Singh." "Anuda what??" I guessed the Maharishi had led him to an "ashram" in India. For real! Bobby's younger sister shared his email and phone number with me. I nervously called Bobby— or Anunda. We chatted for over an hour. I told him about the poem I had written for him. I sent him the book it was in and the CD it was featured on. We tried to connect when I was in LA since he was living in a mobile home in a national forest in northern California. Unfortunately, we never managed to meet in person. One recent Christmas, I received a package from him containing a "Windproof Zippo Lighter." The note read, "I stole this from you in the 60s, and I've felt guilty about it ever since. I tried to find a replacement, so I searched all over. I finally found this one. Please accept my late return." Wow! Well, I thought, I never did get to see Bobby Rusch again, but I finally received a windproof lighter that I can't use since I quit smoking in 1981.

So, old Bobby first introduced me to Al Kooper's music. From that point on, I always bought Al's new solo albums and CDs. In late summer of 1998, I heard an interview with Al Kooper on Terri Gross's *Fresh Air* program on our local public radio station. Being an avid, longtime Al Kooper fan, I listened closely to the detailed interview about his career at the time and his forthcoming memoir. What caught my attention was that Al was a professor at the Berklee School of Music in Boston. At that time, I was running the YMCA Writer's Voice in Downtown Detroit. When I heard Al was teaching college, I thought, *Hey, I teach college too!* In my mind, we were no longer hero and fan, but colleagues instead. Who knew? To that end, I looked up Kooper's email at Berklee and invited him to visit Detroit to read from his then-new memoir (Backstage Passes & Backstabbing Bastards) when it was released. One thing led to another, and Al suggested that he also perform a one-man show in Detroit while he was here. I quickly organized "An Evening with Al Kooper" at Alvin's Twilight Bar on the Wayne State University campus. Some young hipster kid designed a very cool 60s-style poster for the event, which Al still has hanging in his music room at home in Somerville. So, now we had a reading and signing set up, along with a performance. I also suggested that he hit Ann Arbor, as it was a musical and savvy city. He agreed, so I arranged a reading through my friends there with a post-reading Q&A at Shaman Drum Bookstore. Al understood the performing aspect of the visit, but as a literary author, doing "readings" was a horse of a different color for him. I told him I would walk him through the literary reading scene.

On the other hand, his one-man show in Detroit introduced a new style of performance for him. He shared stories about his own history along with the writing of his many popular songs. Since then, he has refined this act and performed it from California to the East Coast with great success. To do this type of show, Al needed a special computer-based keyboard, a Korg 88, so I ordered one. The kid at the music rental store said, "Sure, we have one." When he arrived at the campus club for soundcheck, he showed up with a red Farfisa organ, which I remembered seeing the 1910 Fruit Gum Company play in black and white on *American Bandstand* in the mid-60s.

What the heck! I thought to myself. The kid insisted this was the best he could bring. I remember Al yelling at him, "That would have been useful news… YESTERDAY!!!" We both told the kid to take that piece of junk organ back. He reloaded, jumped in his van, and was gone in seconds.

Al began to panic, and I felt the same way. Eventually, he contacted the U.S. Korg offices in New York, as he was the national spokesperson for the Korg 88. Within moments, they ordered one for him at no charge from a Guitar Center in Franklin, Michigan. I sped down the freeway to pick it up. They handed it over without any questions and even helped load it into my minivan. With the Korg in hand, I was on my way back to Alvin's. In the end, the show went well. We had a couple hundred people attend, and even over two decades later, I still hear from those who talk about it today. Al signed numerous books, albums, and CDs, and he took photos with fans.

After loading the Korg back into the minivan, we drove home. Al popped a cassette of new material into my player and mentioned that he was working on some new songs. I thought this was great and found his lyrics to be quite poetic. During our long weekend together—hanging out, visiting used record stores, and exploring Detroit—I realized that Al Kooper was not a typical "rock star." I considered him well-read, very much a poet, and a great friend. I loved talking to Al about music, and I think he liked me for that reason. I enjoyed all his stories and connections in the music biz. One of my favorite stories is about a night he was working overnight in the Los Angeles studio. After finishing, he walked to his car and was driving down Santa Monica to the 405 when he spotted Bill Withers pumping gas around 6:00 a.m. He pulled into the gas station, circled back to Bill, rolled down his window, and said, while pointing at Bill, "I know I know I know I know," before speeding off.

Since then, we've shared many fun and humorous times together. He performed his one-man show again here in Dearborn a couple of years later. Shortly after that, I managed to book him and his entire band to play the Main Stage at the Detroit Festival for the Arts. For this big full band show, he reserved the Korg in advance, so I went out to retrieve it once more. That performance was incredible. He played all his well-known Blood, Sweat & Tears songs as well as many from the *Super Session* album and *Live Adventures*. The audience went wild for each masterful piece. He received an encore, and the band packed up and flew back to Boston.

One slightly odd adventure in Detroit occurred a few years later. Al and his band were scheduled to perform at several blues festivals in Canada, starting in Windsor, Ontario (just across a bridge or tunnel from Detroit), then moving on to London, Ontario, and finishing up in Toronto. I was set to accompany him on the short tour, but when he arrived at the first stop in Windsor, Al had requested special equipment that would make it easier for him to work by touch, as he is legally blind. When they arrived for soundcheck, the necessary hand-operated pedal instead of a foot- operated one was missing. The promoters hastily tried to obtain the required equipment but came up empty. Al was very displeased, so he canceled the entire tour and called me to come and pick him and the band up from a hotel in Windsor. I drove my minivan to a small hotel on the outskirts of Windsor to pick up a group of downcast musicians heading back to Boston. We loaded my van with guitars, amplifiers, and some luggage, which we strapped to the roof. I drove the band to the Detroit airport, and Al stayed with me for more record shopping and discussions.

Another funny time we spent together in Detroit was when Al's wife called me during a snowstorm that affected both here and Boston. Susan, Al's wife, called to say, "Al can't get back to Boston on a flight from gigs in Tokyo." Since Detroit has a direct flight to Tokyo and I have made that flight several times, I was familiar with it. She explained, "Al needs you to pick him up and take him home for the night. A couple of band members rented cars at our airport and drove back to Boston." While Al and I ordered Thai food, we chatted in my warm St. Clair Shores house as the snow fell outside. That might have been the night we decided to create a poetry and music album.

Al wanted me to send him poems recorded at a local studio so he could score them, just like he had done for several films and television shows. When we met again in Boston, he took me to his home studio and played it for me. It sounded amazing, and I couldn't believe the richness of the sound.

A few months later, when I was in New York City for gigs, Al invited me to a professional studio in the East Village where he was mixing his first Blood, Sweat & Tears album, *Child Is Father to the Man*, for 5.1 Sensurround. While I was there, he wanted me to listen to our CD in that format, and it sounded even more incredible. We were both excited, as were the guys in the studio. Kooper had just signed with Steve Vai's Favored Nations label. He was deciding whether to release "Poetry Score" or include some of those tracks on his upcoming album. Neither happened, and the album sat on our shelves until 2023 when Jett Plastic Records planned to issue it as a special Record Store Day vinyl in November 2023. Ultimately, the album never made it to vinyl and remains in my private collection on CD.

Kooper and I have spent a lot of quality time together over the past 25 years. We visited a bookstore near his home in Somerville, and I joined him on a European tour with his Funky Faculty to Italy, Norway, and Denmark in 2006. We had many adventures and fun moments during that trip. We stayed in first-class hotels, and Al always requested a top-notch meal at a local restaurant in the cities we visited. The first stop in Italy was just outside Milan, where I flew in and met the band at the airport. The club where Al was scheduled to perform had featured my old touring and recording buddy, Country Joe, the night before. I went with the band to see Joe while Al chose to stay back at the hotel.

During that tour, I worked as Al's informal press agent and handler. He participated in radio and television interviews in Italy and Norway, which I enjoyed listening to while hanging out with him.

In 2008, we played several gigs across every part of Spain imaginable. Al referred to it as "The Spanish Castle Magic Tour." We performed in every major city and region of Spain, enjoying the same perks as in 2006: five-star hotels, gourmet meals, and covered transportation throughout the country. We flew in and out of Madrid as our hub. I counted something like 10 flights and two bus rides in just eight days. It was crazy!

We have shared laughter and engaged in serious discussions about music, politics, and baseball from Detroit to Somerville, Milan to Bergen, and from Copenhagen to Malaga, Barcelona, and Madrid.

I believe it all began with a kid from my Lutheran church named Bobby Rusch, his pet Vietnamese spider monkey, and a cute redhead with an epileptic brother just two streets away from me. From old Bobby Rusch, I gained a lifelong friend in Al Kooper, and Bobby finally returned my windproof Zippo lighter that he borrowed during our teenage years as a Christmas gift in 2017. Who knew? What a guy. It's a blessing that can only be explained by Al's song "I Love You More than You'll Ever Know."

M.L. with The MC5's Wayne Kramer | The MC5 © Leni Sinclair

MC 5

You know the Motor City is burning baby.
And there ain't a damn thing in the world I can do.

—John Lee Hooker

I've always deeply loved God and Christ, much more than any of my other friends did at the time. Understand me; I wasn't "bigger than Jesus." I just loved Him a lot, and I still do. My grandparents made me attend church and Sunday School as a child, but I always took those lessons seriously. Yes, it's true; I would sometimes skip Sunday School and use my offering money to buy candy at the corner store, but I still loved Christ.

In the late summer of 1967, I made a Molotov cocktail in my garage with my good friend Jeff. We jumped on our bikes and rode up to my church. I was the only kid in my neighborhood who attended the Lutheran Church. Jeff was Catholic. We rode our cheaper Schwinn Sting Ray knockoff bikes. Jeff and I pulled up at my church one Sunday afternoon with our homemade explosive. I'm not sure what I was thinking, but with the direction the country was headed in with Vietnam, I felt I needed to release my growing political and cultural displeasure and angst somewhere. Since the church was seen as an authority figure, it represented the "old" America of my displeasure, I took out my fire violence on them. No one saw us do it, and in the end the only person hurt by my actions was me. When I hurled the small Coke bottle filled with gasoline from my grandfather's lawnmower canister stuffed with an old white gym sock, I felt like I was releasing everything bad in my life against everything good. I loved the Lutheran church that I attended for Sunday School and services, but it had, in a way, interfered with my growing anti-authoritarian beliefs: hostility (I've struggled with that ever since I first saw Elvis on *Ed Sullivan*) and my "kick out the jams, motherfucker" anger.

"You know the Motor City was burning baby.
And there ain't a damn thing in the world I can do."

Those words by John Lee Hooker had barely left Rod Tyner's mouth when my war against "the Man" began to take shape. I wanted to tear down and destroy everything I loved or once enjoyed and cared for in America. Anyone or anything that got in my way became my enemy. I deeply regret many of those choices now.

I gave up baseball because it was too American and wanted nothing to do with it. But I love that game and always have. I could have stayed in the field across from my house and played all day until dusk; many times, we did. I'd play with anyone who happened by. "Come on, Nancy, just pitch me a couple, would ya? I'll go get them after I hit them." Nancy was the only girl on our street.

One of my school buddies had a great saying about that: "He who hits it goes and gits it!" or I'd say, "Billy, I know you're only six but just let me throw you a few while you try to bat!" I really loved that game. I kept a 1960 *Baseball Digest* in my nightstand by my bed. I'd often pull out the one with Roger Maris on the cover and fall asleep dreaming about the game. Even during my anti-American days, I'd sneak a peek at Roger before going to sleep.

In the spring of 1967, after returning from my first concert at Ford Auditorium on the Jefferson bus line, I bought a copy of my first Fifth Estate right out front. During the bus ride home, I read about an upcoming MC5 single ("Borderline"/"Looking at You"). The article included a picture of the five bare-chested musicians with White Panther buttons stuck on their chests as it appeared inside their debut Elektra album, recorded at the Grande Ballroom in late 1968. I remember carefully cutting that picture out of the newspaper and rolling it to fit inside one of my uncle Charlie's old glass cigar cases. That picture represented the new world I was about to enter. The MC5 sang about politics and cultural issues that would soon fill a political void inside me. They sang about the evils of government, the horrifying war in Vietnam that I was becoming obsessed with ending, race relations in Detroit, and even revived an old standard with fresh youthful sexual energy in the song "Ramblin' Rose." Additionally, they recorded a song by a guy whose name alone blew my mind back then, and his music still amazes me today—the great interplanetary Sun Ra. I was starting to dive deeper into America's dark heart.

Just like when I was four with Elvis, the music pulled me in, the drugs deepened my understanding, and the course of my politics, life, and education was taking a hard left. As Big Steve Parrish of Grateful Dead roadie fame said, "No left turns un-stoned." I was alive, but it was also a painful time of war, civil rights, white hatred, and a new anxiety in America. It was all unfolding in the same America that had given me a glorious working-class home with two amazing Elvis-loving grandparents and "Holy Baseball." But things were starting to come unglued, just like my youth. In thirteen short years, I went from Elvis to The Beatles to Dylan to The Doors, transitioning from penny candy to Chum Gum and from The Beatles to Cream. One thing led to another, and before I knew it, I was growing my hair and ratting it to resemble Rob Tyner of The MC5. All I wanted was to "kick out the jams, motherfuckers!" I couldn't kick out enough jams to save my life. I had finally discovered the music and the band that matched my growing interest in national politics, infused with anti-American sentiment. Was it The MC5, coupled with the neighbor boy's death in Vietnam? Or was it the death of that boy's mother from a "broken heart" a couple of years later? I was 13, and someone or something was going to take the blame for the pain I felt inside due to the tragedies of war. Ultimately, it would be my country that I would punch and punch until 2008 when Barack Obama was elected to show me another side and an alternative possibility. Man, that was a hell of a lot of teenage angst to carry inside me into my late 50s. I supported the SDS (Students for a Democratic

Society), started at the University of Michigan by Tom Hayden and others, with assistance from Wayne State Board of Governors member Millie Jeffries (whom I later knew). She helped secure the UAW camp (now Lakeport State Park), where the SDS wrote their iconic 1962 "Port Huron Statement," which I have always admired and supported. The first line stated, "We are people of this generation, bred in at least modest comfort, housed now in universities, looking uncomfortably to the world we inherit." I was all in on the SDS. I later related to their offshoot group, The Weathermen. Someone gave me a .22 rifle that I carried in my 1964 Chevy Nova trunk. I am not sure what I thought I would do with that. Oh, Youth!!

Long after 1967, I first met The MC5's drummer Dennis "Machine Gun" Thompson. He was the musical programmer for the robot rock 'n' roll characters at a large pizza chain called Major Magic's All-Star Pizza Revue, a local rival to Chuck E. Cheese. In a way, I suppose "Machine Gun" was still part of the music business. He seemed a bit bitter then and didn't want to talk much about the Five or any of his later musical adventures. However, he did provide a complete explanation of how these robots were programmed and how he created the music himself for their "Happy Birthday" rants whenever a kid's mother informed the manager it was her son's or daughter's birthday. I had seen The MC5 perform at the Crow's Nest, a very trendy club near my house, in 1969. I remember being captivated by Dennis's live performance and how forcefully he attacked his drums—shirtless and dripping with sweat. I thought that was how all drummers were meant to play, yet I don't recall ever seeing Ringo drum shirtless on Ed Sullivan.

Many years later, I met Rob Tyner and became friends with him. He was the MC5 hero of my youth and truly embodied the Future Now for me. I met Rob through my underground broadcasting hero and later friend, Dave Dixon, from WABX radio, one of America's first underground freeform radio stations. Dave was one of my earliest cultural heroes, and I often called him my "music professor" from my youth. Dave and I quickly became friends after he introduced me and my Magic Poetry Band at one of the early Live at Sam's Jams shows in 1990. He was friends with Sam Milgrom, the founder and original owner of the Magic Bag, and the current purveyor of rock art and photographs at his Sunset Avenue shop named Mr. Music Head.

Consequently, Dave had the task of introducing my poetry band at this weekly event inside Sam's Jams Record Store on 9 Mile Road in fashionable Ferndale.

Dave was a living legend in the history of countercultural radio in Detroit. I first met Dave and another broadcasting hero, Harvey Oshivsky—who later became a friend—at a Teach-In Against the War in Vietnam held on the University of Detroit campus in 1970. I remember that Dave and Harvey served as the coordinators and MCs for each panel discussion, and I recall seeing them both running around the university halls in their white socks. I wasn't sure what it meant, but I have wanted to run around Wayne State in my socks ever since.

Anyway, after Dave returned to Detroit from Florida in the mid-1980s, we became friends, collaborators, and colleagues on his groundbreaking television show that brilliantly showcased music, film reviews, poetry updates, and interviews with cultural icons. The innovative concept was truly ahead of its time. The show served as a 30-minute precursor to Elvis Costello's Spectacle and Live at Daryl's Place, but it was much cooler than the competition provided by Detroit talk show hosts like Lou Gordon, Bill Kennedy, and Joe Pine.

Later, Dave transitioned to an AM radio talk show and brought me along. He dubbed me "Detroit's Culture Czar," and I provided weekly updates every Saturday evening on poetry readings and unique art events across Metro Detroit. Occasionally, I invited special guests for engaging interviews. Throughout his show, I featured many notable guests, including Ken Kesey, Al Kooper, Country Joe, Ed Sanders, and others. Kesey performed magic tricks on the radio, and Country Joe played "Tricky Dicky from Yorba Linda" live at mine and Dave's request.

Hip hip-hip hurrah.
He walks, and he talks, he smiles, he
frowns, He does what a human can,

It was Tricky Dicky from
Yorba Linda,
The genuine plastic man.

After another show with Kesey, Ken wanted to swing by a bowling alley near the radio station to roll a few frames. Someone took a photo of us posing for the camera while holding bowling balls. I titled that picture "Take the Acid Heads Bowling!" During the time I spent with Dave until his passing over Memorial Day weekend in 1999, we laughed, challenged each other on Detroit trivia, and talked endlessly about music. He had been my music professor for many years from the age of 13 onward. Being part of Dave's show and his world always gave me a brief glimpse back at Detroit radio history during those early broadcasts from 1967 to 1969, high atop The David Whitey Building on WABX—when Detroit underground radio was new and distinctly vibrant.

In addition to Dave, members of The MC5, John Sinclair, and Pun Palmondon were among my heroes. Through my Wayne State topics classes, Pun and I became good friends. The enduring question of that decade about Pun was, "Did he or didn't he" bomb the Ann Arbor secret CIA office? Pun will never reveal the truth. He was my political hero and a champion of the White Panthers. In fact, the idea to name their organization was born from Pun's admiration for the Black Panthers in Oakland. Pun's passion for radical politics always inspired me to get involved in public activism against the war, for civil rights, freedom, and all power to the people.

When I started teaching my "Motown: What's Going On?" class at Wayne State, I always invited Pun to join us regularly. My students adored him, and they were consistently captivated by his stories about beginning as a union organizer, finding himself at the Detroit Hippie Epicenter (and our Haight-Ashbury-Detroit Style) on Plum Street, and meeting Detroit legend and The MC5 manager John Sinclair along with his entire badass crew. At that time, Pun was eager to find a community to belong to, and the lively hippies of Plum Street, Sinclair's activism, and The MC5's mission all resonated with him deeply. He got involved in making sandals and candles on Plum Street, eventually moving into the Detroit Artists Workshop and later the White Panther Headquarters was located on the Wayne State Campus at the corner of the John C. Lodge Freeway and Warren Avenue.

In 1968, due to ongoing harassment by the Detroit Police Department at the Wayne State campus, the Panthers and The MC5 operations relocated to the now-famous Hill Street compound in Ann Arbor, Michigan. Shortly after the formation of the White Panther Party, they changed their name to the all-inclusive Rainbow People's Party reflecting their progressive outlook. Just after their arrival in Ann Arbor, on the cool fall night of September 29, 1968, around 11:30 p.m., a bomb exploded in downtown Ann Arbor. The blast damaged offices in a two-story building that was later discovered to house an illegal CIA office. The CIA's charter prohibits it from operating within the United States. Nevertheless, the CIA frequently recruited students on college campuses, including the University of Michigan.

On that late September night, a loud explosion echoed for miles, originating from the office at 450 Main Street in Downtown Ann Arbor. How strange! About a year after that bombing, a federal grand jury in Ann Arbor indicted three members of the White Panther Party. Their indictment included White Panther Minister of Defense Pun Plamondon, who faced charges for setting off the bomb, while White Panther Minister of Education Jack Forrest and the legendary John Sinclair were charged with conspiracy to commit the bombing. John Sinclair, a good friend of mine and fellow traveler along the literary highways of Detroit and across America, was already in prison, serving ten years for possessing two marijuana joints at the time of the incident. John was the White Panther Minister of Information and the MC5 manager, a counterculture icon, and a celebrated superhero of the Detroit counterculture scene (or so the establishment believed). He coined the White Panther's slogan: "Drugs, Rock 'n' Roll and Fucking in the Streets," which became the rallying cry of 1967. However, by the time the actual bombing indictment was issued, John was already incarcerated, serving a 10-year-to-life sentence for those two joints.

Pun, meanwhile, went underground for over a year. He was eventually taken in by Black Panther-in-exile Eldridge Cleaver at his northern Africa compound. Eventually, Pun returned to the Detroit area and was arrested on I-75 heading north with friends. One of them threw a beer can out the window, prompting the police to pull them over. Bingo! The fuzz had themselves a real-life fugitive.

The remainder of Pun and the White Panthers' story provides a fascinating look into American counterculture during the late 1960s and early 1970s. However, dear reader, you will need to delve into their memoirs, history books, legal texts, or online resources for that. I should mention that Pun, Jack, and John's case was tied to Nixon and the Watergate break-in. The Supreme Court ruled in favor of these three Detroiters because the government violated wiretapping laws by not securing a warrant at that time. Ironically, this is how Nixon got caught and was almost impeached for the Watergate break-in; his wiretapping essentially got his own dumb ass in big trouble. Nuff said.

I have been friends with both John and Pun, living members of The MC5 and the Detroit Artists Workshop community since the early 1980s, and I genuinely treasure our long friendship. Over the years, many cultural heroes from Detroit have visited my Wayne State classes, including John Sinclair, Rodriguez, Hugh Masekela, and many others. We've had great discussions with my students as they shared essential insights about campus life at Wayne State and in Detroit in the 1960s. Rock 'n' Roll Fire and Kick Out the Jams, "I done kicked 'em out!," and I threw that unloaded rifle in a trash can somewhere

Pam and M.L., 1972

PAUL McCARTNEY

"Maybe I'm amazed at the way I really need you."

1969

"I'm going to marry your cousin!" I excitedly told my best friend Jeff one sunny summer day as we sprawled out on the grass at our favorite hangout spot—the elementary school court just across the street from my house. From sunrise to sunset, we immersed ourselves in laughter and fun, munching on juicy watermelon, grooving to WABX underground radio, and trying out all the quirky improvisations we picked up from *The Jonathan Winters TV Show*, which we adored. Our time together was often split between the court and leisurely walks through the charming streets of St. Clair Shores in the evenings, where we scavenged for unique props to inspire our improv performances like our idol. It could be anything—a bicycle casually left on the side of the road or our friendly bald neighbor enjoying a Tigers game broadcast by the legendary Ernie Harwell on his little AM radio from the comfort of his porch. Some days, we'd dazzle our friends with impromptu skits that could last for several uproarious minutes. With a simple toss of an object (like a pencil, a quarter, a tissue, or even someone's sandal), we'd spark 20 minutes of laughs and creativity! Our joyful journey even led us to establish the Ridgeway Arts Collective back in 1974, and we still gather to create spontaneous art pieces, continuing to embrace the spirit of improv into the 21st century.

Now in our 70s, we may not stroll the streets anymore, but our hearts remain full of cynical fun and laughter as we delight in our improv performances together in the 21st Century!

My plan had always been for me to marry Jeff's cousin Pam Morrill and for us all to move to New Rochelle, New York, where both Jeff and I would live and write for *The Alan Brady Show*, just like our hero, Dick Van Dyke. This was our employment plan following junior high and high school. Never mind that we had no idea back then where New Rochelle was or that *The Alan Brady Show* was merely a fictional sitcom. We both dreamed of working with Buddy and Sally, with a little Dick on the side. This was the only job we aspired to as kids. We knew we needed to find employment after high school or perhaps after college because I had to somehow support Pam.

So, *The Jonathan Winters Show* became our education. We watched that show as if it were our religion. It embodied our comedy and humor. We were always slightly apprehensive about the outcome because we had heard that he lost his sanity earlier in his life and was found sitting in a tree in his yard back in Ohio, his home state. That was close enough to Michigan, and we felt a deep connection to Jonathan.

Ah, a touch of youthful paranoia (like Jonathan) was good for the soul in retrospect. This was around the same time we began experimenting with marijuana, so "bad craziness" felt just around the corner, or so we thought, having read about it in the newspapers we delivered daily. One of the first hippies in St. Clair Shores lived on our street and was our friend. He knew a real, honest-to-God "pusher." We only knew this pusher as "Dave," and our neighborhood hippie friend was more than happy to share the holy hemp with his childhood buddies. All hail the holy bud! I might consider this another miracle, but it eventually took me to the brink on more than one occasion; see the chapter on The Doors.

Another great spot for improv after getting a "nickel bag" was in our backyard pup tent. We'd sleep outside in one of the backyards during hot summer nights and smoke large amounts of weed, creating even weirder, more surreal improv on our way to working with Buddy and Sally. None of their parents or my grandparents were aware of our new devotion to the holy smoke.

Back then, marijuana was considered a felony. There was even a strange movie, a cult classic, we'd seen titled *Reefer Madness*, often subtitled as *The Burning Question, Dope Addict, Doped Youth,* and *Love Madness*. We wished the part about "love madness" was true for our marijuana experiments; it never seemed to happen. Oh—those deceitful adults in the 60s. Pot was a big deal to carry around back then since it was a felony. Often, when we had pot, we'd walk around with our little nickel bags in our pockets. If we thought we saw the cops (almost every car from a distance looked like one), we'd toss our plastic nickel baggie onto a lawn and scurry away. Every car and every headlight seemed like it had to be a cop car. As a sidenote, it rarely was.

As a Hollywood sidenote, I've been working a lot of time in Los Angeles recently, and I pass by Morey Amsterdam's old house on Hillcrest in Beverly Hills. Each time I visit, I stop at the curb for meditation, prayers, and to pay homage to my youth. My trips to Morey's house feel like attending church in Hollywood.

During our junior high years, I asked Jeff to arrange a meeting. He did, and we all met on Jefferson between Furton and Garfield. I guess I thought of this meetup as a "kicking of the tires" moment. I hate to think of myself as that much of a sexist, but hey, I was only thirteen. I wasn't "woke" yet.

But let's get back to my story about meeting Pam. It was during my late elementary school years and early junior high when I first decided I wanted to marry her. In the summer of 1967, I asked Jeff to arrange a meeting between us. I remember we met on Jefferson Avenue, a major road that runs along the shoreline of Lake St. Clair. I mainly wanted this meeting to see his cousin Pam up close, rather than from a distance as I had seen her as a child riding her bike up and down Jeff's driveway on Fifth Street. This was the only view of her I'd had since spotting her at ages seven or eight.

Pam was beautiful—blonde hair, little granny glasses, and a Sassoon haircut. Thus began my love affair with that look and that girl. Full disclosure: I still enjoy looking at cute blondes (young or older) with glasses. She was sweet and innocent, which I liked, but

I suppose I wasn't so innocent myself. See pup tent pot-smoking marathons and Jonathan Winters's shtick above.

When Jeff asked, "Well, what do you think?" I probably made a Larry David-type expression, nodding, "Hmmm-Ah… I'll think about it." But I couldn't get this girl out of my mind. At that time, I was in 8th grade, and she was in 7th grade. Still, I thought about her day in and day out. I dreamed about our future married life, having kids (I could never have imagined us having two kids as cool as our Shane and Shelby, though), and living our whole lives together, which is exactly what we ended up doing. We have been married for 50 years now and together 57 years.

At that time, I couldn't shake this dream of a future life. Finally, on March 31, 1969, I asked Jeff to call his cousin, using my grandparents' old dial rotary phone in our living room, while I listened with my hand cupped over the mouthpiece on our kitchen phone. I asked him to find out if she would "go steady" with me. I said, "Tell her I won't take 'no' for an answer."

In the drama of those brief minutes and seconds, I heard her say, "Yes." Whew!!! Then I thought, *Now, what do I do?* I didn't even know what "going steady" meant. I learned the term from Zelda Gilroy on the old *Dobie Gillis Show*. Zelda seized every chance to "snag" herself a Dobie. Well, I just "snagged" me a Pam, and now I had to figure out what the heck that meant.

That was March 31, 1969, and since both of us were Beatles fans (hey, they were still a band at that time), we had heard about Paul McCartney working on the first "real" Beatles solo album, simply titled *McCartney*. It was released about a year later on April 1, 1970. But before that, we were blessed with one final Beatles album that seemed to come out of nowhere in September 1969. It was *Abbey Road*. Just when the word on the street was that The Beatles were breaking up, this tasty and now immortal masterpiece appeared. We had all heard and read in *Circus* magazine the horror stories of The Beatles trying to film themselves making an album. The movie ended up portraying The Beatles going through a divorce. Oh—that hurt! It was, and still is, painful to watch the bickering and backbiting in the last film *Let It Be*. Of course, the full nine-hour version of the 2021 *Get Back* put to rest the negative perceptions everyone had about the "rooftop" film. Still, Abbey Road gave us all a sense of hope for the future in the new decade. "Come Together" became our fall anthem, and "Something" became my love song for my beautiful girl Pam. The lyrics were spot-on for us

Something in the way she moves
Attracts me like no other lover
Something in the way she woos me

I don't want to leave her now
You know I believe and how

Yes, I certainly "believe and how," and I still believe in love all these years later. It was everything we needed back then, and it's all the world needs now to save itself, to save each other, and to save America. We were in love ("LUV," as the J. Geils Band sang at Detroit's old Cinderella Ballroom). Pam seemed to fill a significant void in my life, and I understand that now. I had been searching for something that I just couldn't find until I met her. Pam has been a wonderful friend, lover, and dependable companion, and she is, quite simply, one of the finest human beings on the planet. She is kind, loving, understanding, and very smart. Plus, she still looks like my dream girl from over 50 years ago. She is like a fine wine that gets better with age. I needed a partner like her to tame my wild side and to save my life when I let things get out of hand during a drunken New Year's Eve bender when her cousin Kenny and I snuck in Jägermeister and Red Stripe beer to the Detroit Symphony for the Annual New Year's Eve Vienna Holiday Concert. After the concert, we headed to the Soup Kitchen Blues Bar near the Detroit River. Once there, I started drinking shots of Jack Daniels. I remember I tried to drive back to St. Clair Shores by way of the sidewalks along Jefferson on the lower eastside. That did it! Pam got me out of the driver's seat and secured me in the passenger seat. I almost ruined everything and lost my dream that night. Shortly thereafter, I realized that this kind of drinking and partying had to stop, and it completely ended a few months later. I've never looked back or missed those days of "wine and roses."

Pam has always been aware of and understood my panic disorder, which began when I was 17 years old. My panic attacks persisted until 1991, but before that, I went through a peculiar phase of agoraphobia where I avoided going out in public and engaging with others. On that day in March 1969, I realized I never wanted to be apart from this girl. I was right. There is a God, and this was the fourth miracle of my life, one I have joyfully continued to embrace. My disorder didn't make things easier for Pam, but she significantly enhanced the quality of my life. Pam has become a fantastic mother, a wonderful aunt, a loving grandmother, and still my best friend.

When my life began to gain public attention in 1989, she remained, thank God, unfazed. By 1994, when I started working with Jason Shinder at the National Writer's Voice Project, I knew my life in my cherished St. Clair Shores was about to undergo a dramatic change, involving extensive travel both nationally and internationally. I remember reflecting on this after I hung up the phone with Jason that afternoon. Jason asked me to be in Pittsburgh the next day for the Associated Writing Program (AWP). This new venture seemed to be the one I had worked toward my whole creative life. I was working in the field that made me the happiest in my number one dream job of teaching at Wayne State.

After I quit drinking, I found myself unexpectedly on the cover of our local weekly arts publication, the *Metro Times*, in 1989, as well as in both of Detroit's major newspapers, the *Free Press* and the *Detroit News*. My face was all over Detroit. One of the leading and most popular columnists at the *Free Press* during that time was Bob Talbert, who referred to me as the "backbone of Detroit poetry." How could I possibly live up to that? We hadn't even entered the '90s yet. I was honored, to say the least, but I didn't believe I had done anything remarkable to deserve such praise.

In addition to the press coverage, I found myself on the radio more than your average poet and began traveling across America like a nomad while Pam held down the fort at home with the kids. I was determined to provide my children with the same stability that Grandma and Grumps had given me, and I thought it would be even better since we were their "real" parents. The main difference was that I wanted to be honest and open with my kids. No, I didn't want them calling me by my first name like some of my liberal academic friends, but I also didn't want to create a fake reality for them. Everything was mostly out in the open, and our children knew how deeply we both loved them. Except for the times I had to hit the road for poetry-related events and to earn a little extra money for the family, we were a very close unit, just like I had been with my grandparents. Instead of just the three of us, it became "the four of us." We went everywhere and did everything together. I even started taking my kids on poetry tours (which often turned into baseball and fishing trips) when they were four and five years old. My son Shane traveled to New York and Woodstock with me when he was ten. This was wonderful because both he and his sister gained real-world experience, and, most importantly, they both learned to love and appreciate the fine art of baseball. All hail the Detroit Tigers and the "No Lights at Wrigley" Chicago Cubs.

But back to my love story, minus Ryan O'Neal and Ali McGraw. In April 1970, one year after our love for each other began to blossom, McCartney released a solo album in which he played all the instruments and sang. The last song on side one was "Maybe I'm Amazed." That quickly became my song for Pam, and whenever I hear it today while driving, flying on a plane, or even in a hotel elevator, I flash back to a time that was innocent, filled with hope, and offered us eternal freedom. As the years go by, these lyrics still ring true for us.

Maybe, I'm amazed at the way you love me all the time,
And maybe I'm afraid of the way I love you.

Maybe I'm amazed at the way you pulled me out of time,
You hung me on the line.
Maybe I'm amazed at the way I really need you.

"Truer words have never been spoken," as Grandma used to say. McCartney really nailed it for me in this stanza below:

Baby, I'm a man, maybe I'm a lonely man
Who's in the middle of something
That he doesn't really understand.

I am grateful and glad to have lived during the time of The Beatles and the 1960s in America, even though these were not easy times. The Vietnam War was tearing apart the fabric of the America I once knew as a hopeful kid in the late 1950s and early 1960s, and then the world became difficult for many of us. The mild drug use that began in the spring of 1967 eventually turned into a painful epidemic. Before long, LSD, opium, speed, and even a bit of heroin entered the scene. Some friends lost their minds on acid, others became addicted to needles, and a few ran away from home, never to be seen or heard from again. I can't fully explain the depth of pain and loss experienced by the children of the 60s, but it was undeniably present. I lost several friends to overdoses, suicide, and terrible addiction.

My good friend, a fellow Mountain band devotee and Catholic school hockey player, fell victim to heroin in the spring of 1970. A few years later, my other close buddy from the drug culture died in a rundown mobile home court on Lake St. Clair, where I had broken my front teeth in the 8th grade while trying to impress a girl by jumping on the rocky shoreline. Other friends quietly faded from my life, and I later discovered that some had died under tragic circumstances. Despite the dangers, I was easily led down a bad path, but I truly believe that Pam saved my life, and she continues to rescue me from myself every day. She filled the void of loneliness and fear that I initially tried to fill with drugs and, later, alcohol. The 60s, along with my close connection to the hippie scene of that era and my own self-medication for anxiety and panic, must have pushed me to the brink.

I wanted more from this life. I longed to be comfortably high on life and at peace with myself without resorting to substances. Pam showed me that this was possible and gave me the opportunity to enjoy life and the world around me. Before Pam, in the spring of 1969, I realized that I was indeed caught up in drugs, alcohol, radical politics, and the sweeping cultural changes of the 1960s, feeling "in the middle of something I didn't understand." I was genuinely amazed by all the good she brought into my life. I still am, and I am grateful for her love and friendship. She's still my rock and my girl!

Jeff Ensroth & M.L. Contemplate What Happened at Kent | M.L. on Blanket Hill at the site of the Kent State shootings. Jeffrey Miller was murdered at the bottom of this hill (as seen in the famous John Filo photo of the girl screaming over Miller's Body)

NEIL YOUNG

Grandma, Vietnam, Four Dead in Ohio,
& a Game of Hippie Baseball

1970

After the invasion of Cambodia, I gave up baseball for a few years. I somewhat regret that now because I love the game so much, but I could no longer support anything American after that. The 60s were tough on all of us—from the older neighborhood boys who were drafted to serve in Vietnam to the kids playing on baseball fields and mud lots across America. Everyone made sacrifices in one way or another. In a sense, it was a cultural sacrifice, different from the sugar and gas our parents were used to. For me, American ways and traditions had to go.

Cambodia and Kent State marked the end, the limit, the close of my youth. I gave up apple pie and baseball, but I couldn't give up Grandma. I wanted to, but she had made such a strong impression on me with her constant reminder to kiss her before leaving the house because she might not be alive when I returned. After hearing this throughout my childhood, I couldn't toss her out with the mitt and the Hostess Fruit Pies, worried about carrying her death on my shoulders late into my mid-life, when I should be dealing with other problems and crises: my hair turning gray and falling out; my wife finishing her menstruation and complaining at me; we'd both be having hot flashes, and damn it, my grandmother's ghost would be screaming at me, "You S.O.B. (her favorite initials), you gave me up with baseball and Hostess Fruit Pies. I told you to always kiss me before you left the house, but after this darn Nixon and his Cambodian thing, you S.O.B., you stopped with the kissing! And understand this, young man, your grandfather is upset too! I guessed he would be." Well, I couldn't live with that, so I kept Grandma close to me always.

However, this story is only partly about that. It's really about life before Cambodia and Kent State in May of 1970. This is a tale of my hippie days and my love for baseball. Before the hippies, there was nothing but baseball. A whole lot of it—baseball from morning until dusk. As long as there was enough light to see that little round object, usually secured with electrical tape, there was baseball. I remember days so hot that grasshoppers would fry when they jumped onto the aluminum siding we used as a backstop, yet we still played baseball. Once, we played for so long in the blazing sun that I was sick for a week. But during that entire week, I dreamt about Roger Maris, Mickey Mantle, Al Kaline, and Hank Aguirre. My grandmother kept me in a dark room with a fan blowing. She said her brother Andy once suffered from sunstroke due to too much baseball and sun exposure. I lay in bed, extremely worried, wondering if what my great- grandpa might have died from was sunstroke or a heart attack. I had heard both mentioned in the same breath as my deceased great-grandfather's name. After the sun "left my brain," as my grandma put it, I was back in the fields playing ball.

This all happened several years after I played in the Lutheran Church league and illegally in the "Catholic" Little League. I loved baseball so much that I asked my Catholic friend to take me to the St. Gertrude Church Little League. I felt guilty for not being Catholic. However, when Mike Platte asked the Dodgers' coach if I could play even though I wasn't Catholic, the coach told one of his assistants, "Give this kid a bat and let's see what he can do." I smacked the first pitch over their outfield fence. I heard the coach yell, "I don't care what religion that kid is; he's on our team now!" All I had to do to secure my spot on the team, which I did for the next three seasons until I turned 13, was sell the required number of candy bars and keep my mouth shut about what church I attended. When I turned 13, I played in the Lutheran Pony League and returned to my home church. By the time I turned 14, I had been confirmed in the Lutheran Church, which allowed me the freedom to make decisions about my faith.

I want to emphasize that what we played was "hard" ball. We took immense pride in anything with the word "hard" in it. We were giggly adolescents, and "hard" ball represented something far more exciting than "soft" ball. "Hard" ball was what we played with. Those "sissy" kids always used 'soft' balls. That was Cal's favorite joke. I promised him I would use it in a story if I ever became a writer. Well, I'm a writer now. That's for you, Cal!

Now, this point might seem minor, but it genuinely marked the beginning of the divide between the "cool kid" baseball players and the "goofy kid" baseball players. This also represented the division that was starting to emerge across the country, and some people believe that life isn't symbolic. That's what my college professor said when he claimed I "didn't know a symbol from a tit!" I told him that if I ever became a writer, I would expose his sorry ass in my story. Well, I'm a writer. You're exposed, dude!

Anyway, this division probably became more noticeable when we started stealing records from the Woolworths store. We figured there were all sorts of groovy records by Hendrix, Cream, Grateful Dead, Jefferson Airplane, and others, and that the guys running the store didn't know anything about the new hip culture. So, we thought it was better for us to have them than for the capitalist pigs to sell them. We had just begun hearing about capitalism and the mess it created, thanks to the new underground radio stations in town. It didn't sound cool. The radio was always talking about capitalism and our parents' generation. Well, I had a whole family of sorry folks to prove that it must be a sick system. From Uncle Andy to Aunt Ruth, my family was a pretty sad bunch. I wanted their love; they handed me their money instead. I understood the underground message. So, we kept ripping off the dime store. We listened to these new records while the other kids, the "soft" ball kids, stuck to watered-down California pop stuff. That made sense. "Always a day late and a dollar short," that's what my grandma used to whisper about some of those kids. She also added, in hushed tones, since she was friends with their parents, "If you ever mention any of this in public, I'll tear your heart out—because you'll break mine." What she meant was that she would be embarrassed because she revealed her truest, innermost feelings in public. God forbid. I learned about this crap, too, after Kent State.

Anyway, the division began, and throughout the sixties, it expanded. In early spring of 1970, between the last Hendrix album, aptly named *Cry of Love*, the final Cream record, aptly titled *Goodbye*, and spring training, several of us stumbled upon the "soft" ball boys playing in a muddy lot across from a field where we smoked most of our pot. Maybe we were smoking that day, maybe not (a documented side effect), but there they were, and there we were, standing in the warm spring air, dressed in wide bell bottoms and Levi jackets adorned with patches proclaiming things like "Woodstock," "Peace," and "Power to the People." Everyone had one of those little Rolling Stones "lips and tongue" patches. So, we approached those kids and asked if they wanted to join us for a game of ball. Those "short-haired, yellow-bellied sons of Tricky Dicky," as Lennon described their type, just smirked. The pudgy one, whose hair was as short as mine was long, shouted, "With you guys? We'd kill ya!" Logically, they probably should have. We'd smoked too much dope, read too much Che, listened to too much MC5, and tried too hard to connect with our "spiritual selves" to win a baseball game. But my brother chimed in, saying, "Come on, you little bo peeps. Are you afraid to play with a hard ball?" We laughed. "Hard," hee-hee—it still made us giggle even as hippies. We may have been hip, but we were not fully mature.

The only greaser in our group perked up; he loved the talk about dicks and motorcycles. He wore his leather all summer long, claiming only a "real man" could handle it. We thought that only a dickhead would even attempt it. He should have been in the other group when the split happened, but he smoked cigarettes, and they wouldn't allow it. These other guys were hardcore Brady Bunch types. One even had a nose like Alice's, but that's a story for another time.

So, the greaser, whose last name was Forge (which I thought was pretty symbolic) said, "Come on, you chickenshits, play us a game—the losers get the shit beat out of them!"

I looked at my brother with a twisted face. I shouted, "Hell no! I want to play for something worthwhile. You might be a greaser, Forge, but we're hippies. We don't beat no shit out of people, you jerk. Let's play for a joint!" The "soft" ball boys glanced at each other.

Then the one with the slightly crossed eyes said, "Oh, forget you guys. All you ever think and talk about is revolution and dicks."

Huh? I thought. "Was that supposed to be an insult? If we lose, do we get your joints?" And he grabbed himself between the legs.

I immediately switched to my best negotiating voice while chuckling to myself. "No, I mean a smokable joint. You know, pot-grass-blow-weed-marijuana—you know?"

They turned red, and the youngest towhead sheepishly said, "We ain't never done that before. We don't smoke that stuff."

I quickly realized my mistake and said, "OK- OK, how 'bout if we lose, you guys buy us all a Hostess Berry Fruit Pie?" Now, they could get with that. Everyone loved those turnover-looking pies filled with delicious berries, chemicals, and glazed.

"OK!" the towhead said, and the cross-eyed kid agreed.

Then, a voice of hidden authority emerged from the back of their group. You know, the kid who always looked like a Marine even at ten years old? The one whose brother signed up instead of being drafted for Vietnam? He said, "You guys can't play baseball in Beatle boots and bell bottoms."

Well, that really upset the greaser among us. He said, "Listen, you motherfucker, I don't wear no tennis shoes. They make my fuckin' feet stink, and I don't want my fuckin' feet stinkin' when I go to my fuckin' chick's house. Now, if you ain't got no fuckin' chick to care about your fuckin' stinkin' feet, then don't fuckin' tell me about fuckin' wearing Beatle fuckin' boots with my straight-legged jeans to play this here fuckin' game. You bastards are so worried about fuckin' balls: baseballs, footballs, basketballs. Why don't you get some fuckin' balls and stand up for what you fuckin' believe in?" I knew this took the greaser over the edge. He was never very political.

However, he did have a touch of politics in his voice that day. Still, his rant confused the hell out of me. Yet the "soft" ball boys must have understood it because they quieted down, and we played. We did well.

We scored many runs, and my half-brother Ron hit every pitch over Mr. Stayshook's fence (symbolism again) for a home run. We also learned that day how important clean-smelling feet were to Forge. No one ever mentioned that greaser's old Beatle boots again. In fact, he's likely still wearing them now as we head into the 21st century…unless he's dead. We lost track of that guy.

Anyway, we won, and that really upset those guys. We enjoyed the fruit pies with the delicious berries and glazed crust, reminiscing about all our baseball memories, which were some of our most cherished childhood moments.

In fact, these were the deepest memories that the damn war in Southeast Asia kept eroding from our minds. Then, in May of the spring of 1970—WHAM! Kent State!! Kent State marked the invasion of Cambodia (which I learned later). I heard about the shootings in my 11th-grade Political Science class in high school. It stunned me. The teacher walked into the room after lunch. He looked as pale as a ghost. He then proceeded to tell us that he had just heard that four college students had been shot and killed at a college in Ohio. What the hell? I was furious. All the philosophy and all the pot in the world wouldn't bring these four kids back.

Five years prior, the neighbor boy's brother, the older kid who enlisted with the Marines for Vietnam in the fall of 1965 right after high school, was killed in action in December during the first major battle early in the Vietnam War, the Battle of La Drang. Following Kent State, the division in America deepened within our once "wholesome" suburban world and in the nation's heart. I gave up baseball and apple pie. I would have given up Grandma, but she soon shifted her stance on the war question. There was hope for healing, yet I still can't shake off all the pain from Kent State, even now, more than 50 years later.

I visited the campus for the first time to commemorate the 20th anniversary of the May 4th killings in 1990. My lifelong friend Jeff joined me on the trip to Kent. As we drove along the hilly roads leading to the Kent campus, The Beatles' song "The Long and Winding Road" played on the radio. That day, the song took on a completely new meaning for me.

Many times I've been alone
And many times I've cried
Anyway, you'll never know
The many ways I've tried
And still they lead me back
To the long winding road
You left me standing here
A long, long time ago...
(Lennon & McCartney)

The warm spring day I spent at Kent was filled with speeches, a peace march along the route of the student protesters, and an all-day poetry marathon featuring some of America's best-known poets. Everyone sat around listening to poet after poet—local, regional, and national—at the legendary Brady's Coffeehouse. Brady's was an iconic venue for anti-war meetings, draft resister organizations, and community counseling in the 1960s and early 1970s. After that period, the place was often filled with music and poetry on most evenings. Brady's was the kind of place where regulars washed and hung their own cups on a large board above the serving area.

As I listened to poets reading their poems, I looked around the room and spotted the great American poet Alicia Ostriker in the audience. After I read my poem, she approached me to express how much she appreciated my work and the effort it took to drive all the way down from Detroit. It was a literary "Elvis Moment" for me. I was familiar with her book, *The Mother/Child Papers*, which contains poems about the Vietnam War. That day, I also met several special people and poets who have since become my lifelong poetry buddies. The Appalachian poet Maggie Smith was the Poet-in-Residence at Kent, and I admired her working-class poems. I owned her first book in the Pitt Series, *Cold Comfort*. Maggie introduced me to her friend and comrade, Maj Ragain, a student survivor of May 4th, who became a wonderful new friend. Like Maggie, I connected with Maj immediately; it felt as if we were twin brothers from different mothers. We became fast friends and stayed in touch, visiting each other often until he passed away in 2018. Maj told me many of the students from 1970 are still living nearby or in Kent. It seemed to me that they just couldn't bring themselves to leave. That place was the scene of the crime that had scarred their lives since that May 4th. Maj Ragain was a wonderfully warm and kind soul. He introduced me to his close buddy from Cleveland, Daniel Thompson, whose book was titled *Famous in the Neighborhood*. Until his death in 2004, Daniel collected blankets for homeless veterans throughout Cleveland. These Ohio poets truly walked the walk, just like their Cleveland poetry peer, the great and legendary D.J. Levy. I was impressed. Maj also introduced me to another person who would become a lifelong friend: Brooke Horvath. He was a great poet, scholar, and professor at Kent State, as well as a huge baseball fan like me. We both loved the nuts and bolts of the game: counting pitches, looking for trends and patterns, tallying balls and strikes, and counting curveballs and sliders. Oh, it was a religion, dear readers. Trust me

These kind folks eventually made me an honorary citizen of Kent, and just a couple of years later, Detroit's Chapter 9 of the Vietnam Veterans of America honored me and Country Joe McDonald by gifting me a beautiful silk baseball-style jacket with my name on the front. I always wondered whether I should tell one group about the other. I kept both honors to myself.

Since May 4th, 1990, I have made many trips back to Kent State. I've taken my Wayne State students in my Vietnam War through Literature class on a walk through the tragic site, which we followed with an honest and open discussion. I still feel wounded and heavy with sadness when I stand where Jeffrey Miller was shot and his blood ran down the curb, and I can still see their 1970 class photos, which look more like high school pictures of

Jeffrey Miller, Sandra Scheur, Allison Krause, and Bill Schroeder, as if they were my own family members. I will never forget May 4th as long as I live.

Every year on May 4th, I remember the four students who were murdered. I replay the moment when Mr. Crabtree entered the room as if he'd seen a ghost. He slowly pulled out his chair and sat down, carrying the weight of this new world on his shoulders. In a somber voice that I've rarely heard from a teacher, he said, "They just shot four kids in Ohio for protesting the war."

Neil Young quickly penned a song and called Crosby, Stills, and Nash to the studio to record the now-famous track "Ohio." I cannot think of May 4th without thinking of Neil Young singing that sad, sad song

Tin soldiers and Nixon coming
We're finally on our own
This summer, I hear the drumming
Four dead in Ohio

Since that day, Mr. Crabtree, eleventh-grade Poli Sci, Neil Young, Kent State, and four dead in Ohio have remained vivid in my memory and will continue to do so forever.

M.L. in his Letters from Earth, Student Literary Org at Oakland University, 1974 © Gregory Booth Hallock

GEORGE HARRISON

(Ja Guru Dev) The Dead Word (or How I
Learned Transcendental Meditation)

> *All things can wait except the search for God.*
> —George Harrison

1976

Why would I ever learn a word from a dead language just to be at peace with myself? A mantra? Transcendental Meditation. Really? How could this mysterious word, this non-meaning word, help me concentrate when I already had a hard time remembering when to eat lunch, a necessary biological function? George Harrison introduced me and everyone I knew to the concept of meditating. He got all the Beatles and their friends doing it. Nowadays, everyone in this crazy, fast-paced, "ever-changing world in which we live in" knows about and has tried some form of contemplative or Buddhist prayer. If you're young, you turn to Buddha. In my case, my meditation has shifted from mantra to contemplative or Centering Prayer. Still, I was grateful to have practiced TM for ten years before discovering my adopted Catholic faith's practice of Centering Prayer as a method. I use the Aramaic word "Maranatha," which translates to "Come, Lord Jesus." While practicing TM, I used a Sanskrit word. I don't remember the word, but I saw an episode of *Curb Your Enthusiasm* where Larry David pleaded with his friend Richard Lewis to lend him his TM mantra. In that episode, Larry accidentally revealed the mantra, and I couldn't believe it was the exact same one I had. That means everyone had the same "secret" word that was supposedly given only to me. Son of a gun!!

However, in the mid-1970s, this mantra was all my college friend seemed to want to talk about during the last semester of my senior year. He told me I had problems. He said I owed it to myself to find nirvana or to have a satori to deal with all my panic and anxiety disorders. I can't quite remember which one now. Nirvana? Or satori? Both? I didn't think it would make any difference. I was sure I couldn't have one. I told him "I always seemed to have a hard time with metaphysics." I laughed to myself. If you can't smell it, I don't want it. Imagine—a freaking satori? What a strange guy my school chum was. Up until that time, I thought a satori was a specific star or maybe a member of the British Parliament. My friend was a science major, and he was taking a course in astrology or one of those related hard sciences, so why not consider a star?

But he got me thinking: Do I have problems? Is this guy kidding? Well, after five years of schooling—on top of the first fifteen or so—putting up with annoying teachers who refused to teach our generation the rules of grammar (the foundation of our language), having crushes on girls, getting caught for spitwads at first and dope later, discovering I needed to use a rubber on my weenie the first time I did it, after waiting as long as Moses did to find Canaan, moving away from home to starve for an education, get a job, and worrying about being drafted, how can anyone go through all this and not have a few problems? OK! OK! So, I have problems. So how will this mantra thing help me? I never trusted that "star" stuff. In fact, I hated that star stuff. I didn't understand that guy with the pointy ears trekking everywhere. What was his deal anyway? I also hated cartoons, fairytales, and musicals. In fact, I still haven't seen the three biggest musicals of all time: *West Side Story, Gone with the Wind,* or *Star Wars.* I know! I know! Some aren't musicals, but to me, they might as well have been. I haven't seen them.

If you can't smell it, I don't want it. Imagine—a damn satori! "Okay—Alright, Mr. School Chum Man! Take me to your guru or your leader. Take me to your Moonie. Take me to your "star."

And he replied in a soft, calm voice, "You've made the right choice, my tangled brother." "Tangled brother?" What??? I wanted to punch him for saying something so ridiculous. "Tangled?" But I suddenly caught myself and remembered that I was experiencing what kids nowadays call "the Imposter Syndrome." If that's a real thing, I can say that coming from the working class into a more intellectual college world, I didn't feel confident that I belonged there. I had spent much of my life feeling average and nothing special. I think Grandma taught me that. She would say, "You're better than no one, and no one is better than you." I still believe this, and I don't think I was taught correctly grammar anyway. Was "tangled" an adjective? Or a verb? An adverb? See? What the hell is an "adverb?" In my panic, I recalled the names of every grammar teacher, from Mr. Badachevski to Mrs. Wilson. I told my friend that I wanted "to find nirvana to cure my neurosis." I tried to act as calm as my friend. Soon, we were off to his center, which was in a dental office building on 13 Mile Road in Roseville. *Oh no—back to Mudville,* I thought.

When we arrived at the center, my friend introduced me to one of his teachers. What a joke this guy was! He was running around in bedroom slippers, trying to figure out where someone named "Bob" had put the clean handkerchiefs, fresh fruit, and flowers. I heard him yell, "Where's the rice?" from the back room. He claimed he was just about ready to start. This got my mind racing again. I was nervous once more.

What did this guy want to start? He had a damn hanky, a piece of fruit, and flowers and was screaming for rice, for God's sake. What was I getting involved with here?

I envisioned a world where everyone wore slippers, twirling handkerchiefs, and tossing fruit and flowers. I thought to myself, *Nice place you Moonies have here.* My calm friend overheard me and stepped hard on my toe. I wanted to smash his face, but I quickly remembered I was on "the road to bliss."

After the teacher found his belongings, he appeared serene and calm. I noted how nice and peaceful everyone in this cult was. As the teacher passed me again in the hallway, I made a mental checklist: one fresh handkerchief (not soiled), fruit (yes, two apples and a plum)—a plum? Is a plum a fruit? Okay, I guess it is. Flowers (pretty) and a one-pound package of Ann Page rice. *How thrifty,* I thought. Why are these calm types always thrifty? My grandmother called it "cheap." My friend was whispering something to another guy in slippers, and I was getting agitated.

No one had told me to bring slippers, and then it hit me. Oh no! A cult has kidnapped me. Those slippers meant that people stayed all night. I was going to have to stay all night? All night long with rice, flowers, a plum, and my slippers? I would be trapped with many calm, quiet men in slippers. I grew even more anxious. I had to escape. How had I let this happen? I had seen all the films, TV shows, PBS documentaries, and public service announcements about this kind of thing. But here, like a complete fool, I sat, trapped. In my senior year of college—damn it, a senior—and it was my last semester of school—forever. And what had I allowed to happen? I let some slipper-wearing cult kidnap me. My grandmother was going to be furious because, as far as I knew, the cult was not Lutheran. Grandma would say that after all that money for a liberal arts education, I should know the difference between a cult and a religion.

I was probably going to be expected to wear slippers all day and shop for stupid rice. Maybe I could convince my grandma that her clueless grandson was a sales rep for Ann Page products; after all, Ann Page is A & P, a major grocery company that my grandma completely trusted and respected, along with her beloved Sears. But no! It would all be a huge lie. I'd be a Moonie searching for meaning, and I had no idea what a Moonie was. My grandfather was an auto worker—UAW all the way. He understood unions, but he would never understand this. My ship would be sunk with my grandparents!

While my mind raced toward the finish line, my friend suddenly turned to face me. He seemed unusual. No, not just then; he simply looked peculiar. He appeared like a nerd. That's why he stayed calm—good grades, a Fred MacMurray-type father, and a mother as sweet as Donna Reed. What a charming TV family. I was sure I felt envious. But more than that, I was scared and quite jumpy. He stared deep into my eyes and asked if I was "ready." In a nervous twitch, I blurted out, "I-I-I only like rice for breakfast!"

He looked at me, puzzled, and said, "What?" I felt a little comfort: at least I wouldn't have to shop for rice right away. "Are you ready to learn your mantra?" he asked. I glanced at the door, aware it was locked. I just knew it—even if it wasn't! This place was likely tightly secured. There was no escape.

At that moment, the door opened, and the postman walked in. Just like that, he stepped inside. He dropped off some mail and turned to leave. This was the test. Would he actually be able to walk away? For a few seconds, I pictured buying rice, cutting flowers, and chanting mantras with a postman. Then, I recalled my grandmother saying, "You know, most postmen are alcoholics!" My God! I would spend the rest of my life chanting a mantra with an alcoholic mailman. My mind was racing! But before I could finish my nightmarish daydream, the mailman was gone.

My only chance for escape lay in the mailman's mailbag, but he had disappeared!

"Okay," I said, "Give me that stupid mantra." My hands were sweaty. I was breathing fast and hard. My friend asked me to follow him and the teacher to the back room.

He said, "Walk this way; it's easy, you'll see." I thought about how nice simple sentences were. Maybe I did learn a little grammar in school but screw it.

He took me into a dark room. He lit some incense and pulled out two apples and a plum from a drawer in the dark. I whispered, "I've seen that fruit before." He told me to try not to talk. He took a pinch of rice and placed it next to a small container of water. I wondered if it was holy water. Oh no—holy water meant Catholics. My grandma was really going to kill me. Not only was I in a cult, but I was also going to be a Catholic. That was even worse in her eyes.

I could almost hear her screaming, "There has never, ever been a Catholic in this family!" I curled my toes in fear. The teacher then began with some mumbo-jumbo that sounded like background dialogue from the movie *Gandhi*. I didn't understand it. He finally reached a word that must have had significance because he kept repeating it. Then, he asked me to say it softly and reached for my hand. *Shit*, I thought. Could this be a gay men's Catholic cult? I could hear my grandmother in the back of my mind.

But there I was in a room filled with incense, rice, holy water, fruit, flowers, a handkerchief, and a man in slippers asking, "to hold my hand" and chant a word that sounded something like "sha- woo." I didn't know what else to do, so I held his hand and started chanting, "sha-woo-sha-woo." However, the chanting created quite a decent rhythm, and I felt serene. It was working. It was simple. "Sha-woooooo." I was initiated.

When it was over, I watched with curiosity. The teacher then led me to a room and asked me to sit quietly, alone; my heart thumped in my chest like a hamster, and he told me to "keep saying the word sha-woo until you feel complete inner peace." As soon as he closed the door, I opened one eye and started to plan my escape. I felt good because I didn't think I had been brainwashed yet. In fact, I felt a serious sense of relief. But how would I get out? Could a guy who had just spent time in the dark with a man in slippers chanting sha-woo be sane enough to escape on his own? *Why not*, I thought; crazy people escape from mental institutions all the time. I was determined not to let my grandparents down. They had paid good money for my education, and if I could get through finals in one piece, even though I had problems, I would be happy, and they would be proud. On the other hand, if I couldn't escape or if I was brainwashed, where would I spend Thanksgiving Day, Christmas, and Easter? There was no way in hell my grandma was going to let a Catholic live in her house for any holiday. She would say, "I have my morals, you moron!" I would probably end up a vegetarian or, worse, a vegan. Aren't all these cult guys anti-meat? That would really piss my meat-and-potato grandpa off. He would tell my grandma that they had failed by sending me away to college and that college had turned me against a good Delmonico steak. What a darn shame this generation is, he'd think!!

I sat quietly for a moment as my calm friend slowly opened the door. He told me I had done well and had just given birth to my true conscience, which set me on the path to satori. I asked, "What about nirvana for my neurosis?" He replied, "That comes after you're dead!" I mumbled, "You mean when my grandparents find out about this when I go home?" He gave me another puzzled look.

I asked if I could leave the center. "Sure, anytime. In fact," he said, "I have an exam to study for now—bye!"

I had just dedicated my life to a cult, and he had an exam to study for. I thought these guys were all pretty slick, "smooth operators," as my grandma would call them. Kidnap a poet, brainwash him, and send him back into the world to recruit—all of this with "a dead word." At that point, I could see how easily people could stand on freeway ramps selling flowers or at shopping malls or concerts. Son of a gun—they had me!

Shelby & Shane Liebler during House Husband Years

Fela in Detroit (photo by Leni Sinclair)

JOHN LENNON

Fela and the Little Children

I'm just watching the wheels go round and round
—John Lennon

1981

For many summers when our children were young, I was a stay-at-home dad. I changed countless diapers, fed many bottles of Gerber's, packed numerous lunches, and spent many days enjoying fun times. We loved winter days at museums downtown by Wayne State, often drove around Belle Isle to see the deer, watched icebergs drift down the river, or strolled through the old streets of Detroit in the basement of the Detroit Historical Museum. I had become what my hero John Lennon transformed into in 1975—a stay-at-home dad. I wasn't trying to imitate John Lennon, but in retrospect, that's exactly what I had become, and I loved it just as he did.

One snowy, cold day, I decided it was time for the kids to enjoy a quality visit to the local record store, Car City Classics, in St. Clair Shores, one of the best in all of Metro Detroit. My kids and I spent many happy weekdays there afterward. I documented this first experience because it was a hilarious incident shared with my son and daughter. I often read this essay during readings in the early years, and my children loved hearing their names in a story.

For them, it felt like they had a part in a movie or their favorite cartoon. They giggled, or "chortled," because they remembered that day as I've recorded it here. So, here is the incident in question. A former editor remarked it made me seem like a bad father, but I believe Shane and Shelby would disagree with that assessment. It was a typical fun day together for us back then.

It's 7:30 a.m. I'm abruptly awakened by a loud scream from the living room. "Leo the Lion! Leo the Lion!" I'm furious. Horoscope signs flash in my mind; I recall that I'm a Virgo, and then I wonder why. Once more, "Leo the Lion!" I want to go back to sleep. I wish to resume my journey to satori, my pilgrimage to bliss, my path to God; my damn dream interrupted by some

S.O.B. named Leo. I hear my son chortling in the living room. I think about how I've always wanted to chortle. But I never truly understood what it was. I thought it was something only Lewis Carroll's characters could do, but now I'm not so sure. This kid is sitting in my living room, chortling. My first concern is that he doesn't wake his baby sister with his chortling. "Stop your darn chortling!" I yell from my bedroom. I lie there for a few more minutes, pondering why I'm suddenly using the word "chortle" on a weekday morning at 7:30. But it seems like a great word, and after all, it's my job to appreciate good words; it's an excellent word! Again, another shout of "Leo the Lion!" Okay—that's it. I jump out of bed, one eye pointing down, the other pointing up. I pause for a quick look in the bedroom mirror. I think I look just like Red Skelton doing one of his Gertrude & Heathcliff skits. I poke my head out of the bedroom door and yell down the hallway, "Shut up! Do you want to wake your darn sister?" I glance at the floor and chortle to myself.

"Dad," my son says, "will you play Leo the Lion with me?"

"Will I play with you? I thought you wanted to watch a cartoon."

"But Dad! I'm a raisin, and I live in Chicago." What? I wear a perplexed expression and think to myself, *These modern kids—they're all surrealists.*

Alright, I decide to humor him. "Why are you a raisin today?"

"Well, Dad," he replies, "you drank wine in Chicago with an obvious bird—didn't you?" Now, I am completely confused. I want to chortle just to channel Lewis Carroll. Eventually, I make my way to the living room to turn on the TV. Just as I find the channel for *Leo the Lion*, my son asks, "Dad, after this show, can I watch *All My Children*?"

I respond, "You are all my children!" Then he mentions that he likes bananas sometimes. I simply say, "Good—OK." At that moment, the baby starts crying in her crib. After scrunching my face, swearing to myself, and stomping around the living room table a bit, I muster the courage to enter her room and confront the poopy situation that will inevitably be in her overnight diaper. She has never let me down. Sure enough, the diaper is filled to capacity, and I'm the only one around to change it. I say, "Thank you, Lord," and get to the smelly task.

The next point of order is to make oatmeal, which is the house specialty. Just before I start cooking the oatmeal, I remember having quite a few poems to revise and a poetry reading to attend at 8:00 p.m. But none of this matters to these hungry "oatmeal heads." Just as I take out the saucepan, the baby pees her first diaper. I say "shit," but I quickly recall how important it is for me to breathe in the smell of pee every morning to make my day go right. And it does every time; it's like smelling salts for me. Once back in the kitchen, I fill the saucepan with cold water. As the water slowly boils, I begin pouring salt into it. At that moment, out of nowhere, I hear, "That's not enough salt, Dad." I quickly turn my head to find the source of the squeaky voice. I start to boil over, "What do you know about salt? You're only 3½ years old! Who do you think you are, Julia Child?" The kid gives me a look that could piss off a cabbie in New York City.

After the oatmeal is cooked, I put the baby in her highchair and the boy in a chair at the table. I ask my son what he wants on his oatmeal, and he tells me he wants honey. I tell him we've got no honey, and I fling open the cupboard doors to see what we can use to sweeten his breakfast. His eyes dart quickly to the top shelf; he spots the pancake syrup, and I spot it, too. I know exactly what this kid is thinking, and I yell, "No, you don't put pancake syrup on oatmeal!" He responds, "I know, Dad; I was only kiddin'." I feel defeated and mumble for him to "eat your darn breakfast," then I look over at the baby and say emphatically, "You too!" She blinks and looks at me, "I don't know what you're talking about, and I don't care."

After everyone is fed, I shower and attempt my now-famous one-eye-open meditation. I try to make the most of my mental solitude. I always ask God for strength first and peace second; I rarely get either. Somewhere near the end of my meditation, I get this crazy notion to visit the record store later if the day goes well. I mumble to myself, "God, why do you give me such a wild thought when I'm stuck with two kids all day?" It occurs to me that the devil might be behind this plan. Right after meditation, I find myself anxiously dressing two seemingly untamed children. I tell my son, being the older one, to put on his own jacket and shoes while I dress the baby. Just as I neatly get the baby tucked into her snowsuit and snow hat, she poops. "Damn it!" I scream. "You always poop. Why do you eat so much?" She blinks at me again, looking as though I'm the real turd. Finally, though, we manage to get everything together, and we're ready to go. I get everyone in the car, make sure the seatbelts are snug, and off we go. A short while later, we pull into the parking lot of the record store. I warn the kids not to act up and embarrass me at a hip place like the record store where cool people shop. The baby just blinks, and my son promises, "Yes, Dad!" I open the door with a big smile and walk in like a cool and relaxed father. The owner looks at me as if I'm just another record junkie with two brats. I start to lose confidence, but I smile and say, "I'm just in for a quick Fela stop. Did you get any Fela records today?" He walks away, apparently not wanting to deal with a chubby guy with two kids looking for African music. I make my way, with the two kids in tow, toward the international music section. I scan the aisle until I spot the African music. As I begin to thumb through the section, the baby wanders into the comedy section. I can still see her, so I don't worry. Remember, I'm used to pointing my eyes in different directions from my daily practice of Transcendental Meditation. Anyway, at that moment, my son spots a Fela album cover that we already have at home. His vision transports him into a tribal dance he once saw on a special edition of Sesame Street. A guy with a cowboy hat and Levi jacket peers over from the Country Western section.

He gives me a look like I'm just another "bleeding heart liberal" for letting my son do an African-style dance like that in public. I'm puzzled by his expression for a moment, but—oh crap—now I've lost the baby in "Comedy." I panic for a second until I hear her mumbling. She strolls around the aisle corner with a Phyllis Diller record in hand. I shout at her to "put that thing back." I remember again that she doesn't understand me. She seems glued to the record. My boy takes his dance on the road over to the "T's" in "Rock." I chase him, yelling, but I remember to look at a T-Rex album I've wanted to replace since my brother-in-law lost the original at an "End the War" party in the 1970s. I find *Electric Warrior* in the bin, but it's now a collector's item, costing an arm and a leg. I quickly wonder if the cowboy in Country Western is into buying black-market babies. The baby gives me a strange look, and now I feel guilty. "Can she read my mind?" I remember how I once read about a mind-reading baby in my aunt Ethel's *National Enquirer*. Anyway, I glance back at the record and start to mumble. I swear under my breath about my incompetent brother-in-law and how I'll never lend him another record. But he was in his 40s then and only listened to dentist-office music.

I shrug and drag the two kids up to the irritated guy at the cash register. He looks at me, then at the album by Fela, then at the kids, before looking back at the album and craning his neck for a closer look at the title. I say, "Yes, it's what you think it is." He snarls the title at me, "*Confusion? Part 1,*" then stares at my son. "And *Part 2?*" he asks, looking at my baby daughter. He looks back at me again. I shove $10.00 toward him and smile. He rings up the bill and hands me my change. I thank him with a smile and head for the door, using my usual hip walk and confident manner.

After the trip back, I pull into the driveway. The kids are just as anxious as I am to hear the new record. They squirm to free themselves from their seatbelts. As soon as we step inside the house, I put the record on and sit down to finish revising my poems. The two kids burst into a wild dance around the living room while I tap my foot and type. Suddenly, my son leaps onto my daughter's head. At that moment, I realize this is too much fun to be real. Right in the middle of this sibling chaos, the baby poops again. I'm irritated, but I also feel that justice has been served to her occasionally obnoxious brother. I giggle to myself; I'm on my fourth poem revision and my fourth diaper change of the day. Something makes me believe this is a divine revelation. I don't know right away what to do with this revelation, but I think it might inspire a story or a poem later. As I read through this draft, I feel I was right.

    In the baby's room, I carefully change her diaper, and try not to get any mess on my jeans or under my nails. After all, I still have a reading to attend. I shout to myself and my kids that I just can't write another line of poetry. Turning off the typewriter, I head to the bathroom to clean up for my poetry reading. The kids don't notice me; they are glued to the Disney Channel. I quickly grab a glass of Mr. Juicy (cherry flavored) and a handful of salted peanuts for dinner. My wife pulls in from work. I kiss her and the kids, then head out the door and into my car. I'm off!

    Again!

    I arrive at the poetry reading a little late. The emcee has just introduced a somewhat academic-looking poet. I think to myself, "God, I've changed too many diapers for this crap!" He begins a poem about a dead cat, a dead poet, and a "live cat that will never know kittens." What the heck? I look at the ceiling and then slap myself on the forehead. Phyllis Diller comes to mind, and I slowly and methodically rework one of her skits that I remember from the old Steve Allen Show. I chortle to myself. The people in front of me turn in unison and give me a nasty, snooty glare. I remind myself that, with two kids, I'm used to looks like this. They give me another dirty look. I try to ignore them and the academic poet, continuing to rework the skit until the end.

    It has been a long day, and I need to laugh—not to think. Driving back home after the reading, I recall the lyrics from John Lennon's "Beautiful Boy" on his final album: "Life is what happens to you while you're busy making other plans," and it truly is.

M.L. Preparing for first Public Radio Reading
at WDET in Detroit 1975 © Gregory Hallock

M.L. in his one-act play/film *Beneath Man's Integrity*, the start of
The Ridgeway Collective, Spring 1974 © Gregory Hallock

M.L. with Leni Sinclair and Dennis "Machine Gun" Thompson of the MC5 at Wayne State University

M.L. through the high school years 1969–1971

John Sinclair, Ed Sanders, and M.L.
after Book Beat Reading © Cary Loren

L-R: Bill Hulet, Peters Lewis (of Moby Grape), M.L.,
and Jeff Reynolds recording *The Coyote & the Monk* Album 2010
in St. Clair Shores at Detroit Radio Co. Studios.

M.L. in Munich 2015 with his German Coyote Monk Band with Detroit Monk Charlie Palazzola (center) © Leni Sinclair

M.L. on his way to Jail for Justice during the 1995 Detroit Newspaper Strike © Damon Hartley

Eminem Publisher Joel Martin and M.L.
in his backyard pool in Laurel Canyon, CA 2025

M.L. with English singer/songwriter
and Dead Ocean Recording Artist Bill Fay in North London

M.L. & Pete Brown (British Beat Poet and Lyricist for Cream) after a reading at the London Poetry Society

M.L. and Pete Brown in Abbey Road Studio's Canteen

M.L. with Michigan Poet Laureate Melba Joyce Boy

M.L. with Timothy Leary at William S. Burroughs' Birthday Celebration Lawrence, KS

HÜSKER DÜ

Candy Apple Zen Arcade & Beatniks in Kansas
with 10,000 Maniacs

1987

The year marked a pivotal turning point in many ways. As I boarded a plane to Kansas after a couple of quick cocktails in the Detroit airport lounge, I had no idea that a long, drunken weekend lay ahead of me—and shortly thereafter, the end of my alcohol consumption. This change wasn't solely a result of my time in Kansas; rather, I was approaching the end of my self-medication phase for my panic disorder. Redemption, if not recovery, was on the horizon.

I was heading to Lawrence, Kansas, after receiving an invitation from William Burroughs and Edie Parker-Kerouac to participate in Burroughs' River City Reunion. I was on my way to a weeklong event featuring many of my counterculture heroes. All the "talent" for the festival stayed at the Park Inn in Lawrence. The list of invitees included Allen Ginsberg, Robert Creeley, Timothy Leary, Anne Waldman, Ed Sanders, Jello Biafra, Marianne Faithfull, Stan Brakhage, Ed Dorn, Jim Carroll, and the house band for the week was Bob Mould's Hüsker Dü.

I became friends with Bob there because he was closest to my age and shared a genuine love for baseball. Punks, Beats, and baseball were my passions. We made tentative plans to catch a

Tigers game when the band played in Detroit shortly after the Reunion in Kansas.

This was intended to be a week-long party and gathering for hundreds of people. I was scheduled to give a reading at Kansas University during my stay, with events and performances happening at various venues throughout town, including art galleries, theaters, and clubs. Most people were friendly and welcoming. However, Jim Carroll turned out to be unpleasant. I ran into him at the university bookstore and excitedly told him that I was teaching his *The Basketball Diaries* in a Fall 1987 class I created at Wayne State University called "Beats, Hippies and Punks." His response was, "So?" I immediately fell silent out of embarrassment. Later that day, I called the campus bookstore in Detroit to cancel his book and instead added Ed Dorn's classic, the newly republished *Gunslinger*. As early as 1987, I began to express my displeasure with egomaniacal and unstable individuals, which I later realized was more the norm than the exception.

During this otherwise incredible reunion, I bumped into Allen Ginsberg on the street while looking for a bar to catch the Tigers' game. We had met a few times before, and he was always kind and open. But on that gray day on the street in Lawrence, he was a total jerk. A colleague at Wayne State was a huge fan of Ginsberg and asked if I could get his autograph for him. I confidently replied, "Sure—that's easy!" So, the opportunity presented itself nicely on a side street in Lawrence on a cloudy, warm fall Saturday afternoon. I approached Ginsberg holding a poster of one of his poems. I greeted him as a friend of his good friend, Edie Parker-Kerouac, to which he replied, "So?" He did sign the poster for my friend, but he quickly fell to the very bottom of my "shit list" until the day he died. This was probably unfair of me, but it was how I coped with "stars" like him. I have always struggled with people who are supposed to be or seem like one thing only to turn out to be another.

I suppose this reflects my J.D. Salinger upbringing. Once I read *The Catcher in the Rye* in seventh grade, there was no going back to the "phonies" in the world. From that point on, I felt I could sense them from a mile away. This led to my eventual reluctance to meet some of my heroes like Bob Dylan and Van Morrison. I loved them both so much that I feared great disappointment from a face-to-face encounter. I came within a couple of feet of meeting Van the Man at a Detroit concert in 2006 after being introduced to his longtime guitarist, John Platania, who created the iconic "Domino" and "Wild Nights" guitar licks back in Van's Woodstock days. I met John at a friend's Professor Louie and The Crowmatix Show. Louie was the person who revived The Band by producing, managing, and performing with them in 1993, and he was Rick Danko's touring companion and close friend. Professor Louie and his band invited me to a benefit show for a Connecticut community radio station that also featured John Sebastian and Artie Traum. Platania told me backstage that Van was a genuinely nice guy and that, in another life, Van wanted to be a comedian. I thought that was the strangest thing I'd ever heard, but John knew him well as he still tours and records with him. John then suggested that I come backstage to meet Van the following week at his first Detroit show in years.

In an unusual historical turn of events, Van almost grew up in my hometown of St. Clair Shores. Van's dad's sister lived in the Shores, and Van's dad came over to get a factory job and then send for his family. However, George, Van's dad, missed his family and Belfast too much, so he went home. I could have been competing against Van Morrison for Poet Laureate of St. Clair Shores. Insane! Upon leaving the Masonic Temple, I passed by a door with a sign reading "Back Stage." I pushed it open but quickly retreated. I thought, *Nope! I am not going through this door. I love Van too much*, and then images of Ginsberg and Carroll flashed in my mind. I wanted to keep my memories and ideas of Van Morrison pure, even if they were false. This lesson has held me back many times, but, clearly, there have been occasions when I opened that door to befriend my heroes. I've carried a working-class attitude that we are all equal in this life. I wanted to be as honest and truthful as possible with everyone I ever met and worked with in my life. I engaged with everyone, from students to strangers, from famous folks to locals. I listen to whatever they are discussing. It is my thing. When someone, whether after a class or a reading, is talking to me, they become the focus of my full attention. I'm not sure where I got this from, but it likely came from my grandma. She was kind to everyone and always said, "Michael! We Lieblers are lovers." I took that saying to heart and made it my life's theme. This may seem sentimental in my narrative, but it is true.

Anyway, I arrived in Lawrence, Kansas, in a purple haze of adrenaline and alcohol. We rented a car and headed to the River City Reunion to read, perform, and meet many of my Beat heroes. I brought two working-class friends from Detroit, Killer and Rudy. Killer flew in from Los Angeles, while Rudy and I traveled from Detroit to Kansas City. When we got to the Park Inn in Lawrence, we found it fully booked with all the reunion talent for the week. In the hallways, I would pass Allen Ginsberg, Timothy Leary, and Marianne Faithfull almost hourly. I remember the morning of my first breakfast sitting in the dining room, glancing around and seeing Ginsberg eating with Ed Sanders, Marianne Faithfull engaged in an intense conversation with Anne Waldman, and I ended up having my eggs with Fernando Saunders, the legendary bass player for Lou Reed's recordings and live shows. Fernando has performed all around the world with music legends such as Marianne Faithfull, Joan Baez, Slash, Tori Amos, Jimmy Page, Jeff Beck, and even the great Luciano Pavarotti. He was at the Reunion as Marianne Faithfull's accompanist. It turned out that Fernando was from Detroit and had attended Wayne State. My world was getting smaller and smaller.

I did my first reading for a large audience on Friday afternoon at the university. I performed some of my early poetry accompanied by a tape-recorded music track. I walked around the vast ballroom reciting my work. People received the performance well. In fact, I was both humbled and surprised by their response to my work. I was reading to all the elite beatnik hipsters of the world, gathered in a small town in Kansas. It all seemed to come together for me. I received many lovely compliments from notable guests like Ed Dorn and Ed Sanders. I was in Beatnik Hipster Heaven, so we headed to the bar, of course, to celebrate my good fortune. Are you, dear reader, noticing a drinking pattern developing here?

Anyway, as we were leaving the Kansas U Student Center Ballroom, we bumped into Timothy Leary. He was warm and friendly, so we invited him to join us at the bar, which he gladly accepted. That's when we found out that bars in Kansas were actually "clubs," and patrons had to be members. So we paid for our membership dues, including Mr. Leary's, and then started drinking and playing pool with some locals. Over time, I recall buying several rounds for the House. I may have misunderstood then, but as I remember, the beer and well drinks were quite cheap. Eventually, we had the entire bar singing along with the jukebox selections, using our pool cues as guitars and microphones. Leary joined in, too. He perked up when "Kick Out the Jams" (the clean 45 rpm version) played on the jukebox. Leary took Wayne Kramer's lead part on his pool cue. After the song, Leary told me he loved The MC5. In fact, he said they once played a house party at his California home. He asked if they were "still playing." He also inquired about John Sinclair, who had become a good friend just a couple of years earlier. I updated him on Sinclair and the Detroit scene. Then Leary perked up again and said, "Shit—I'm on a program at a movie theater here with Jello!" I thought to myself, *Is he talking about Jello Biafra of The Dead Kennedys?* Jello was their lead singer and an anti-censorship troublemaker. Yep! That's exactly the dude Tim mentioned. When he let us know, I looked up the program in my bag to see when it started. Oh shit! We had less than five minutes to get to the theater we'd never heard of because "we are NOT from Kansas!!" In the car, we talked endlessly. I remember glancing in the rearview mirror several times, watching and listening to Tim, "The Acid King," yammer on about politics, drugs, censorship, and the wonders of LSD. Our eyes locked during one of my glances in the rearview mirror, and it struck me, *Fuck—I'm in a car, drunk, in Lawrence, Kansas, with Timothy Leary?*

At that moment, I thought The Moody Blues were liars when they sang years ago, "Timothy Leary's Dead." *Dead?* I thought. He's in fucking Kansas right now. How is it even possible that he is "dead?!" This guy was more alive than you and me at that moment, and acid or no acid, he was as funny as hell. We pulled up in front of the Liberty Movie Theater in downtown Kansas. We saw the huge marquee announcing a "Lecture Today at 3 p.m. with Dr. Timothy Leary and Jello Biafra on Censorship in America." I noticed the guys in the backseat were trying to sober Leary up with a joint. I pulled up to the curb, the rental car door flopped open, and out rolled a stoned-to-the-bone Dr. Timothy Leary. He said, "Hey—aren't you guys coming in for the show? You can be my guests."

We replied, "Have a good show, Doctor." Someone slammed the door, and we returned to "the club" until closing that evening. When we arrived back very late at the Park Inn, the halls were packed with Beatniks, hippies, and punks gathered outside various doors holding court. Ginsberg was by one door reading a new poem he had just written, Leary and Jello were complaining about censorship to a stoned mini-audience, and I found myself squeezed into a hotel room next to Bob Mould of Hüsker Dü. Hüsker Dü was the house band, just as The Grateful Dead had been at the On the Road Kerouac Reunion in Boulder five years earlier. They played nightly at the town's hipster-punk club. Bob was newly sober, as he told me, and he was engaged in an internal battle with the band. He seemed sincere, honest, and very real to me.

I remember thinking, while inebriated, that I wanted to join him in sobriety for my children's sake, for my wife's sake, for my students, and most importantly, for my own sake. I was starting to hate the feeling of losing control and those awful cottonmouth hangovers in the mornings. Bob made sense to me that night, but even though I didn't quit right away, I was only six short weeks from deciding to end my self-destruction with alcohol. Bob seemed sharp and clear-headed, and he wanted to talk about literature, too. I liked that as well, but I had the weight of the drink shoved deep into my mouth. Damn it! Alcohol was once again interfering in my life. I feared I was becoming a bumbling fool in front of a Dü. I could certainly sense Bob's genuine warmth. I clearly remember him mentioning that things were rocky with The Hüskers. I assured him it was just a typical band phase. Hell, I was loaded—what did I know?

The biographical fact is that Hüsker Dü broke up following the sudden suicide of their manager, David Savoy, right after the Kansas gigs. They were set to start their Spring Midwest tour, which was scheduled to take them to Detroit later that fall. At that time, I had only their album, *Candy Apple Grey*. However, I loved discussing poetry, music, Husker Du, and our mutual friends in Minutemen, fIREHOSE, DC3, and others from their small indie LA label, SST Records. I also recall having a great conversation about our shared passion for baseball. It turns out Bob was just as big a baseball fan as I was. We planned to catch a Tigers game in the weeks ahead at the Old Tiger Stadium when the Dü was set to perform at St. Andrews in Detroit, the still-cool alternative venue for music. The baseball game never happened, and shortly after the River City Reunion, Hüsker Dü ceased to exist. I was disappointed to hear they had split up, but I thought this might free Bob since he seemed quite troubled by how poorly things were going in late September 1987. It was over for them as a band, and alcohol was soon to be over for me as a poet.

    Thank God! Thank you, Bob Mould, for inspiring me to kick the bottle once and for all that warm night in Kansas. You never know who might end up saving your life.

Robbie Robertson of The Band © John Mathew Smith, Creative Commons
Gene Clark and Rick Danko in Detroit © Frank Pettis
Poet, Author, Jack Driscoll © Creative Commons

ROBBIE ROBERTSON

with Gene Clark, Jack Driscoll, & J.D. Salinger

> *Who else is gonna bring you a broken arrow?*
> *Who else is gonna bring you a bottle of rain?*
>
> —Robbie Robertson

1988

By Christmas Eve of 1985, I was a 32-year-old man filled with anxiety, unable to heal myself or rely on anyone else. I was exhausted from feeling sick and tired. My drinking was genuinely starting to trouble me, and I was certain it bothered my wife as well, who had been my best friend since I was 15. It made me feel cheap, irresponsible, and out of control. She was close to ending the marriage, as she later told me. I sensed it, I guess. It was time to grow up, be a responsible father and professional, and begin practicing what I preached to my students: "Analyze and know thyself."

One major thing I couldn't accept about myself was using alcohol to self-medicate for my anxiety and panic. I had recently been rescued by *The Phil Donahue Show* while being a stay-at-home dad, cleaning the house and changing countless diapers. I was making the bed with a slight hangover, as I recall. A "slight hangover" is like having a "slight heart attack." Is there really such a thing? My children were only 5 and 2 years old. They didn't really know me yet. I had our portable TV set on the dresser in our small bedroom. It was tuned to Phil's show, and the sound was low. As I made the bed, I heard the guest discussing some of the same experiences I had been facing since I turned 17. That summer, I was turning 32. Almost half my life had been spent in terror and fear of the unknown. I genuinely believed I was having the dreaded (and often discussed in my youth) "LSD acid flashbacks." How could I explain this to my grandmother?

We didn't keep anything stronger in our house than black licorice or Butterfingers. She'd never understand pot or, for God's sake, an "acid flashback." No one in my family would have comprehended that back then. So, I developed my own ailment. Everything became, "my sinuses are making me dizzy." Always horrifying dizziness just before slipping down the rabbit hole of life and the universe. Dizziness became my primary symptom of "anxiety" or "panic attack." I learned all this from Phil. I had no idea. No one did. There was an older woman doctor in the UK named Claire Weekes. She wrote a book about this new phenomenon now widely known as "panic attacks and panic disorder." I had to wait through the Hostess Bread commercial and a Dial soap ad to learn her name and the book title. The book was titled *Peace from Nervous Suffering* (1983). I quickly packed up the kids, placed them in their car seats, and raced to New Horizons Bookstore in my neighborhood. I ordered the book. I wanted to know more about this affliction that I had experienced since my teenage years and that I had been self-medicating with alcohol. I knew there had to be a better way to cope with this than having drinks. When I drank, honestly, I didn't know if I was dizzy from the alcohol or my anxiety. I thought that alcohol could be my ticket to a long, happy, panic-free life, but it was not!

Panic was an ongoing battle for me. I prayed, I meditated, and I bargained with God to relieve me from depression. I told Him that if He made me a famous writer and freed me from alcohol and panic attacks, I would write poems for Him for the rest of my life, making Christ the centerpiece of my work. "Blah, blah, blah." I'm pretty sure that was His response (for liberal readers, it was Her response). However, I'm convinced God made that dismissive gesture with His hands every time I spoke on this topic. I sank deeper into my depression each time I used alcohol to calm my nerves and stave off my panic. I felt like Holden Caulfield, viewing myself as a big "phony." With two young children, I felt like Ray Milland's character in *The Lost Weekend*. I didn't like that grimy feeling of having a hangover while watching my kids.

Another serious issue I had with drinking was my feeling of being a "big phony" in the classroom. I never drank on the job; I never felt the need or urge to do so. I built my classes on being honest, open, and serious in our discussions about who we are as people. I used stories, poems, and creative nonfiction to open doors and help us all explore who we were as humans living in this complex and uptight world. I always tell my students that after reading a good piece of literature, we should be asking, "Who am I?" and "What should I now become or do?" My class discussions always center around these two questions. The drinking crutch, I felt, made me less than honest with my students, my readers, and myself. I didn't like it! I know many teachers don't see it this way, but I take being a role model for my children, my students, and my audiences very seriously. J.D. Salinger damaged me as a young teen. I hated anything phony, especially since I was a big phony myself. Marijuana only intensified my Salinger complex as a post-*Catcher in the Rye* teen. Every time I smoked a joint in my early adult days, I noticed phoniness in others and in the rampant societal issues of the 60s, but funny enough, I didn't see it in myself. "I was blind, but now I see." It became clearer with every drink I consumed to combat my overwhelming panic.

Finally, I reached my lowest point on Christmas Eve 1985. I broke down around 2:30am. I felt lost, dejected, lonely, like a fraud, and a dreaded "phony." I was preaching one thing and doing another, so instead of asking God to help me write poetry for Jesus, I completely collapsed, realizing the former wasn't working for the Lord. I totally caved and cried out, "God, save me! I don't care about writing this poetry nonsense. God, what does a working-class kid raised by factory-working grandparents know about poetry anyway?" Then I leaned back and said, "Take it away! God, I don't want it." Save me from this panic, the self-medication with alcohol, and the loneliness and misery I felt, and I said "Lord, I will serve only you. I want to surrender everything to you, and I'm willing to give up my poetry too. I don't care about these things anymore, God!"

Strangely, and I swear this is true, God responded to me clearly, saying, "You don't have to give up your poetry, you asshole!" He whispered, "You just needed to realize that you aren't the one in charge, and this life isn't about you." He asked, "M.L., would you just let go and allow me to handle these things from now on?" Then He promised, "Would you let me take care of all the nonsense, and you just do the work that matters?" I could almost feel the "Christmas Eve alcohol" being flushed from my blood by the Holy Spirit. I sobered up, recited the Lord's Prayer by the light of the early morning Christmas tree, and quietly slipped into bed, leaving behind my "old self." I finally left it all behind forever that early Christmas morning. I left the old, tired me in the alcohol dream of the ghost spirit under our family Christmas tree.

I didn't completely give up drinking right away. That would happen on Halloween Eve 1987 while hanging out with Mike Watt and the fIREHOSE boys at Paycheck's in Hamtramck. I never got drunk from alcohol again after that Christmas Eve, and—best of all—I never experienced another hangover. Saved? Amen, I say, Amen!

I have been liberated beyond all expectations, and I'm never going back down that shit-covered road, a paved rabbit hole of doubt, despair, loss, and chaos again. I have long desired to be free of any substance that had control over me: cigarettes, drugs, alcohol, and eventually food. It's not going well on the food front, but the others are only distant memories that I struggle to write about now. The long and short of it is: no one ever heard of an M.L. Liebler before 1987. After my final lovely drink at the Union Bar in Hamtown, my literary star rose beyond my expectations.

My longtime friend Tim McGorey recently mentioned he saw my face on the marquee at the Music Hall in Downtown Detroit. He asked, "Did you ever think one day you'd be up on a major theater marquee?" I told him, "Hell, Tim, I didn't think I'd be alive now."

Three things contributed to my full recovery and my moment of self-actualization. First and foremost was my deepening faith in God and Christ. The second factor was my friendship with my hero, poet Jack Driscoll from Interlochen in Upstate Michigan. I had the chance to see Jack read alongside the esteemed American poet W.D. Snodgrass, another poetry associate I met years later when I hosted him in Detroit. Both Jack and W.D. delivered remarkable readings. A couple of years later, I ran into Jack in Royal Oak at The Poetry Resource Center, where he gave another outstanding reading.

After his performance, we sat down for an engaging one-on-one chat. Jack, a recovering alcoholic himself, shared with me, "M.L., once the alcohol washes out of your body, everything you see, feel, touch, and taste will become poetry—real poetry!"

The final spiritual piece of the M.L. puzzle came from a man named Robbie Robertson. I didn't meet him until many years later when I included him in my Detroit music poetry anthology *R=E=S=P=E=C=T.* Robbie Robertson was part of the iconic Woodstock group The Band. On his self-titled solo album released in 1987, Robbie sang about redemption, faith, saving grace, and the richness of life. In tribute to Robbie's contribution to the M.L. puzzle, I partially used one of his lyrics from that album for the title of my 2000 book, *Written in Rain: New & Selected Poems 1980-2000*, published by Mifanwy Kaiser's Tebot Bach Press in Los Angeles.

Robbie's lyric in a beautiful song he wrote in memory of his bandmate Richard Manuel, after Richard committed suicide, expressed something like how he "didn't believe it was all written in sand." It was then that I realized that my life had been "written in the rain," where that rain represented both the washing away of my past mistakes and pain through the metaphorical baptism of the Holy Spirit. Amen again!

Now, my life was ready to take off. During the summer of 1988 (long after my last drink), I heard The Byrds were scheduled to perform at a small bar near Wayne State's campus. I had always loved The Byrds, so after my early evening class, I went to see this version of the band. It was Gene Clark's group using the name The

Byrds. After that summer class, *I thought, Oh, hell, I am going to see The Byrds.* I drove to the venue, parked, and went inside. By that point, I was completely done with drinking. I watched closely as my longtime Byrd hero Gene Clark performed songs from "Turn, Turn, Turn" to "Mr. Tambourine Man" to "Eight Miles High" to "Silver Raven." I stood at the back of the small venue, and it felt as if Gene frequently looked at me throughout the show. It began to seem like he was focusing on me more than a performer typically does with a member of the audience. I thought about it, but I didn't dwell on it too much. During his performance, Gene spoke very positively about God, Christ, the Holy Spirit, and love between songs, especially toward the end of the show. I later learned that he had gotten sober in 1987 and was a Catholic. To close the lengthy set, he performed an extended version of "Knocking on Heaven's Door," which included quite a bit of preaching. When the show ended, I felt fulfilled. It was a fantastic event, as I had always been a huge fan of Gene and The Byrds.

The bathroom in the small venue was just behind the stage. As I navigated through the crowd to head to the restroom, Gene grabbed my arm and placed his hands on my shoulder. He looked me in the eyes and said, "You know what I've been talking about all night, don't you? You know exactly what I meant."

I did. I replied, "Yes—yes, Gene, I actually do know what you were talking about."

He exclaimed, "I knew you did!" I was amazed, stunned, and slightly in shock, but I really had to pee.

I said, "Gene, I really have to pee now, but we'll talk when I come out." When I exited the bathroom, he was surrounded by fans seeking autographs (cell phone cameras didn't exist back then). I quietly squeezed past, thinking we would connect again somehow down the road.

I was "feelin' a whole lot better" as I walked to my car. To me, it was one of my early "God Moments." It meant a great deal. Not too many years later (1991), I read in the paper that Gene Clark had passed away. I felt a pain in my soul, but I will never forget that time in a small music club in Detroit when Gene Clark "set me free" that time.

M.L. with Edie (Frankie) Parker-Kerouac

Tom Waits Public Mural by Dan Dalton for DanDaltonArt.
Photo © Gregory Booth Hallock

TOM WAITS

Jack & Neal, Edie, Tom, & Me

Wasted and wounded, it ain't what the moon did.
—Tom Waits

1979

I hate health food, but my wife loves it. So, what was I doing in an Eastside Detroit health food restaurant called Ruby Taboo? I had been there once before, so I agreed to join my wife and her best friend for dinner. That year, I was working on my M.A. at Oakland University, which gave me plenty of time to hang out, drink wine, and not worry about where the night would lead. It started with something I dislike (health food), and then I unexpectedly met a Beat hero I knew little about, and it all happened entirely by chance.

We were seated in the owner's exclusive back room, reserved for friends and regular patrons like my wife and her friend, Mary Jo. We had ordered our squash apple vegetable dish—it makes me nauseous just to think about it—and we opened the bottle of wine we were permitted to bring into the restaurant. I was gazing at the walls in Ruby's back dining room when I remarked, "Man, this place looks like somewhere Jack Kerouac might have hung out."

"What did you say?" the chef-owner inquired.

I simply responded, "With all these vintage black-and-white photos from the 1950s on the walls, the whole vibe could be straight out of a Kerouac novel."

First, a bit of background. I knew very little about Jack Kerouac and the Beat Generation during the early to mid-1970s. I remember hearing the Detroit poets of that time mention his name often. I recall thinking to myself, "I don't know who this Kerouac guy is, but if these lousy poets think he's good, he must be just as bad!" Wrong! My best friend and my wife's cousin, Jeff, had studied the Beat Generation and Kerouac in his Contemporary American History class. Many years later, he suggested that we take a closer look at Jack and Neil, mentioning that they were pretty cool guys. He handed me his paperback book, *Kerouac: A Biography* by Ann Charters, which I didn't properly read until later that night after a gallon jug of cheap red wine.

So, the chef-owner says, "It's really funny that you mentioned that because Edie Parker is in the front room, eating with her friend Henry Kingswell," a well-known cutting-edge journalist from Detroit in the 60s who wrote for *The Detroit Free Press* and edited the then-hip, recent *Metro Detroit Guide Book*. This book was the precursor to something like Andy Linn's *Belle Isle to 8 Mile: An Insider's Guide to Detroit*.

Anyway, the chef asked if I would like to meet Edie and Henry. I was stunned. I knew of Henry and his connection to the underground press first, and then The Detroit News later, but Frankie Kerouac? Really—Jack Kerouac's first wife is in the front? I thought, How can this be? Now, keep in mind, I knew very little to nothing about Kerouac and the Beats—other than what I gathered from Tom Waits's songs and seeing many of his live shows.

I mustered as much courage as I could and said, "Sure! I would love to meet her." I was thinking this guy must have added too much "cumin or turmeric" to his dishes—or maybe too much pot out by the dumpster in back? "What in the world would Edie Parker-Kerouac be doing in an eastside Detroit health food restaurant?" I wondered. "Okay, this is weird, but let's go meet this alleged 'Jack Kerouac's first wife.'" I made imaginary two-fingered quotation marks in my mind. I gulped down another glass of the wine we brought in under the then-trendy BYOB rule at the restaurant, and we left the backroom's seclusion to head to the main dining area to meet a living, breathing Kerouac. "This is insane," I mumbled to my more-than-slightly inebriated self.

The chef, Victor, gently touched Frankie Kerouac on the shoulder and said, "This is Detroit poet M.L. Liebler, and he'd like to meet you and say hello."

Frankie turned around and, with a warm, inviting smile, replied, "Nice to meet you, Detroit poet M.L. Liebler. This is Henry Kingswell."

Since I had heard of Henry and his journalism background, I was thrilled to finally meet him in person. Henry pulled the cheap jug of wine up from under the table, and the old-school Beat gathering began just as it likely had in *On the Road*, or so I imagined with my limited understanding of the subject. I remember we talked for hours that night until the restaurant had emptied. Then, Victor (like Rocky Pioggi, the bartender in The Iceman Cometh) swept around our table, seeming more than ready to turn off the lights and lock the front door.

Frankie invited me to her guest house the following afternoon, which was situated behind the renowned Dupont Mansion on Lake Shore Drive and Fisher Road, an exclusive park in Grosse Pointe. When I visited her the next day, she showed me photographs, letters, and a painting by Jack. As our friendship developed after our initial meeting, Frankie became a part of our family. Since she did not have children, our two kids became hers. Over the years, Aunt Frankie gifted them wonderful presents, stuffed animals, and more.

In 1982, I helped Frankie put together a book featuring photos and drawings of Jack Kerouac, along with writings from other living Beat Generation figures through my Ridgeway Press.

Frankie had been invited to participate in the 30th anniversary of *On the Road* at Naropa's Jack Kerouac School of Disembodied Poetics in Boulder, Colorado. We created a charming little chapbook titled Save the Frescoes that Are Us, inspired by a poem by Frankie within the book. Ridgeway resident fine artist Jeff

Ensroth designed a striking cover for this limited-edition chapbook. Frankie was invited as a special guest and close friend of Allen Ginsberg to speak at the conference. Her old gang from Columbia University was there too: Herbert Huncke, Lucian Carr, Gregory Corso, and William Burroughs, along with Ken Kesey, with whom I would later in life take bowling after we did a radio show in Michigan.

When we left the radio station that evening, Kesey said, "Let's go bowling." I thought what the hell? We bowled for a while and mugged for the camera. I remember telling the guy taking our pictures to capture a shot of us with our bowling balls, and I titled the photo "Take the Acid Head Bowling."

Alongside Edie's old friends were her new friends, including Lawrence Ferlinghetti, Diane di Prima, The Grateful Dead, and many others. The week was filled with classic Beatnik fun and antics. The film *What Happened to Jack Kerouac?* was filmed there that week, and all the usual gang, including Edie, were interviewed for the film.

So, Edie sold 300 copies of our chapbook at the conference for $20 each. The book was well received by the Beats and the audiences; in fact, she sold out. The book is currently an expensive collector's item on eBay.

Shortly after Edie returned from Boulder, I introduced her to the music of Tom Waits. Tom Waits was a poet and musician my buddy Jeff had first shown me in the early to mid-70s. One day during our janitorial shift at Sears in the Macomb Mall, he told me he had seen this guy on *The Mike Douglas Show* the day before, who had a gravelly voice and performed with just a sax player. Waits did a song about "Small changes being rained on with his own .38." That resonated with me at the time. I had been wanting to combine music and poetry to inspire more people. I always thought that if a blue-collar, unrefined guy like me could write it, anyone could. I still believe that everyone can and should write poetry.

Anyway, Jeff told me about this guy, then he demonstrated, "It went something like this, in his best Louis Armstrong slurred voice, 'Small changes got rained on with his own .38.'"

I was stunned. I was completely sold on this guy without even hearing him. I immediately ran to the local record store and bought Tom Waits's Small Change album with the half-naked stripper on the cover. Holy crap! This was a Beat dream come true for a newcomer to the Beats' history. Soon after, Jeff and I wanted to see him live. We heard he was playing at the non-restored Michigan Theater in the spring of 1975 in Ann Arbor. My cousin was attending the University of Michigan, so we had her get us tickets, and we began counting down the days until the show. We had very close seats, and as I recall, only about a third of the theater was filled, but Tom was truly amazing live. I became a fan and Tom's advocate right away.

I remember trying to introduce the great Detroit public radio broadcaster Martin Bandyke to him in the early 1980s when I was on one of his shows. I asked him to play "Kentucky Avenue" from his 1978 album *Blue Valentine*. I thought the lyrics fit the theme of my poetry. At that time, he said he wasn't "that into Tom Waits." That was all Martin played after he heard *Frank's Wild Years* in 1987. Hmmm. Things change.

Shortly after *Rain Dogs*, I lost interest in his work for a period. I wasn't fond of all the clanging and electronic sounds accompanying *Rain Dogs*. I sensed that shift with *Frank's Wild Years*; it could have been one of those moments when everyone uncovers your secret (like when we first heard the album Boys and saw U2 in concert in 1979). There were "Nobodies" who swiftly transformed into instant somebodies, and die-hard fans often drift away from bands during such times.

Anyway, before his style changed, I took Frankie to see and meet Tom. It was clear from his lyrics and demeanor that Waits was a huge fan of the Beats, and we saw him perform at The Royal Oak Music Theater. This was well before *Rain Dogs*. At that point in his career, Waits was still the Beatnik, gravelly-voiced singer with streetlights and gas station pumps on stage. We passed a note backstage after the show through a roadie, hoping Frankie could meet Tom in person. I thought Tom would have many questions for her about the Beats' early days. However, that was not meant to be. One week later, Frankie received a letter from Tom apologizing that the theater staff did not deliver the note to him sooner. He mentioned they would meet at his next stop in Detroit. Frankie got the impression that Tom was my "best friend." I told her we had never met and I was just a fan.

About a week later, Edie gave me Waits's letter, and I wrote back to Tom at his address in Los Angeles. Soon, Tom sent me a note saying he was moving to New York City with his new wife, Kathleen Brennan. He mentioned they were working on a new play called *Frank's Wild Years*.

He described the story and score as a blend of Jacques Brel and *The Flintstones*. Tom provided his new address on 3rd Street in the West Village and his phone number. He invited me to call him if I was ever in New York City. Amazing! This was a few years before my New York City poetry reading phase.

I ended up seeing *Frank's Wild Years* when it premiered at the Steppenwolf Theater in Chicago. It was a one-of-a-kind play, to say the least. It felt like a musical poem featuring actors and was inspired by Waits' life and adventures. Tom was in the cast, and I hoped to meet up with him in Chicago, as he lived there for some time during the previews and the run of the play, where he played the lead role, Frank. At that time, I was participating in several readings in Chicago, which made me quite familiar with the art scene in the Windy City. My Chicago poetry friends mentioned that Tom and Kathleen were quite visible around the city.

Many years later, I began participating in multiple readings throughout Los Angeles and Orange County. One venue I connected with and continue to be involved in annually is Beyond Baroque, which serves as LA's counterpart to New York's St. Mark's Poetry Project. I discovered that Tom Waits started his career by participating in poetry open mics there. I think of this every time I share the stage at that fantastic venue in Venice, California. In many ways, my numerous Beat experiences can be traced back to my close friend Jeff and my dear, beloved Edie "Frankie" Kerouac.

Shortly before Edie's passing in October 1993, she was involved in the release of the Beat Generation box set by Rhino. Rhino hired her for a promotional signing at a location in Detroit. Edie invited me as her guest to interview her, read some of Kerouac's work, discuss the Beats, and hold a question-and-answer session with her. We did this at a new concept: a "coffeehouse" in Royal Oak; this was long before Starbucks became ubiquitous and before Royal Oak transformed into a chic and popular place to hang out. It was a wonderful evening. The café was packed; everyone wanted to see Edie. She had become a local legend.

At the end of the program, as we sat alone at a table, Frankie pulled out her only copy of *Save the Frescoes* from her purse. She said, "I want you to have my only copy." I had long since lost my own copy, so I graciously accepted it. I brushed aside thoughts that Edie might know something about her health that I didn't. Edie passed away shortly thereafter.

As it turned out, one of my Beat-inspired students at Wayne State, Paul Trombley, took care of her in her final days. He called me the night she passed away from St. John's Hospital in Detroit. He said, "Our Edie is gone." I was grateful that he was there with her at the end. He was a good kid. I remember going downstairs to my library to hold and look at my small, treasured, stapled chapbook that the two of us worked feverishly on putting together in the Spring of 1982 for the Summer Kerouac *On the Road* conference in Boulder. All hail the good, the bad, and the freakiness of the Beats—now and forever!

Ray Manzarek of The Doors & Michael McClure

THE DOORS

Ten Feet to China

"Break on Through to the Other Side"

1991

By early spring 1991, I was done. I was fed up with two major aspects of my life. While my teaching and poetry career was cranked up to eleven on the volume knob of eternity, my anxiety and panic levels overwhelmed my mind, pushing my life past 20. My indecision and reluctance to commit to Catholicism felt like both bashing my head in and kicking my ass, both physically and spiritually. I had been sober for nearly five years by then, but I couldn't find a way to enjoy the proverbial fruits of my labor. I needed to find "shelter from the storm" somehow, and I needed to embark on that long road back to freedom and liberation—and, most importantly, to myself.

I longed for the Alan-Watts-style-life—minus the alcoholism and other demons I discovered much later. Since 1967, I had been attempting to establish some form of spiritual security in my life. I wanted Watts' "bliss" and the "natural" high he expressed in his talks and philosophy.

Alan Watts' blend of Buddhism and Christianity became my personal koan. Someday, I hoped and prayed to feel high just from living my own life without external influences. I aimed to move beyond drugs, alcohol, and cigarettes. That seemed to be what Alan had achieved. Alan was my underground radio hero on Sunday mornings. He was both an Episcopal pastor and a Zen master. That's what I mean by referencing the 60s. Picture that nowadays. No—skip that. Don't picture that nowadays. I don't want my parish priest to also be a Zen master. OMMMMMMMMEN!

Help me Jesus! I wanted to fill my cup with spiritual enrichment and peace without using anything to alter my mind. By Christmas of 1969, I had stopped my experiments with the LSD Acid Tests after one final dose of psilocybin just before the holidays. At 17, I had experienced highs beyond what any mind-expanding drugs made by man could provide. O beautiful false reality—I bade goodbye and good riddance that Christmas to acid trips…or at least until 1972.

In spring 1972, I took half a hit of pure Windowpane LSD while diligently working on the McGovern campaign in March 1972. I was 18 years old and had just been elected as a Democratic precinct delegate for my area in St. Clair Shores. I was on my way to changing the system from within. Yeah, right! I later learned in party politics that this wasn't possible. But that's the beauty of youth. Everything seems feasible until reality kicks in, pushing you to reinvent a fresh approach to change, or at least that's how I faced life. But back to that crisp, sunny spring day spent on a windowpane, munching on Burger King Whoppers and discussing political, cultural, and national change with my one good tripping buddy, who could only wrap his head around "Summertime Blues" by Blue Cheer for hours on end.

Man, this life was going to be a drag with several decades of life left, and I am stuck expanding my mind with a moron listening to pre-pre heavy metal music. That moron would die a few years later from a heroin overdose in a rundown trailer park in St. Clair Shores. I should have stayed in the McGovern campaign office that day, but I enjoyed some of the trip (except for the Blue Cheer). I realized life was far from enjoyable after spending over ten hours tripping my brains out while reading and re-reading Dr. Richard Alpert's (Ram Dass') book, *Remember - Be Here Now*, which I had bought at a trendy bookstore on the east side of Detroit, across from the old Harper Theater (now Harpo's—a heavy metal club). Wow! That friend was really ahead of his time all those years ago.

After ten hours of that nonsense, I taught myself that I'd sure as hell better "heal thyself." Baba Ram Dass, Alan Watts, and Timothy Leary would not save me from anything, least from myself. *Oh well*, I thought (and still do), *back to my search for God after McGovern's clock-cleaning election loss.*

All of this is part of the larger story of how I ultimately found God and gained full control over my anxiety and panic in 1991. I transitioned from being able to walk only 10 feet without experiencing a panic attack in my psychiatrist's parking lot to traveling solo all the way to China and exploring this vast world many times since then. The unusual soundtrack for this chapter of my journey was R.E.M.'s "Losing My Religion." Although the song discusses "losing my religion," I was truly blossoming into my own redemption.

Three significant events occurred in 1991 that seemed interconnected in various ways, bringing my life full circle. First, I finally decided to heed my family physician's advice and see a psychiatrist for my panic disorder. He referred me to Dr. Walter Guevara. The wheels of grace were already turning when I discovered that Dr. Guevara's special research area at Wayne State was in "Anxiety and Panic Disorders." At that time, this was a new area of concern and study. It was, akin to the current fashionable mental illness of bipolar disorder. Along with ADD, these are the major issues many people seem to struggle with in 21st-century America. In a few more years, we'll likely discover a new disorder for young people to grapple with—sort of the peanut allergies of their time. I don't know exactly what it will be, but it'll probably be a combination of the cell phone merging with the flesh of their hands, manic depression, Tourette syndrome, and Asperger's all rolled into one. They will be so attached to their cell phones that they will become an extension of their reality; they will experience manic depression (not in the good Jimi Hendrix way—which would really rock!), and their sole focus will revolve around their devices, texting, tweeting, and whatever the latest underground Facebook coding is. They'll know every ringtone in existence, yet remain clueless about who the president is, why Republicans took away their healthcare after years of having it, or anything that truly matters to their pursuit of happiness and liberty. They will be able to recite their friends' emails, associated ringtones, and trending topics on Instagram. Oh sweet progress—what have you done? And I was worried about a silly little panic back in 1971.

In retrospect, an old-fashioned panic attack might be just what the doctor ordered for many kids today, considering the immense lack of attention, knowledge, and future hope generated by this new mania. It could be called some name that Maury Povich, Dr. Oz, and Dr. Phil will invent.

None of these TV characters are real doctors, by the way; Phil is merely a lawyer, for heaven's sake! Dr. Oz promotes untested health products and has a strange emphasis on decent crudité, while Maury is simply your average Povich hoping to be the next Jerry Springer, becoming the authorities on all our issues. They'll be diagnosing Oprah and this new generation. They'll find Oprah's struggles with her weight to be pretty small potatoes compared to this bizarre new trend, all of which occurred before fascism came to America.

So, I went to my first appointment, and the good Dr. G asked, "M.L.... How far do you think you could walk by yourself on my sidewalk toward the main street without having a panic attack?" I pointed to a spot about 10 feet from his window. Okay, good; he noted it in my chart. He prescribed an anti-depressant that's somewhat outdated these days, like those hoops kids used to wear for braces when I was in elementary school in the 60s. You know, I don't see them much anymore, but it seems like everyone has braces now.

Dr. Guevara mentioned that new research indicated that, for some unknown reason, this antidepressant altered the chemicals responsible for releasing fear in the human brain. If my issue was a chemical imbalance, this could restore my brain chemistry to its original state. I wasn't sure if that was a positive thing, but I wanted to take that chance. I was tired of spiraling out of control, trying to escape from myself, and drinking too much beer to numb and self- medicate. I had come to realize that Rilke was 1000%

correct when he wrote, "You must change your life." I prayed that "a change was going to come," to quote Sam Cooke. The change finally arrived in the spring of 1991 when I met Dr. Guevara at his Roseville office, and I never would have imagined a place like my old Mudville could save me. But why not Mudville? This is where it all began. I was raised there for a couple of years, but I consciously forgot old Mudville.

However, I do remember my fondest memories of kissing, or at least trying to kiss, Mary Hawes behind her odd, old, doorless shed. Once, when Mary wouldn't kiss me at six years old, I found some stick matches and kept striking them on the box, throwing them into that old, always-open shed door. Soon enough, the piles of newspapers and rags caught fire, and the whole thing went up in flames like a stack of hay. I guess I was trying to "light my fire," so to speak, many years before The Doors and the church door Molotov Cocktail incident in 1967, but it makes sense in hindsight. I ran into the woods behind the shed where I had attempted to kiss Mary. She freaked out. So, in my juvenile mind, I thought I was showing this five-year-old a true sign of my affection by burning down her shed. Indeed, she'd see how much I loved her at age five, and she would want to kiss me. Boy, that was a terrible idea to try to win this girl's heart. Then it hit me that attempting to kiss a playmate wasn't a good thing to do to an apparently unwilling kid.

My psychiatrist set me on the path to reclaiming the person I was before the panic attacks started at age 17. He explained that my issue seemed to arise from the chemistry in my brain, and this one antidepressant, Tofranil, appeared to balance those chemicals to prevent the dreaded panic attacks. I was on the road to recovery and a normal life— well, as normal as a poet, activist, type A busybody could be.

It was around this time that I began to consider something a good Lutheran would never think about or even remotely contemplate. I decided I could accept being Catholic. I had avoided the "C word" all my life. Catholic was a word never spoken in our home. My grandparents had a very old-school approach to religion, even though they never attended church. For them and their generation, a Lutheran marrying a Catholic was akin to interracial marriage. My uncle married a Catholic and converted, which nearly broke my grandma's heart. Then my half-brother married a Catholic, and good old grandma spotted a cross around his neck under his T-shirt.

One day, she pulled me aside and whispered, "Do you think he has become Catholic?" I told her I didn't know and that I had never thought about it. She insisted, "If you know, Michael, you better tell me."

I found all this religious stuff oddly interesting, especially now in the 21st century. Still, my grandma made me go to Sunday School, get confirmed in the Lutheran Church, and attend church every Sunday. Throughout my life, my grandparents attended church only once, on Christmas Eve when I played the Inn Keeper in the service play that December 24th. Now that I think about it, I'm not sure they attended my dual confirmation and baptism; I hadn't been baptized as a baby. What I remember about that Christmas Eve service is part of one of my two lines: "There's no room here tonight!" I could hear my grandfather's voice in the congregation doing his version of whispering—which was him talking in his normally loud voice. Whenever he opened his mouth to speak, the whole congregation would look his way with scowls on their faces. I didn't care what those people thought because my grandfather was finally in the place that grandma had made me go to every Sunday, and I loved that man more than if he were my own father. Now, I'd give a year's salary just to hear his "pseudo-whisper" in church or hear my grandmother's voice again anywhere in this world.

My mind felt like it was healing and finding balance, and I was becoming mentally stronger and more confident in avoiding panic attacks each day. It was certainly "better living through chemicals."

That summer, I told my wife I was going to formally convert to Catholicism. Of course, she was thrilled. Catholics always get as excited as hell when someone mentions the C word (Convert). I confided in my wife that I couldn't take the usual RCIA route since we were regular churchgoers at the Catholic church in our neighborhood, and I had been taking communion every Sunday for over five years. During those years, my wife lived in fear that I'd be discovered and outed as a Lutheran improperly and fraudulently taking Communion at each Catholic mass. It was the senior usher (who later was shamed from the parish for "schtupping" (as Grandma would say) the Catholic school's librarian—but in fairness, I'd say she was a pretty hot blonde, so who could blame that old geezer fart? The "old geezer" asked us one Sunday on our way out the door if we'd consider being Eucharistic ministers. I was honored, but my wife was panic-stricken. Her nightmare had come to life. Her lying, cheating, no-good, communion-taking Lutheran husband would be shamed in the very church where she had grown up.

I whispered in my grandfather's loud whisper, "What the hell are we gonna do now?" I even said it as if it were her fault. I remembered that my wife had some cool, decent, and active liberal Catholic friends (who have since gone down the QAnon rabbit hole). I called the former liberals and asked how a heathen convert becomes a Catholic without having to endure a year of Sundays and leaving before communion, especially since everyone had already seen me take communion Sunday after Sunday for over five years.

Our friends advised me to contact Father Albert at the Franciscan Monastery of St. Bonaventure on the east side of Detroit, the home of the soon-to-be saint, Solanus Casey. I called and nervously asked for the monk they recommended. I explained our self-created dilemma that was causing my wife to lose sleep. He was very warm and kind, much like Clarence the angel from *It's a Wonderful Life*. He invited me to come down to meet with him, which I did right away.

He handed me a contemporary catechism—not the Baltimore version—and said, "Read this, call me when you're done, and we'll meet to discuss any questions or concerns you have about our faith." I thought, *Wow, that was easy!*

I was on the path to Catholicism. I read the book in about two weeks. I scheduled my return appointment, thinking I would complete several of these before being confirmed as a Catholic.

When I met Father Albert again, he calmly asked in his contemplative Franciscan voice, "So Michael—what are your questions, if any?"

I replied that I only had three questions I couldn't fully grasp. These three issues were significant points of contention between Catholics and Protestants: Mother Mary and the Saints, Purgatory, and the Rosary. I told the priest, "First, you can't tell people they can pray to Mother Mary or the Saints and still get to heaven. They either give themselves completely to God or they don't! There's no such thing as purgatory." I also mentioned that he shouldn't tell people that such a place exists because it doesn't. He told me that I didn't have to accept it if I didn't want to. I thought to myself, Damn straight, brother (with "brother" meant casually, not in the Jesus-loves-everyone, family sense).

Father Albert asked, "Okay, what is your second question?"

I said, "I don't believe in the Rosary, Father! You must tell people that praying on beads won't get them into heaven or anywhere near it."

He explained the brief history and purpose of the Rosary, reiterating, "You don't have to believe it or practice it if you don't want to." I realized I was really appreciating this guy. I had finally met an open and honest Catholic or Christian. He fielded every question I threw at him and responded thoughtfully. "What is your third question, Michael?"

I blurted, "Purgatory! You cannot, must not, tell these poor souls that they can go to a middle-earth kind of place called 'purgatory.'" I insisted that there was no such place, stating that people either believed in Jesus Christ as their Lord and Savior or they didn't. Those who did had a trip to heaven awaiting them in the afterlife, while those who didn't went straight down, passing "Go," collecting only lots of hot, hot heat.

He explained the theological reasoning behind purgatory. I didn't remember exactly what he said, but again, he remarked, "Believing in purgatory is not mandatory, Michael." I thought, *Crap, now I'm really liking this chubby little monk.* I was beginning to think my grandmother had these people pegged all wrong—very, very wrong. They weren't half bad, in my opinion. This guy seemed open, honest, understanding, and kind. I later learned that Father Albert was one of the rarer priests who embodied all these qualities, as did many of the Franciscans at the monastery. With that, he asked if I had any more questions. I did not. He suggested we schedule my confirmation into the Catholic Church and my official Catholic baptism. Again, I thought, *Holy shit, that was easy!* I liked this lack of bureaucracy and red tape. I could get used to this. And I didn't even have to shame my family or my beautiful, innocent Catholic children, who attended the Catholic school connected to the church.

A week later, my family visited the monastery in Detroit. I was confirmed and officially became a Catholic. I felt the earth shift slightly as my grandparents turned in their Lutheran graves. I still sense the ground rumble when I drive by Gethsemane Cemetery on Gratiot and Connor on my way to Wayne State. Now that I was officially a Catholic, I did what most Catholics—or Christians, for that matter—never do. I immediately joined the Left Wing-oriented Catholic Worker Movement to carry out the works of mercy for all people as prescribed by the biggest bleeding-heart liberal, hippie, peacenik, freak of all time—a certain Mr. Jesus Christ:

- feed the hungry
- give drink to the thirsty
- clothe the naked
- offer hospitality to the homeless
- care for the sick
- visit the imprisoned
- bury the dead

While I still fall short every minute of every day, I actively seek and pray for God's grace to understand these works and to continually keep my focus on them.

In the early fall of 1991, I received a call from someone promoting a show in Ann Arbor featuring Ray Manzarek and Michael McClure. He had seen me perform some of my poetry and asked if I would open for Ray and Michael during the early show, while John Sinclair would open the later one. Naturally, I immediately said yes. Why not? I had overcome my panic attacks and had just found God on a "Moonlight Drive." To top it off, I would be sharing the stage with one of my favorite '60s recording artists and one of the most astonishing Beat poets, who recited the *Canterbury Tales* in Middle English at The Last Waltz on Thanksgiving 1976.

This event would be incredible. I was excited to finally meet Ray Manzarek in person. His band, along with Jim Morrison, had helped bring me "out of the closet" as a young poet and hipster at 13 when I first heard "Horses Latitude" on their *Strange Days* album.

The venue booked a lovely hotel room for my wife and me. We arrived in Ann Arbor early that night. I was on the first show, while John Sinclair was scheduled for the late one. When I got to the club, the promoter greeted me and asked if I wanted to meet Ray and Michael before the show. I broke out in a cold sweat and made some sound that must have resembled "yes." He led me to the green room, where the great Ray Manzarek was sitting alone, eating his dinner and reading a magazine in the quiet space.

Ray said, "Oh, Michael is eating some wild boar or some sort of wild game upstairs in the restaurant."

The promoter said, "Ray, I'd like to introduce you to a Detroit poet who is opening the first show. His name is M.L. Liebler."

Ray turned around, flaunting his long lamb-chop sideburns and flowing hair, a huge smile spreading across his face. He exclaimed joyfully, "I love poetry!"

I stumbled over my words and replied, "Me too!" Fumbling, I added, "Ray, I haven't seen you since May 1968 at Cobo Hall."

He said, "You were on that show too?"

I responded, "No, my grandparents drove me to the show to see The Doors."

He then seemed to ponder those days, stroking his long sideburns, and said, "Those were some fine days, M.L." Ray then handed me his copy of the new Atlantic Monthly that he had been reading on the plane. It featured the now-famous essay "Can Poetry Matter?" by the illustrious California poet Dana Gioia, whom I later met a few times in the poetry world when I directed the YMCA Writer's Voice Project.

I had him read for my online program during the pandemic. As it turned out, Dana's dad was from Detroit. Many years later, I told Dana that I had discovered his famous essay through Ray. He expressed his wish to have met Ray or any members of The Doors, as he loved them dearly. It was Ray who encouraged me to read Dana's essay in The Atlantic. He had been reading it on the flight to Detroit and insisted it was a fantastic essay on poetry that I needed to read "immediately!" He gave me his copy of the magazine, and after I read it, it blew my mind because Dana articulated everything I had long believed about the meaning and importance of poetry in the public sphere. It was an art form for everyone, not just the academic elite and snobs at universities. I ended up teaching Gioia's essay in my Introduction to Poetry classes at Wayne State in the early 1990s.

Since that evening, I have had the opportunity to know and collaborate with Michael McClure multiple times. I liked him and his artist wife, Amy, very much; they have both treated me kindly over the years. I bumped into Ray several times at airports across the country, and we enjoyed warm, cordial chats about life on the road and literature. Becoming friends with these two was something I could never have imagined—it felt organic and genuine. To add to the excitement, I had the chance to meet and befriend the Doors' drummer, John Densmore, through our mutual friend and Zappa-produced musician, Rubén Funkahuati Guevara. Rubén organized a Zoom reading for my online Living Room Literary Series, which I started on Easter Sunday, 2020, bringing poetry programming into our new COVID-era online world. In April of 2021, I hosted John and Rubén. John was an excellent guest—warm and engaging. We agreed to do some gigs together in Los Angeles once the pandemic finally ended. Ultimately, I met two members of The Doors whom I respected and appreciated greatly.

Having long moved past panic attacks and "High Anxiety," I set off alone in 2000 to teach and give poetry readings in China. This journey further nurtured my poetic spirit. In many ways, I was aided along the way by two Guevaras (Rubén & Walter), three members of the Doors (Ray Manzarek, John Densmore, and Jim Morrison), and Jim's close friend, the legendary Beat poet

Michael McClure. Eventually, I became a world traveler, circling the globe multiple times to advocate for the importance of poetry in everyday life. My travels took me from China to Germany, England, the West Bank, Israel, Afghanistan, Russia, and finally to France, where I had the opportunity to pay my respects at the grave of the first poet I ever admired, Jim Morrison. I took the Metro to Père Lachaise Cemetery, embarking on my pilgrimage to connect spiritually with Jim. There, I visited his gravesite and expressed my gratitude for teaching me in 1967 that poetry belongs to the people and can be conveyed in countless ways and styles. My journey would not have been the same without my exposure to The Doors and "Horse Latitudes."

At heart, I may still be a shy kid, afraid to share my thoughts and feelings, but I will always be grateful to Jim Morrison for his spiritual and literary companionship from my early teens to my adult years. In many ways, it was my poetry companions in The Doors who significantly helped me start my public poetry journey at 13. In 1967, they aided me in "breaking on through to the other side" spiritually, poetically, and musically. I haven't looked back since.

Sun Ra in Detroit © Leni Sinclair

M.L. Liebler with Ridgeway Co-Founder Carl Ra Aniel at Dr. Evermor's Art Park, WI ; founding members of The Ridgeway Artists Collective

(L-R) Jeff Ensroth, Carl Ra Aniel, Gregory Hallock, Larry Wilson, and ML under Bogey

CARL RA & SUN RA

The Ridgeway Years: 50 Years of Dada Hijinx

"Space Is the Place"
—Sun Ra

Space became the place for us, and it all started in my first creative writing class at Macomb Community College with Professor Lawrence Pike. He later became my poetry mentor and a close friend until he passed away from lung cancer in 1995. Pike introduced me to Carl Ra Aniel, saying, "M.L.! I want you to meet and work with that student in the far corner of the classroom. He's a poet and filmmaker, and I believe you two have a lot in common. His name is Carl Aniel; now go say hello and create something, Liebler—go and create something!"

So, Professor Larry Pike sent me to the other side of the classroom that day to work with a hippie-looking guy named Carl. I glanced over and saw a lanky kid with long, shaggy hair and a headband. This guy reminded me of the type of people I had spent my first post-high school years trying to escape. I didn't want to be reminded of what I used to be. My "Be Here Now" moment had long passed. By the mid-70s, I was more of a "Been There, Done That" kind of kid. I had recklessly cut my hair, grown a beard, and tried to disappear and hide out at a community college on 12 Mile Road. The 1960s were long gone for me by early 1974. I had stopped smoking pot and taking LSD, and I had no interest in revisiting the long hallway to my past, which he represented to me. He could have walked straight out of a Zap comic book.

"Geez! Really? Do I have to meet him and work with this guy, Pike?"

"Yes, it will be good for you," he said, turning back to sit at his desk and ignoring me.

In my smug, smartass way, I thought, *Okay, I'll play this stupid classroom game and meet the post-hippie screwball. Why not?* So, I walked to the back corner and extended my hand to say, "Hello." This was the big bang beginning of the Ridgeway Artists Collective and my 50-plus years of friendship with one of the hippest, coolest guys I never wanted to meet, but I'm damn sure glad I did.

Neither of us could have realized that one day in a community college classroom on 12 Mile Road in Warren, Michigan, we were about to join the Ridgeway Artists Collective and remain connected for 50 years. After Carl and I became friends and creative troublemakers, I invited two emerging artists and another high school journalism friend to join our new group of young "smartass" hipsters with "anti" attitudes and a negative worldview. I guess we were punks before "punk" was a thing. We were also anti-academic. Maybe it was the working-class side of us all. None of us seemed "born to follow," to quote The Byrds, in anything, from clothing to culture to our unique taste in music.

Carl Aniel was the son of a disabled factory worker living in a working-class, union neighborhood in Roseville, which had previously been known as "Mudville" in an earlier chapter. He attended Burton Junior High School on 11 Mile Road, east of Gratiot. Burton was a typical working-class junior high school. I knew some kids who went there, and they were in a popular local band called The Tidal Waves. They had a regional Metro Detroit hit, all under 15 years old, with a cover of the classic 1959 song by Don & Dewey titled "Farmer John." That's what I remembered when he told me he had gone to Burton, though it seemed he didn't know that. This was probably part of my early obsession with music. Even though I have known Carl for 50 years, I am not sure what pulled him into jazz and avant-garde jazz. I later found out he was just as obsessed with Detroit's public radio station (WDET) and host Judy Adams and her Morphogenesis Show as I was with rock 'n' roll. Judy was an acclaimed Detroit broadcaster who, coincidentally, played piano on one of my later albums. Additionally, I know Carl didn't own any Beatles albums until he purchased The Beatles' *White Album* from a Chicago Salvation Army store at the age of 40 in the early 1990s.

Ironically, the five of us shared a lot in common. We all enjoyed breaking norms in art, politics, and "American" culture. Carl was radical in everything, especially politics, as was I. However, he took his music to another level by listening to avant-garde jazz (Sun Ra, Pharaoh Sanders, CJQ, Coltrane, and others), while the rest of us preferred The Beatles, Jimi Hendrix, Cream, The Doors, and Dylan. Greg represented the other end of the avant-garde spectrum with his Bonzo Dog Doo Dah Band, Hot Tuna, The Monkees, Nice, and similar groups. Carl was a talented filmmaker for a 19-year-old kid from Roseville, and that was his aspiration. After all, he was that kid in school who worked in AV and set up classroom films for the rest of us to watch. As a student at Macomb, he created many cool little videos.

Macomb College had a three-camera studio and professional editing capabilities, which Carl first utilized, followed by the rest of us, for many video and film projects. The first film we created was a challenging production of one of my one-act plays, inspired by my high school teacher, Norm Levinson, who once performed a soliloquy from The Iceman Cometh in my Economics class right in front of our strait-laced teacher, Mr. Brown. I wrote a short one-act play titled "Beneath Man's Integrity." It was my tribute to Eugene O'Neill and, secretly, to Mr. Levinson. Carl agreed to direct and produce the film, which we shot on location at an Eastside restaurant where Jeff and I had worked as teenagers. Naturally, I invited my best friend, Jeff Ensroth, along with two other childhood friends, to play background characters in my one-man play. This little one-act play ended up connecting Carl with Jeff, Greg, Larry, and me for the rest of our lives. I don't think anyone anticipated so much from that spring day.

After shooting the one-act, we all took part in Carl's other insane and entertaining television productions. We recorded *The*

Late Show with M.L. Liebler, where I interviewed unsuspecting community college students and the Campus Queens—which had a completely different meaning back then. Carl also filmed a fantastic live show in Macomb's Student Union featuring Detroit avant-garde trumpeter and legend Charles Moore and his Shattering Effects band from the famous Strata Gallery in Downtown Detroit. I had never heard music like this before.

Another major act that Carl recorded was the great rebel, Los Angeles poet Charles Bukowski, who became somewhat of a regular visitor to Macomb College. However, Buk was eventually banned from Warren (and Macomb) for smashing tables in a drunken rage at our local college hangout bar across from the college.

Carl taped student poetry readings, and once he pressed a button on the system, we all appeared on every television in every classroom on campus simultaneously.

We held our first Love Art Fest, creating Warren, Michigan's first-ever campus Dada Art Show at Macomb College South. Things got a bit out of hand when Carl suggested we tie up the entire audience with spools of Christmas ribbon we had brought, surrounding the "grassy knoll" on that warm, blue-sky suburban spring day. College students in 1973 (post-60s and pre-Reagan) didn't quite appreciate our sense of humor and artistic antics. Some people began smashing the artworks, like the "candle in boot" on a pedestal, and they further wrecked our already broken dinner plates on display. We aimed for a Duchamp vibe reminiscent of his famous "urinal-on- wall." While the exhibit seemed cool to us, it certainly irritated many students and some of the less hip faculty members.

Later, Carl infused his leftist politics into his art by organizing a protest at the McDonald's across from the college. He invited several students—some like- minded and others not so much—to march with signs that read, "Free the Potatoes," "Give Idaho Back to the Potatoes," and "Ban the Fries." Customers and workers wearing those funny white paper hats couldn't understand what was happening out front, prompting the manager to call the Warren

Police. They arrived, just as puzzled as the customers and protesters. In fact, no one understood the meaning behind it all.

The police instructed the Ridgeway impromptu gang to "please leave the area NOW!" We all complied, laughing all the way back to the Macomb College Student Union. Carl instigated many art events like this over the years and pursued his filmmaking ambitions during those early times, which eventually led him to Columbia College in Chicago.

One of my favorite art events that Carl organized was the now-legendary "Amazing L," a massive inflatable letter L contraption made from clear plastic bags, tape, and a vacuum cleaner that filled it with air, as several hippie-looking individuals tossed it around the center of campus. Many passing students stared, both astonished and utterly bewildered, as the plastic (and amazing) letter L floated through campus.

Another installation of Carl's, which we all participated in, was the famous "Water Ballet," held at one of Carl's friends' houses in Warren, not far from campus. It served as an art gift for a birthday celebration. Carl assigned us to different houses where we hooked up hoses with various sprinklers attached to the ends. When Carl gave us the signal, we turned on all the different sprinklers. We blasted Charles Moore's "Shattering Effects," the Macomb jam we had recorded earlier, from my 1971 yellow Volkswagen Bug using my 4-track tape player.

It seemed that the five of us had nowhere to go but toward Dada. Dada was an anti-art movement of the early 1900s that began at the Cabaret Voltaire in 1916. It emerged after the devastation caused by WWI, spreading from Europe to Russia and New York City. Dada drew inspiration from 19th-century artist Alfred Jarry's political, satirical, and highly profane play Ubu Roi at the time. These artists became our heroes, along with Hugo Ball, Tristan Tzara, Man Ray, Jean Arp, and others. Their movement captivated us as Beat suburban community college students.

By the summer of 1974, we started The Ridgeway Press, which blossomed into a nationally and internationally recognized small press publisher by 1980. We began with Carl Aniel and Jim Jarvies's *Thundershowers Rain on Me Supreme* in a limited-edition run of ten stapled books, each featuring different covers. After Carl's book was released, we published my first chapbook, *The Martyr of Pig*, followed by two handmade and subversively printed anthologies: *Kitana Po* and *Earth Walkers*.

At that time, double-sided Xeroxing hadn't yet been invented. Carl conceived the idea for us to lay out our poetry anthology *Kitana Po*, assign a Roman numeral to each poet (so we couldn't be traced), and present the booklet to the college printing building as a project for one of our poetry professors, Larry Pike.

Once it was finished, we returned to pick it up for Professor Pike (I'm not sure he ever knew about our devious plan, but I think he was included in the anthology). We collected the books, and since double-sided printing didn't exist back then, we ended up with a poem on one side, followed by two blank pages, another poem, two blank pages, and so forth. It was the best we could do with the technology available at the time. Then, Carl and Larry hand-lettered and pressed printed the covers. We went to a local Speedy Printing place to print single sheets that displayed the numbers and corresponding poets. For example, I.

M.L. Liebler, II. Carl Aniel, III. Larry Pike, IV. Donna Pici, and so on. We then penciled in a price inside the cover to mimic their other books. God had not yet invented barcodes or a method for counting inventory. We took them to local bookstores in St. Clair Shores and executed a "reverse steal." Instead of stealing books, we placed our Ridgeway books on their shelves in the poetry sections. Since computerized inventory didn't exist back then, we checked back at each bookstore periodically to see if any had sold. If they had, we secretly slid more Ridgeway Press books onto their shelves. Our philosophy was more about getting our work out there than making money. What did we care about money? We were 18 or 19 years old. Macomb College's printing department was unknowingly covering the production costs. As I mentioned, we didn't care about money back then, and I don't think any of us do today. Working-class roots, I guess. Work hard, never look back, and take no "capitalist" prisoners.

From this auspicious start, Ridgeway would go on to publish well over 100 authors' chapbooks and paperback books that included everyone from Country Joe McDonald to Faruq Z. Bey, Faye Kicknosway, Stella Crew, and eventually Ron Allen, Geoffrey Jacques, Jim Gustafson, and Ed Sanders. But before all that happened, we were just a quirky group of bored suburban kids from St. Clair Shores and Roseville with a bit of talent and a love for the arts. Holy crap!! The next thing we knew, at least in our minds, we had become our own art movement!

Over the years, what began in a community college classroom 50 years ago has evolved into lifelong friendships and many wild art happenings, from the Jack Pine Christmas Tree Giveaway Reading (which didn't actually involve a Christmas tree) to a boxing match called "Poetry on the Ropes," where poets literally boxed the crap out of each other to primal scream underwear shenanigans. There were countless art happenings and even a public hanging... of me!

In the spring of 1974, five of us kids, fresh out of a suburban high school and unfamiliar with the concept of college, embarked on something unique and meaningful to us. I didn't know anyone attending college; no one in my family ever did, and my grandparents never fully understood why I would pursue my education after high school. Ridgeway marked the start of a long decade of friendships filled with love, anger, war, peace, and eventually the insights of old age among friends. We shared countless laughs and drunken artistic sessions. Now, we meet bi-monthly on Zoom for two hours to create radio plays and catch up on what's happening in our lives.

The Ridgeway has journeyed from St. Clair Shores to Chicago, then to Madison, and back again. We transformed from naive kids inspired by poetry and film to participants in Dada and Surrealist art happenings. The original Ridgeway Collective was made up of an unlikely group of characters. We adopted new names: Jeff Ensroth became "Jert," Gregory Booth Hallock took on the name "G. H Reviewa," Larry Wilson became "Go Back to Canada Larry," and Carl Aniel changed to "Carl Ra" (after his hero Sun Ra), while I became "Milbert." Jeff and I had been friends since elementary school, experiencing love fests, pot fests, Kite-Ins, Love-Ins, schoolyard watermelon-spitting contests, skateboard fests, Crow's Nest-East Rock Fests, and a few fights together.

Greg Hallock lived down the street from us on Lincoln off Sixth Street, and I recall once playfully pulling a souvenir penknife on him. The tiny knife featured a partially nude mermaid on a pearly yellow plate, which I often admired. The mermaid, not the blade!

My grandma had bought that souvenir knife for me in Waikiki, Florida, during our family trip where my uncle, grandma's son, left us stranded somewhere in Georgia because his batshit crazy wife had an issue with Grandma and me. I believe my refusal to drink cheap milk from a horrible plastic container was the last straw that broke crazy Aunt Helen's back. I was simply too much for that lady. Aunt Helen thought I was a spoiled brat, but I couldn't help it if they were Catholic with five wonderfully neat, very clean kids who drank a lot of milk. I was a dirty scrapper who preferred delicious, cold milk in a wonderful, thick, chilled glass bottle—not some molded hunk of plastic. We weren't a large family, so Grandma was more than happy to pay the 10-cent deposit for the glass bottle.

Anyway, after I pulled out my little souvenir knife with the mermaid etched on the fake pearl handle in front of Greg (it was a total joke), his mother was furious with me. I thought to myself, *Geez, lady, it was a penknife, not a switchblade* from Blackboard Jungle! I remember I liked his mom Jill despite the "All the Way with LBJ" Texas hat decal on her front door. Even then, I was no fan of LBJ.

Then there was Larry Wilson, whom I remember as a squeaky-clean white kid originally from Canada, somewhere in Ontario between London and Toronto. He is now a squeaky-clean old white man, and he still hails from Canada. Some things never change. Everyone at school knew that Larry was Canadian. I was his cohort on our high school paper. While Larry had a sly sense of humor, he didn't create any art that we knew of; however, he often contributed funny lines from time to time.

We discovered 45 years later, when he blurted out at a photo shoot in the front yard of the sacred Ridgeway house for our anniversary photo, that he "hated art." That, of course, could have been a typical Ridgeway non-sequitur. However, he was and still is key to Ridgeway as the keeper of the archives of postcards, photos, and whatever else, along with his pal and Ridgeway founder Greg Hallock. Larry is the guy who remembers all our crazy antics. I often worried about where Larry would end up. He was our Ringo, so to speak. I guess I worried about him the most because Greg went to Michigan State after Macomb College, and Jeff and I went to Oakland University. The three of us left Carl and Larry back in St. Clair Shores.

While I thought I had a period of no communication with Carl and Ridgeway, it seems that wasn't the case. Over the three years I believed were lost, many activities occurred. One that stands out to me, as well as to my neck's muscle memory, is the trial I faced with The Ridgeway House Un-American Activities Committee. This was due to my diminishing Dada art energy and resources, as I wanted to concentrate on bigger things: LIFE. I must have voiced my distaste and disgust with America more than once, feelings that grew in late 1965 as I learned more about the Vietnam War following the death of a neighbor in early December 1965. I would later learn that his platoon was involved in the first major battle in Vietnam, known as Operation Harvest Moon, which also took place in early December 1965.

Meanwhile, back at the Ridgeway House, I was charged with high crimes and misdemeanors by the Ridgeway Council on Un-American Activities. I have forgotten the specific charges brought against me, but I suspect it was more for being involved in "Un-Ridgeway Activities" than it was "Un-American Activities." During the trial, they were angrier with me personally. Anyway, as I recall, the trial lasted minutes, not hours, and I was quickly found guilty, and those bastards couldn't wait to put my neck in a noose and hang my ass. So, they tied my hands behind my back and marched me out to a tree on the front lawn or maybe on the neighbor's front lawn. They brought a milk cart out to kick out from under me.

First, it is important to note we were all fairly drunk. I thought to myself that I was going to teach these fools a lesson. I was asked for any last words. I think I said, "Fuck all y'all." Then Carl kicked the milk crate out. I tilted my head back so the rope was at the base of my skull (not my neck) and swung freely from the tree branch. I hung there, playing dead.

Everyone freaked out. "We killed M.L.! No, really, guys. I think he's passed out." I stayed as still as any dead man would. Someone yelled, "Cut him down—hurry up." They did, and I laughed my ass off as I fell to the ground.

There were other activities like this that I had forgotten until recently. Still, I remember that shortly after this, I didn't invite Carl or the other Ridgeway guys (except Jeff, who is my wife's cousin) to my wedding in 1976. I guess I got tired of the Ridgeway's nonsense. I even wrote a short poem, "Ridgeway's On Tour." It went something like this:

When you
said Laugh I
did, but as of
now
I am off this bus.

During my time away from Ridgeway, I focused on becoming a poet. Later, I aspired to be like our poetic hero, Lawrence Pike, at Macomb. I wanted to become a college professor, while Carl and Ridgeway eagerly created hipster, funny jokes and Dada art, much like we did in the early 1970s at Macomb. I knew I would need at least a master's degree to teach, so I committed to attending graduate school and completed my degree in a little over a year as a full-time student.

Shortly after graduation, I was hired by Wayne State University, where I have been since 1980. Larry received an engineering degree from Lawrence Tech and became a Construction Engineer at Wayne State, working in the Civil and Environmental Engineering Department for 30 years. We would run into each other on campus and in the English Department during various engineering projects. It was always great to see my old Dada friend, and I was happy he ended up doing well.

Still, when all is said and done, I fondly remember some of our follies from the old days. Carl's first public happening was "The

Amazing L." For years, I kept that photo framed and hanging on the wall leading into the basement of our first house. As I recall, this was our first art happening. Once we came together as a group of five, we began staging various art happenings all around the MCC campus. I interviewed a potted plant that had recently returned from Bolivia on a television show we taped.

Many years later, MCC decided to eliminate the studio in the basement of the campus library, and all our videotapes were lost or destroyed. Many of these tapes featured famous poets reading in a first-class literary series hosted by the school's resident hippie philosophy professor, Bill Cox. Bill was a laid-back guy with long hair and a calm demeanor. When I once spotted the newest Zappa album on his desk, I knew he was one of us and not "one of them." He curated the best series of readings I have ever seen, bringing to our small suburban campus writers like Robert Creeley, Allen Ginsberg, Ed Sanders, John Sinclair, Robin Eichele, George Tysh, Ken Mikolowski, and even the legendary British beat poet Michael Horowitz and Ireland's Peter Fallon.

Of course, Bukowski came more than once. In fact, Carl recorded one of his readings in the television studio before a student audience. Bukowski drank from a whiskey bottle throughout the reading, and when he ran out, he stopped and said, "I'm not reading another fuckin' poem until I get more booze." Carl kept the camera rolling as someone dashed across the street to a party store to buy an "8 Pack" of Pabst Blue Ribbon in those oddly shaped short bottles. The "8 Pack" slid across the desk Buk was reading at, visible on camera. He cracked one open and continued reading. The first poem after he "wet his whistle" was about love. He said something like, "You kids don't know what love is."

He then read a poem about himself and a "lady friend" who became sick but continued to drink and screw all night. The poem conveyed that by morning, Buk was so constipated that he asked his "lady friend" for an enema. Buk ended up making a mess all over the bathroom floor and all over the "lady friend." By the end of the poem, he remarked that the "lady friend" had "patted his back and kissed his neck."

Buk then turned to us suburban brats and exclaimed, "And that, kiddies, is what love is!" WOW! I thought to my 19-year-old self that this guy was a serious and very real poet. I had never heard poems like his in my young life. Bukowski left an indelible image of "piss love" in my mind forever.

Buk was an old friend of well-known Detroit poet Hank Malone, and I bet Hank's wife was glad to hear about Bukowski's MCC ban, as we heard he had punched holes in their bedroom walls. Oy. Bye-bye, funny, gut-wrenching, drunken, fighting LA poet with a pockmarked face. They gave him his honorarium check when he arrived in Detroit, and he immediately disappeared.

Hank and the gang finally found him in a Highland Park motel with a hooker. They discovered he'd already spent the Macomb College check on that hooker and booze. Oh boy, Buk! We'll never forget you!

We had a few other legendary art happenings at Macomb before we all moved on. One was a staged public poetry reading just down from the grassy knoll overlooking the Student Union. We set up a makeshift stage on a delivery dock in front of the Student Center and mic'ed the poets so they could be heard from the knoll. Just as Macomb's only African American student (I think his name, for real, was John Quincy Adams Washington, or at least that's what he told us) stepped up to the mic to do his reading, a delivery truck pulled up and proceeded to back right in front of our makeshift stage, and John Quincy, continued reading.

His lyrics and rhymes rose over the sound of the delivery truck. As smoothly as the truck backed in, dropped its load, and pulled out, John Quincy Adams Washington kept on with his reading as if nothing happened. The Ridgeway crew sat dumbfounded by the whole event, but we broke into howling laughter that lasted for several minutes. In fact, I'm laughing my ass off right now while I type this memory.

At some point during the summer of 1975, while hanging around the Ridgeway House and Museum, I decided, after several beers and maybe a couple of shots of Jack Daniels, to try Dr. Pangloss's Primal Scream Therapy—a trauma-based psychotherapy made famous by my hero John Lennon. Was it Dr. Pangloss or

Dr. Arthur Janov who created it? I can't remember after all these years. Nonetheless, I stripped down to my "tighty-whities" and, much to the chagrin of the other Ridgeway members, started screaming at the top of my lungs and rolling from side to side.

No one yelled at me. Greg grabbed his camera and started shooting while Carl Ra thought it might be some form of music, as he loved Ornette Coleman, CJQ, and Sun Ra. At that point, I think Larry really wanted to go back to Canada because he must have been wondering, "What the hell am I doing with my life with these crazy-ass Americans?" In hindsight, I guessed Jeff thought I was just being myself since he'd known my antics since childhood, so he continued reading his book. Meanwhile, a public radio poetry show called *Dimensions* was playing in the background.

After the session, I felt liberated, so I decided to call WDET and talk to the host, as I'd heard he had done Janov's Primal Scream therapy out west somewhere. See, it all connects one way or another, and we had built a false narrative about his style of poetry and our thoughts on how "stupid" that all was.

So I dialed the phone and asked abruptly, rather rudely, for "George Tysh, the poet guy host." I said something like, "All that poetry sounds like crap. If you want some real poetry, invite me and the Ridgeway boys down!"

He calmly replied, "Okay, send a couple of poems, and I'll see." Within a week, he called and said, "Sure, come on down next Monday at 10 p.m. and read."

That sure sounded a lot different to me when sober. I thought, *Oh shit—he wants me to come downtown and be on the radio. Oh no! Now what?* At that point, I knew I was a less-than-average and subpar poet, and some of my critics still believe this to be true. I gathered my wits and said firmly, "I'll be there!"

So, I did what any normal, terrified young teen poet would do: I invited all of Ridgeway to attend. We loaded everyone into The Ridgeway's On Tour step van and headed off to Downtown Detroit to WDET FM, high atop the Maccabees Building. Little did I know then that within five years, I would spend my entire life working at the Wayne State campus, with my office in that very same building. All of this happened less than two blocks from where I was born on Woodward, between Kirby and Ferry. How strange life can be. We pulled up in front of this skyscraper, and five to seven of us poured out of the van. The radio studio was on the 15th floor, but the elevator only went to the 14th, so we had to walk up a stairwell.

I banged on the door, and George came to greet us, saying, "Holy shit—who are all these people?" I told him it was Ridgeway. He instructed me that only Carl and I come up. We sent the masses back to the step van to listen on the radio. As we walked in, George was playing this record with a red-and-green label featuring a guy with long hair flowing in every direction. The music was the most incredible sound I had ever heard in my life.

I exclaimed, like a wide-eyed boy, "What is that music, George?"

He told me it was a new record by some guy named Bob Marley. My first thought was of Charles Dickens's ghost, but this was no music created in Victorian England. He said, "It's reggae music." Right then and there, I knew I had to get my hands on that Bob Marley record, Natty Dread. It wasn't easy to find, and there was no online shopping back then, but I finally found it at Harmony House. Thank you, Jesus, for bringing this music into my world. Jah is good all the time—all the time, Jah is good.

Well, that was the night Ridgeway broke into the big time. We were as emboldened as Trump after winning the presidency with 3 million fewer votes than his rival. We took Ridgeway on tour, and the first stop was Michigan State in East Lansing. Upon our arrival, we were informed that we weren't on their schedule. But that never stopped us before. We began loading our quirky art into an empty classroom somewhere on campus. Not knowing our exact location didn't matter. Eventually, someone who appeared to be an authority figure said, "Get this stuff out of here ASAP." We quickly vacated the premises and returned to St. Clair Shores.

Another tour stop was Oakland University, where Jeff and I attended college. We founded a student literary arts group called The Letters from Earth Poetry Series. Through that student organization, we were able to compensate poets and reserve prime rooms in the Student Center Building. We had everything set up: the "Ricky Nelson 'Bring 'em Back Alive'" art piece, "Make Room for Dada," a mounted photo by Greg, a postcard for Larry's famous nonexistent book *Tobacco Row,* and of course, our favorite film that Larry Pike introduced us to during our Macomb days—*Un Chien Andalou,* also known as Andalusian Dog, or as we affectionately referred to it, "that film with the slit jelly eyeball." Everything was finely tuned and ready. We opened the doors to our exhibit, and students slowly and cautiously stepped into the reserved room.

It wasn't long before something we had brought offended the student intellectuals, and this was well before political correctness was ever imagined. Before long, campus police cars began to pull up at the Student Center Building. We were told in no uncertain terms to "get this crap out of here now or we will arrest all of you." I was shocked. I had been arrested when I was 12 for stealing Christmas light bulbs from our neighbor's house. It was innocent and harmless; we just enjoyed how they exploded when they hit the cold winter street. Once I got over the depression of my grandma thinking I was a juvenile delinquent, the St. Clair Shores Police placed me on a full year of probation, during which I had to report weekly to the St. Clair Shores Police Department.

So once again, we were forced to pack up and leave... very quickly. Notice a pattern here? Shortly after, Carl Ra packed his bags and headed to Chicago to attend Columbia College to study filmmaking. I followed him there to polish my national poetry skills in the Big Windy, home of the Chicago Seven and the Cubbies at Wrigley. That's another chapter of the Ridgeway story to be explored in Ridgeway 2.0 in Chicago.

Ridgeway 2.0 in Chicago: The Insanity and Calamity Continues

If we were wild in the early days of Ridgeway, things became weirder and more real in Chicago. When Carl first moved there in 1979, he was squatting in the basement of an abandoned office building in Chicago's Loop. It had a limited trickle of water in a sink for bathing and no bathroom. Outside the side door was the Chicago River, which turned green every St. Paddy's Day but had become yellow from years of urine. The next-door squatters were members of Sun Ra's Arkestra. They often stood by the water to let the music they played flow downstream with the Chicago River while they performed their wild sax solos. On my first night there, Carl and I were coming back from a night of blues on Halstead when the building doors swung open for a Sun Ra Parade. They were playing, marching, and inviting us to join the parade. We did for half a block, but I was still on Detroit time and jet lagged. I needed sleep, so we retreated to Carl's basement bunker. It was a long basement loft. He hung large parachutes from an army surplus store that drooped below the pipes, flaking with lead chips and the occasional running rodent.

Before he bought several parachutes at an Army-Navy store to hang from the ceiling to catch lead chips, Carl constantly woke up at night with a mouthful of lead chips and rodent droppings. I awoke on the first night when I thought I heard something scurrying across the floor. Carl was about a football field away. He had insisted before I left Detroit that I bring a pair of slippers. Of course, I thought he was full of Dada nonsense and didn't bring any. Man, was I wrong! This was not Dada; it was a necessity in that abandoned basement of an old building. After all, it was an uninhabited, boarded-up office building with broken plumbing.

That was my first mistake- assuming it was a "normal" place to live. Alas, it was scarier than it was comforting. Not only could I have been poisoned by lead, but I could have gotten black lung disease to match the color of the floor just by breathing that air. Then, there was the possibility of being bitten by a rat. I thought, *Great—just what this world needs—another rabid poet.*

Fortunately, Carl had a pair of old dime-store thongs for visitors, but one had a broken toe piece, so I had to drag that foot and walk with the other. As I stood up to head down to Carl's end of the bunker, my thongs made a "slap…drag…slap…drag" sound. Carl jumped up in bed, thinking either an intruder was there or one of Sun Ra's band members was sleepwalking.

I woke him up and said, "I can't stay here. Get me a hotel room and a taxi now."

Carl replied, "Now?" in disbelief.

I told him I was getting out of this hellhole. God bless him, he called the closest Holiday Inn and a taxi. He even went with me to help me settle in. At this point in Carl's life, he made it a point to do absolutely nothing normal—like watching television. In fact, he never owned one, and all these years later, I still think he is still televisionless.

Anyway, Sterling Hayden appeared as a guest on Tom Snyder's *Tomorrow Show* that night, and Carl found Hayden interesting, but he refused to watch the television like a normal person. He insisted on keeping his back to the TV, choosing just to listen as I drifted off to sleep in a nice, clean Holiday Inn room with carpeting and fresh sheets: no rats or lead to poison us.

That was the first of many nights I spent with Carl in Chicago. I enjoyed Chicago; it felt similar to New York, which I loved deeply and still do, but Chicago seemed more manageable. Before my first visit, I asked Carl to check if there was an Open Mic scene anywhere. Although it wasn't his genre, he kept an eye out around town. Eventually, he spotted a flyer for an Open Mic in Oak Park at The Book Stall, a small independent bookstore owned by two lesbians with strong literary backgrounds. Carl interned at Charles H. Kerr Publisher, located across the street from the legendary Book Stall. Since the late 1800s, Kerr has been known for publishing anarchist, socialist, and surrealist books. They published notable works on radical labor, including *Mother Jones' Autobiography* and *The Little Red Songbook*, along with various other leftist classics. To reach Oak Park, we had to take the Howard El from the Loop and travel through Chicago's infamous west side to the Oak Park neighborhood.

Chicago presented a cool scene for me, entirely different from what we had in Detroit at that time. It was the second night of my journey when we headed west. At the bookstore, I signed my name on a list. When my name was called, I told the small audience that I was there looking for future gigs if anyone knew of any. I performed my poetry with my boombox music, and people seemed to genuinely enjoy it. The first guy to jump up with his card was a man named Marc Kelly Smith, who would eventually found Slam Poetry.

He said, "I'm thinking of starting a reading series where people read and are rated by judges holding up scorecards like in the Olympics. So, I'll have an Open Mic, a feature (and I'd like you to be a feature), and then this Slam idea." I found that interesting and a bit strange, so I agreed to be one of his first "featured" poets.

The Slam took place in the barrio near what was then a dangerous Wicker Park at Butchie's Get Me High Jazz Bar. I'm not kidding! The spot was about the size of a small library reading room. Butchie only served Old Style beer, and patrons would grab their own drinks and toss a dollar in a coffee can—real working-class Chicago style. The first night I attended, only a handful of people showed up, but they mostly came for the Open Mic and Feature at that time. After I performed my piece, it seemed like people started leaving as Marc cranked up his "Slam Poetry." He was practically begging the small audience not to leave because the "big event" was just about to start, and that's how it went. The second time I participated in the Slam was shortly after Jimmy Carter had been building houses with Habitat for Humanity in that neighborhood. His crew decided to stop by and grab an Old Style at Butchie's. When this news spread throughout the Windy City, the audiences for Marc's Slams grew dramatically.

When I returned for my second Slam reading at Butchie's about a year later, I was joined by people who would become lifelong poetry friends in Chicago and later in New York City. Carl Watson and Sharon Mesmer were among the first to arrive that night. Over time, I became part of the Chicago poetry scene. I was often featured in their poetry calendar in Letter Ex, their literary newspaper, to the point that people assumed I was a "Chicago" poet. Once, a Chicago student enrolled at Wayne State specifically to take my creative writing classes. He told me he had always wanted to take my class, and when he discovered I was teaching at Wayne, he moved to Detroit to attend. He's still a friend and attends our local readings.

As the 1980s progressed, I traveled to Chicago several times a year for readings. I remember doing eleven readings in seven days and attending twelve daytime Cubs games. I had long been a "Die Hard Cubs Fan" since their nearly great but fading season of 1969, so my Chicago ritual became going to daytime baseball games at Wrigley, drinking large amounts of Old Style and Jägermeister, and giving readings every night. After the readings, we often went to B.L.U.E.S. or Kingston Mines for some top-notch blues. It was a grueling yet enjoyable schedule, but someone had to do it. Over the years, I developed close friendships with many Chicago poets. I met wonderful poets like Carlos Cumpian, Cynthia Gallaher, Raul Nino, Judith Parsons Nesbitt, and many others.

I will always be grateful to Carl Aniel and all my poet friends in the Second City who welcomed me as one of their own. Together, we enjoyed a blast of readings and countless Old Styles. A few of my Chi-Town poet friends moved to NYC in the late 1980s and early 1990s. Once they established themselves, they invited me to participate in readings in the Big Apple, and soon, I found myself becoming part of the NYC poetry scene. Through these friends, I had the opportunity to read at The Knitting Factory, City College, La Mama Theater, and many other cool venues.

However, before that, I did several readings in Chicago with my poetry mentor and friend, Ed Sanders. I fondly remember walking around Grant Park with Ed on a cold, gray November day as he pointed out key locations from the 1968 Chicago Police Riot during the Democratic National Convention. This event left an indelible impression on me during my early teen years. He pointed out where he, Burroughs, and Sartre walked, where Detroit's MC5 played (the only band that showed up to perform live, by the way), and where they trained for Zen combat with the police, among other things. It was incredible for me as a child of the 1960s, raised on radical politics, as that convention was a major flashpoint in my youth.

At other times, I read in Chicago alongside the legendary IWW poet and artist Carlos Cortez, my friend and collaborator Faruq Z. Bey, John Sinclair, Errol Henderson, Larry Pike, Edward Moron, and many others from Detroit. We performed at the Guild Complex and Axe Street Arena during the 100th Anniversary of the Haymarket Massacre in 1886, at Linx Hall, and at Chicago Filmmakers with a young Cornelius Edy, along with my first Magic Poetry Band. I frequently read and performed at the Seeley Street Little Theater. I also read at Logan Square Library and the Ginger Man Café in Wrigleyville, where I debuted my performance art piece "Rain Ballet" in 1984, and where Carl and

I caught a rare performance by the great Chicago jazz musician Hal Russell, who showcased his avant-garde jazz while strolling around the bar and swatting flies with his flyswatter. We also read at the Main Chicago Library, during the early years of the now-famous Printers Row Book Festival and anywhere else that would host us and welcome poets.

I remember telling Carl once, amid all these readings and baseball excitement, while we sat in a sparse upper deck seat at Wrigley during our usual day games (Hey, no lights at Wrigley back then). I said, "Carl, if I lived in this badass town, I would build the biggest poetry scene the world has ever seen in the Midwest."

Carl wisely responded that warm day in the upper deck at Wrigley, between pitches, "Well, you don't live here, M.L., so why don't you go home and make Detroit a legendary poetry city and create that scene there?"

I believe this was in 1985, so that's exactly what I did. I came home and soon found myself elected by the late great Detroit poet Henrietta Epstein as President of the Poetry Resource Center of Michigan. This marked the beginning of my efforts to build a celebrated scene in my hometown by directing several literary arts organizations from the mid-80s until today.

Eventually, I helped bring the PRC to the forefront of the Detroit arts scene. I created the "Rock N Read" programs at Alvin's Twilight Bar to raise funds for our nonprofit and support charity. These benefits took off like a rocket and quickly gained momentum. By May 1987, we had a vibrant Detroit literary scene that, by all accounts, continues to grow and thrive in the 21st century.

Thank you for that suggestion, Carl Ra! I embraced that idea, and much programming continues here to this day thanks to that invaluable advice. Even the devastating pandemic couldn't stop us. Others and I quickly pivoted and created various online reading series.

Back in Detroit with Ridgeway in the 21st Century

In June 2019, we celebrated the 45th anniversary of Ridgeway and the 100th anniversary of the Dada Movement. Everyone gathered for one last big hurrah, returning to some of our old antics during our week of Ridgeway fun. We decided on two things. First, we would revisit the scene of the art crime by visiting the little old house on Ridgeway Street in St. Clair Shores for a photo bomb on the poor occupant's front lawn. We pulled up in our "Ridgeway On Tour" camper, sporting various masks (before it became fashionable in 2020) and banging on homemade instruments along the length of Ridgeway from the lake, creating quite a stir. From the back of the camper, I noticed our Sunday afternoon neighbors watching us pass by, likely thinking, "What the hell is this all about?" We all (over 65 years old) stumbled out of the van onto the owner's lawn and posed for outrageous photos. Greg even had his professional camera tripod set up and ready like back in 1974. We topped off the day with a big meal at a local Greek restaurant, complete with plenty of Greek Saganaki to feed our table of 12. OOPAH!

The next day, we decided to return to the scene of our first Ridgeway Dada Festival in the spring of 1974 at Macomb Community College. We weren't welcomed back then, and apparently, we're still not now. Carl called the campus from my house to see if they wanted some free "lazy summer PR." I reached out to a few of my press connections in the local Macomb area to inform them about our plans. The Public Relations team at MCC referred us to the Dean of Alumni. He was confused by our request to stage a few photos, so he connected Carl to Public Safety (back then, we used to call them "Kiddie Cops").

Carl explained that we wanted to commemorate Dada art on its 100th birthday. When he mentioned that Dada was an "anti-art" movement that opposed war, racism, and similar issues, the officer replied, "We are a quiet, peaceful campus, and we'd like to keep it that way, thank you." They planned to connect us to another office, and I told Carl, "hang up! We're going to Macomb's South Campus." We suited up. I wore a wig and a pork pie hat; Carl donned his psychedelic glasses and doctor's lab coat; Jeff sported a Detroit Tigers hat without the brim, making him look Hebrew with what he called "Hank Greenberg's kippa," and Donna dressed normally, as usual. Greg and Larry opted out of the festivities. They weren't feeling quite as adventurous as we were that day.

When we arrived in Carl's old, tattered Wisconsin camper, we were greeted by four (count them: four) Macomb College squad cars lined up in front of the Student Center. We never saw the officers. That seemed typical for the old "MCCC." They showed up because Carl had told them we "wanted to go inside the Student Center to take a few pictures." We imagined they were positioned inside the door, ready to break some heads, flashing us back to our early days during the anti-Vietnam War protests in the early '70s.

We captured our photos and drove to Buscemi's (the pride of Roseville) for delicious pizza and laughter. The anniversary celebration concluded just as Ridgeway began—with sly humor, food, Dada nonsense, and the joy of good old-fashioned, cynical Dada fun. The more things change, the more Ridgeway remains the same after all those years since we first met in a small classroom at a community college affectionately nicknamed "12 Mile High" in Warren, Michigan. It was our Harvard and provided our "real" education. I'm still proud of that place and visit as often as possible. All hail Ridgeway Press, Dada Art, and Macomb County Community College (with all three Cs), where our surreal fraternity Tapa Keg-a-Brew was born. Fifty-plus years is a long time, but none of us has lost our step. Yes, we're older, our hair is gone, and our beards are grayer, yet we remain connected and continue to create unique art and happenings, all with a deep love for one another, just as we did in the early 1970s.

During the 2020 pandemic, we began producing radio plays over Zoom, titled "Welcome to Virusville." Each episode featured a consistent cast of characters performed by The Ridgeway Players and Extended Family & Friends, with Carl back in the Director's Chair. Each week, we would find plant managers Rat and Ruby scheming some devious plot to conceal the horrors and human toll of COVID-19 at a meat plant in Virusville. Some episodes were titled "Rat & Ruby's Flavored Rectal Thermometers," "Make America Dead Again—Again!," "Dr. Dada's Throwing Knives Again," "Arrivederci: Italian Designed PPE," and a series of Christmas Specials for kids featuring Krampus and Pussknuckle & The Sugar Plum Fairies. This demonstrates that "you can't keep good Dada artists down," even now as we enter our 70s. I'm almost tempted to reference the Paul Simon song "Still Crazy…," but nah! Let a sleeping Dadaist lie. Still, we knew then, as we know now, "Space Is the Place!"

Captain Beefheart © Creative Commons)

M.L. Liebler & Faruq Z. Bey © Rebecca Cook)
The Magic Poetry Band (L-R) Brigitte Knudson, Lou DeCillis,
Ted Nagy © Amanda Nowicki)

CAPTAIN BEEFHEART

Breaking the Voodoo While Being as Safe as
Milk with My Trout Mask On

1986 AND ONWARD

In mid-January of 1971, I sneaked out of my job as a dishwasher at Huck's Lakeshore Restaurant on Jefferson and 9 Mile Road. I drove alone to the Eastown Theater on Harper and Van Dyke in Detroit to see Captain Beefheart and the Magic Band. The Amboy Dukes were performing too, but this was long before Ted Nugent became a right-wing, COVID-infected Republican douchebag. He was still a hippie freak back then, wearing a Native American headdress and a loincloth while swinging across the stage with a hatchet and a bow and arrow strapped to his bare chest. It was bizarre then and now, and it felt a bit violent for this hippie teenage boy, but hey, it was the early 1970s, and that was alright!

Anyway, I exited I-94 at Van Dyke and parked in my usual spot behind the nondescript urban grocery store. I walked the two blocks to the theater. Since I was alone, I headed to the balcony where I could sit comfortably, smoke a joint, and watch. Captain Beefheart came on stage wearing a tall, pointed dunce-style hat with a badminton birdie perched on top. The band played at breakneck speed (punk years before punk rock) while the Captain delivered his lyrics at a machine-gun pace. He ripped the pages from their place on a music stand in front of him. By the time the stage was covered in sheets of paper, about fifteen minutes later, he and the band walked off. That was it! He left the audience howling and scratching their heads. However, for me, that changed everything. The image and performance were seared into my memory forever. The following week, I watched the Captain and Magic Band on Detroit's hip underground TV show, *Tube Works,* with my musical mentor and future arts comrade, Dave Dixon, from WABX Underground Free Form Radio.

I didn't want to become Captain Beefheart, but there was something about him that resonated with my connection to poetry and music. I caught part of The Amboy Dukes' set, but I left halfway through their show to return to Huck's Restaurant to wash dishes and punch out. As I scrubbed a few pots and pans until about 1:30 a.m., I reflected on the craziness of my brief encounter with "The Captain."

As a side note, I saw Captain Beefheart again at Harpo's in December 1980 when he returned to recording and performing live shows after several years away from the touring circuit. He released his then critically acclaimed new album, *Doc at the Radar Station.* The show featured many of the same musicians I had seen in the early '70s, but this performance had more depth and a longer setlist than the one in 1971. I don't think his legendary guitarist, Zoot Horn Rollo, was performing at the Harpo's gig, but I might have had one too many shots of Peppermint Schnapps. Still, the Captain was off his rocker and just as enjoyable as ever.

In the fall of 1980, I started teaching at Wayne State University. I was 25 years old and one of the youngest full-time instructors. However, a student assistant was closer to my age. We discovered each other at a Kraftwerk show at a local club, both thinking, "Well, here's a kindred musical soul." The student was Frank Pahl, who would later become a world-renowned avant- garde composer, winning awards for what was, and perhaps still is, called "new music." At that time, we were both huge fans of Ralph Records and the Residents. We bought every Residents, Snakefinger, Fred Frith, Renaldo & the Loaf, Tuxedo Moon, and Yello album we could find. We attended some of these artists' shows in the early 1980s at St. Andrew's Hall. I believe we saw a show featuring Tuxedo Moon and Yello together.

Shortly after meeting and discovering each other's unusual taste in music, Frank and I developed the idea to perform poetry and music live at readings. I started incorporating music into my poetry in the mid-1970s, but back then, I only had access to vinyl records and lacked real musicians. I remember using some of Ornette Coleman's "Soapsuds, Soapsuds" and early tracks from the Chieftains in my initial efforts to create my own sounds. I also tried playing the Silverstone acoustic guitar and a plastic flute, which we used in our fifth-grade class to earn music and art credits. I experimented with this style of performance at early Ridgeway and college readings. I wanted to bring more poetry into the tent, aiming to engage regular working-class kids and adults so they could dig and discover poetry as I had, being the son of an autoworker. At first, I think audiences found my music and poetry somewhat appealing. I didn't get the sense they enjoyed it as much as I did or as much as I hoped they would, but as Kerouac once said, "Walking on water wasn't built in a day."

However, when I met Frank in 1980, he suggested we practice a few pieces for the English Department's Afternoon Literary Series at Wayne State. Frank lived in an apartment in an old building in Detroit's New Center area, behind the old GM building. To avoid disturbing the other occupants, we took his synthesizer keyboard and my bag of poetry into a large closet to start experimenting. We both felt pretty good about it. Finally, the time arrived for our little show in the English Department, in the now-famous Room 400 State Hall. To be fair, there wasn't much poetry or reading happening at Wayne during that time. We had two great writers who would later become internationally known, Edward Hirsch and Charlie Baxter, along with Stephen Tudor, a poet trained in the Iowa Workshop. Still, they were all just teaching in their respective fields: American Literature and Folklore.

Frank and I compiled a brief collection of music and poetry. It was well received, as I recall. Nobody rushed to the podium, but the reception was warm. Later, Frank mentioned that he had a studio in Wyandotte and suggested I come down to record some poetry and music for an album or cassette (cassettes were a new concept back then). He told me I could sell tapes or albums at my readings instead of books. I thought this was a brilliant idea. My dream of reaching and inspiring many people through poetry began to take shape. It was, to say the least, a mustard seed.

    Frank and I played several live gigs around town at Cobb's Corner, Alvin's, and a few literary venues. There weren't many at the time. The poetry renaissance wouldn't start until spring 1987. After a while, Frank said, "Hey man, I can't play all these gigs you're booking; I have my own band and music to create." I was fine with that, but he suggested we record backing music on tape to play behind me at readings on a cassette player. That became my preferred method for a year or two.

    Eventually, some cool anarchist musicians from the Cass Corridor approached me about playing some live shows, and I thought it was an even better idea. Around this time, I met one of my hero poets and musicians, Faruq Z. Bey, though I'm not sure how it happened. Faruq had been part of the legendary Detroit Sun Ra-inspired band, Griot Galaxy. I had seen them live and always admired Faruq as their leader. Someone must have introduced us in the mid-1980s, just as I was starting to make my first cassette. I asked Faruq to join me along with members of popular Corridor bands like The Layabouts and Kuru, fueling my hunger to experiment and combine different musicians and styles to see what would happen. The Layabouts were fronted by the Franklin Brothers (Ralph and Alan), a reggae-rock political band, along with Gerard Smith from the proto-punk band Kuru, who reminded me of Detroit's version of Mission of Burma, in addition to Faruq Z. Bey from the experimental contemporary jazz group, Griot Galaxy. I always said we sounded like "The Art Ensemble of Chicago meets Jefferson Airplane meets Bob Marley." We rehearsed in an old funeral home converted into a music school, located across from the Old Miami at the corner of Alexandrine and Cass. This was the same funeral home where Henry Ford was laid out and where Harry Houdini was embalmed after dying from appendicitis at Harper Hospital. I only occasionally felt creeped out rehearsing there. Sometimes, we had to set up in one of the embalming rooms. It was strange to look at those sinks and think about Houdini and Ford's blood being washed down those drains, but it was a solid place to practice.

We finished the first cassette by early 1986. Before we mass-produced them, the late Nkenge Zola, a well-known broadcaster on WDET-FM Detroit Public Radio, invited Faruq and me to come in and bring our reel-to-reel version of the upcoming recording. We were honored to participate in such a prestigious and respected Sunday evening cultural show.

Faruq and I, along with Ralph and Alan Franklin from the anarchy band The Layabouts, arrived at the WDET studios early Sunday evening. Nkenge interviewed me about performance poetry. She asked what it was and why people should care. I shared the same response I've been giving for several years. By blending poetry and music, I attracted more people to my big poetry tent to discover something new. Then she played a track from the reel we'd brought. I can't remember what it was, but I do recall the phone lines started lighting up. Nkenge told us that people were really digging the recording. One caller asked, "Hey, what's the name of these guys?" Nkenge looked at me and mouthed, "What do you guys call yourselves?" I didn't know what to say since we were a collective of musicians and not a "group." So, I said, tell them "We're The Magic Poetry Band." Boom! There it was, some 15 or more years since my solo visit to the Eastown Theater, where I saw a wild poet-musician with a dunce hat and a badminton birdie glued on top, blast through 15 minutes of spasmodic poetry backed by great music.

From that moment on, we became M.L. Liebler & The Magic Poetry Band. So, what do we do about that? Another caller asked, "Where are these guys playing?" Again, Nkenge covered the receiver and said, "This guy wants to know where you're playing next?" Hell, I had just named the band five minutes ago—how would I know that? I looked at Faruq, Ralph, and Allen and asked if they were available to start booking some shows. They were quite enthusiastic and totally supportive of the idea, so I told Nkenge to let them know we would be playing out soon.

We received positive reviews and feedback on WDET that night, marking the beginning of the journeys and challenges that would henceforth be known as The Magic Poetry Band. One of our earliest performances was part of the Detroit Institute of Arts' annual Borderline program, which showcased American and Canadian writers in both Detroit and Windsor. I was paired with the amazing Diane Wakoski and the legendary Canadian poet Al Purdy at the Art Center in downtown Windsor. Diane and I have been good friends ever since that evening in 1986, collaborating on many projects over the decades. We received a strong response there, motivating us to set up more art-style poetry events. To that end, the Franklin brothers invited their drummer, Mel Rosas, a nationally acclaimed, award-winning painter and art professor at Wayne State, to join us. I asked Faruq to formally participate and brought in an excellent lead guitar player and WSU acting student Gerard Smith to join us. The first Magic Poetry Band had as eclectic a lineup as one could imagine.

Sometime after the band was launched into the public eye, John Sinclair introduced me to the editor-in-chief of *The Metro Times*, Detroit's weekly arts and culture magazine. I believe this was at John's wedding before he moved to New Orleans.

Not long after this event, I was informed that *The Metro Times* wanted to do a major story about me. I thought it was a great idea. I was sober, life was good, my teaching was going well, and the band was a dream come true for this kid who first danced wildly in a 1950s living room to Elvis Presley at four years old. Thank you, Grandma!

Shortly after attending John Sinclair and Penny's wedding, I heard from my old Detroit poetry friend, Jim Gustafson. He occasionally wrote for *The Metro Times* and mentioned that he had been assigned a story about me. He asked me some questions over the phone. A few days later, he called back and said, "Holy shit, they want over 700 words for a bigger story. Tell me some more crap. I now have to find some people who don't like you to balance the story."

I replied, "Whaaaaaat are you talking about, Jim??" The very next day, I walked to my office at Wayne State and found photography umbrellas and bright lights set up in my small office on the 4th floor of State Hall. The acclaimed Detroit photographer, John Sobczak, was getting everything ready.

He said, "M.L., by this time next week, everyone in Detroit will know your face."

"Whaaaaat are you talking about, John?"

He responded, "You are next week's cover story." I was stunned and shocked as John took numerous photos, using terms like "I need several headshots." At that point, those words were unfamiliar to me.

Well, lo and behold, there I was the following Wednesday on the front cover of *The Metro Times* at every newsstand across Metro Detroit. Everywhere I went, I saw myself staring back at me. WOW! And to think all of this began in a closet in Frank Pahl's New Center apartment. What the hell?

After that article, I would appear on the cover of *The Metro Times* another four or five times, but this first time truly piqued people's interest in me and my Magic Poetry Band. Soon, I received a call from Sam Milgrom, who owned Sam's Jams Record Store on 9 Mile Road in Ferndale, inviting me to be featured in his well-known and highly coveted series "Live at Sam's" in the record store, with Dave Dixon assigned the emceeing duties. Dave had been my childhood hero, music teacher, and an iconic Detroit broadcaster. That backstage meeting in 1989 sparked our long friendship, which grew until his early death on Memorial Day in 1999. Dave took me everywhere he went on the radio and television dial, from WDET-FM to his television show and his talk show stint on WXYT-AM radio, where he dubbed me "Detroit's Culture Czar." I appeared weekly with literary updates, sometimes calling in from a rest stop on the highway or from the kitchen of the legendary Tinker Street Café, famous from Bob Dylan, in Woodstock, New York. I was there with The Magic Poetry Band and was surprised to learn, just before I called in, that two members of The Bad Brains were in the audience, as they had recently moved to Woodstock.

We were on fire! We played everywhere. It felt like every series wanted us. We performed at Sam's Jams Record Store, and then the Heidelberg Poetry Slam in Ann Arbor, the second one in the

U.S., invited us. This later led to a guest slot opening for two guys who would become friends: Beat poet Michael McClure and Ray Manzarek (see "10 Feet to China").

As the band's popularity grew, so did what I came to know as "the dreaded band resentment" and "the uber dreaded band meeting." Band meetings felt like executive board sessions where, during these gatherings, "someone is getting fired!" This was all new to me back then, as I was used to being a solo poet, just a guy carrying a bag of poems. Simple stuff! My first encounter with the "dreaded band meeting" occurred when the original bass player (whom I quite liked) became disenchanted due to not receiving as much publicity as I did. He was part of a Detroit anarchist group and collective, leading me to think, "So much for battling the evils of fame and fortune in that grand anarcho way." So, we all gathered at Wayne State's popular Café Detroit.

As we sat around the "dreaded" table at the "dreaded band meeting," everyone seemed somber and quiet, but I was hungry, so I quickly placed my order.

Looking around, I asked, "So, guys, what's on the agenda?" The bass player said he felt slighted, then suddenly got up, pushed the table, and stormed out of the café. I was stunned—no, I was shocked—being a newbie to "the dreaded band meeting." We all just sat at the table, staring at each other. Then, within seconds, Faruq looked around and quickly said, "Does anyone know a bass player?" I thought that was a bit callous, but I replied, "Okay! Does anyone know someone?" I didn't realize it then, but I learned that losing band members wasn't as big a deal to the band as it was to the one leaving. Lesson learned! "Don't let the door hit ya where the dog done bit ya."

This marked the beginning of new members coming and going in The Magic Poetry Band. Over the years, I've encountered people who said, "I used to be in your band." I couldn't remember their names or faces, let alone that they were once a member of "my band." The Magic Poetry Band just kept going. If the band couldn't perform, it was often just Faruq and me hitting the road together: two poets and a one-man saxman.

I would say there were four memorable and significant Magic Poetry Bands from 1987 to 2012. I really enjoyed the first version featuring the Franklin Brothers, Mel Rosas, Gerard Smith, Chip Kipp, and Faruq Z. Bey. That version eventually ended with a frustrated anarchist leaving before 1990.

The second version occurred when we added the incredibly talented Thomas Voiles, who played both the sitar and flute. Faruq and I saw him performing his sitar behind a hippie-slam poet, and we exchanged glances, exclaiming in unison, "We must get him in our band." I asked Tom to leave the hippie poet and join us, to which he agreed that very night. The band then consisted of Faruq, me, Tom Voiles, and Jim Carrey on drums. Later, we added my colleague and friend, Matthew Nikkari, on bass. For a few months, Faruq, Matt, and I performed as The Magic Poetry Trio, using a drum machine to maintain the beat.

In 1997, I committed to making my first "real" CD and formed a completely new band featuring my longtime friend, former student, fellow activist, and baseball fan, Bill Boyer, aka Bill Blank. We brought Steve Bitto on board as our guitarist; he came from Bill's punk political band, The Blanks. Eventually, we added the talented Mike Smith to the group, who played bass and violin. At one point, Majesty Crush's former bassist, Hobey Echlin, joined in on the Magic Poetry fun. This was the band I took to Woodstock and New York. We played Woodstock numerous times—Magic Poetry was "almost famous" on Tinker Street.

Then, just before the turn of the century, I formed what became my favorite version of Magic Poetry, featuring Jim Carrey on drums, Brigitte Knudson on bass, and Ted Nagy on guitar. I truly loved the sound and camaraderie of these three souls. We shared countless experiences, road trips, joyful moments, and plenty of laughs. We often imagined ourselves as a "poetry band version" of Spinal Tap. We performed everywhere together, from Detroit to New Orleans, New York, Seattle, and even in a large cornfield in Oklahoma during the Woody Guthrie Festival.

There were some funny moments, like when I left Ted behind after a museum performance in South Bend, Indiana. We waited and waited for him after packing up the equipment, and I said,

"Let's just go." We drove about 10 miles. The others thought I was a heartless jerk, so I turned around and went back. As we pulled up, Ted came bouncing out of the doors of the Historical Museum. He hopped in as if nothing had happened because, to him, "nothing happened." We all laughed our asses off as we drove on to our Oklahoma gigs in Tulsa and the huge cornfield festival.

We played at the Woody Guthrie Festival in Woody's hometown of Okemah alongside his son Arlo, Country Joe, The Red Dirt Rangers, Slaid Cleaves, John Wesley Harding, and many others. When The Red Dirt Rangers took the stage and performed a country bluegrass rendition of Prince's "1999," I knew I wasn't in Oklahoma anymore; I was in a cornfield in Heaven. People seemed to appreciate our poetry and music. During that tour, we played in Tulsa to a warm and generous audience. Our next gig was in Oak Park, Illinois. I had to fly from Tulsa to Chicago for a Writer's Voice meeting, so the band drove my van and dropped me off at the airport around 2 a.m. for a 5 a.m. flight to Midway Airport in Chicago, where I reunited with them after the meeting in the Loop. We had many experiences like that; this Magic Poetry Band was a group of touring maniacs.

Feeling confident about the band and our sound after extensive touring, we decided to record the album *Paper Ghost Rain Dance* with my longtime musical friend and Cass Corridor brother, Dean Western, engineering and mixing. Dean worked out of Grammy and Oscar winner Luis Resto's (Eminem's musical collaborator) studio in Royal Oak. We had completed most of the album when I had to leave the Lower Peninsula to head north for a residency in the MFA program at Northern Michigan University, located on the shores of Lake Superior in Michigan's Upper Peninsula. I think the band learned something about Ted during my absence that I didn't know; Ted had a drinking problem and had missed several recording sessions. I only found out when he called to say he couldn't play at our album release show at Macomb Community College. I was furious. I had a television interview to do on Grosse Pointe Cable, so I called him from the parking lot of the television studio and proceeded to say the meanest, most hurtful things a person could ever say to another. Then, I fired him. Bill

Blank always said I was "the John Mayall of Poetry" because so many great Detroit musicians moved in and out of my band. I've come to regret, in hindsight, how harsh I was with Ted, and that has haunted me ever since, even though it was back in 2001. I loved Ted, and he was and continues to be, kind to me. We performed that launch in front of a packed audience with just bass and drums. We tried to keep the band together by auditioning a few guitar players. We finally found one who was very good, but he often jumped in front of me on stage. I didn't mind that too much, but I often had to remind him that people were there to see the poet and not the guitarist. Again, the cruel side of M.L. came out.

With this new version of the band, we performed at an event at Jorma Kaukonen's Fur Peace Ranch in southern Ohio, just outside Athens. When my band arrived, since I had come down earlier, Jorma Kaukonen's wife, Vanessa Lillian, asked me, "Who's the old Beach Boy-looking dude?" I replied that he was my new lead guitarist. Her response was lukewarm: "Oh!"

Shortly after joining the band, the new guitarist fell in love with Brigitte. While this was acceptable, they were both married to other people, so their spouses held me accountable for the breakdown of their marriages. It became evident that this version of The Magic Poetry Band was nearing its end.

We played our final gig at a Catholic university in the Bronx, New York City, as part of a major program organized each year by my friend and fellow poet, Rick Pernod. Rick managed the hugely popular Bronx Literary Series, Exoterica, at a radical Irish bar in the Riverside neighborhood. We had performed there a few times with great success, so he included us in his annual literary festival.

The Bronx college festival featured Jim Carroll, who was the friendliest and kindest person I had ever encountered since our rude encounter in Lawrence, Kansas, about 14 years prior. Sadly, Jim passed away shortly after this festival. The festival also included Eric Andersen, Bob Holman, and many others. I participated in a poetry workshop with Eric Andersen, whom I admired greatly. To me, he was more of a poet and literary figure than a musical star. I owned his classic early album, *Blue River*, before we met.

I flew to the Bronx gig directly from the Los Angeles gig, where I had been performing in the poetry garden of Venice at Beyond Baroque. I let the band drive my van to meet me in New York City. The band was being torn apart by the relationship between the bassist and the new guitarist. The drummer, Jim Carrey, told me he didn't want to be in a band like that because he didn't want to get caught in the middle of Oklahoma if their relationship fell apart or if they had a fight on the road. After the Bronx gig, I went back to my good poet friend Barry Wallenstein's place on the Upper West Side of New York. I called Jim to tell him the band was over. He pretty much figured that out and agreed with me. As I hung up, I couldn't shake the feeling that I would never see or talk to Jim Carrey again in my life. I told Barry and that really bothered me. I loved Jim. I tried calling him a couple of times since that gig ended in the summer of 2001, but he never returned my calls.

Years later, Brigitte called to tell me she needed to have open-heart surgery. She expressed her fear and uncertainty about the results, but just in case, she wanted me to know she loved me and appreciated everything we had gone through. Mortality hit me hard after that call. Thankfully, Brigitte came through the surgery and eventually married the "old Beach Boy" guitar player, Randy. They have been happily married for several decades now, so all's well that ends well.

Ted joined AA many years later and has remained sober ever since. His guitar playing has returned to an excellent level, and we continue to work together even today. He is a wonderful human being. Despite all the bad craziness I put him through, he remains a great collaborator and friend.

In 2024, The Magic Poetry Band reformed, adding my "Beatles Forever" band drummer. Brigitte had retired from her position as principal at her high school in White Lake. In the meantime, she received her PhD from Wayne State. We are writing and recording a new album of completely original material, and these folks have never sounded better.

At some point in the early 2000s, Faruq had gotten sober and quit drinking for good. He had developed emphysema but played his saxophone better than ever. Although his doctor advised him not to play, he continued to do so and grew stronger. Finally, his doctor said, "Well, it seems to be working for you, so keep playing!"

Faruq and I returned with a new version of The Magic Poetry Band alongside Alex Lumelsky, with whom I previously traveled for gigs in London and Russia, and my childhood friend Tom Feeney for one last big hurrah.

We played several more gigs between 2002 and June 2012, when I received a call in Casper, Wyoming, where I was a featured speaker at a writers' conference. Lolita Hernandez, my good friend and a fiction writer from Detroit, called to let me know that Faruq had passed away that night at his home. I immediately flew back home. We buried Faruq in traditional Muslim fashion, and I laid The Magic Poetry Band to rest alongside him that sunny June afternoon at his mosque. It was our thing! We started the band in a small studio in Wyandotte and nurtured it for 25 years. It was time to say goodbye to the old Magic band, so I did.

Over the years, between Magic Poetry and my next adventure, I collaborated with my friend Al Kooper from 1998 to 1999. Al scored my poetry in a film soundtrack style, and the album turned out excellent, embodying the type of poetry and music that many devoted fans seem to favor.

However, in the end, the album was never released. For a long time, Al really liked it, even playing a track in an airport for Nick Lowe, whom we encountered during Al's tour of Spain. Nick appeared to approve. Although it was scheduled for a Record Store Day special vinyl release, Al halted production as he had done many times before. The rare album now resides in my Dropbox library, reminiscent of Brian Wilson's lost classic, *Sunflower*. A handful of the short tracks appeared on a CD included in my 2004 New Issues Press book, *The Moon a Box*, which also featured a CD containing my various collaborations with Professor Louie & Crowmatix, Jorma Kaukonen, Mike Watt of the Minutemen, Country Joe, and several versions of my Magic Poetry Band.

In 2002, I recorded a poetry and acoustic music album with Country Joe McDonald titled *Crossing Borders*. We toured for a couple of years with that album. I transitioned Joe from bar gigs to performing at libraries and literary arts venues. We finished by 7 p.m. and were on our way home by 9 p.m., earning the same money he made playing in bars and concert venues.

In 2011, I met Peter Lewis from Moby Grape. He was a poetry enthusiast, so I flew to LA and drove up to his ranch in Solveig, just north of Santa Barbara. We had arranged a poetry music gig at Santa Barbara College through some poet friends of mine, as their campus was close to Peter's home. I stayed with Peter and his family on a small mountaintop just outside downtown Solveig. We rehearsed, wrote new pieces, and enjoyed eggs Benedict every morning at a local diner. The show went well, so we made plans to hang out in Detroit and LA and collaborate further. Eventually, Peter flew to Detroit, and while he was here, we spent a lot of time in Jef Reynolds's studio in St. Clair Shores on the lake, recording new and old pieces. Jef played bass and engineered, while Bill Hulet drummed for our sessions. Peter showcased his lead and slide guitar skills. We ended up recording what I considered a solid album titled *The Coyote & The Monk*. Since we were both fans of Thomas Merton, we began rereading his book *The Seven Story Mountain*.

I had been a serious Moby Grape fan since 1968, when their album *WOW* was released. I was in junior high at that time, but I always loved the fact that Loretta Young was Peter's mother. I've long admired old Hollywood. Peter entertained me with stories of his mother's dinner parties with John Wayne, Ronald Reagan, Joan Wyatt, Clark Gable, and other stars from the conservative side. He told me that his mother once invited Steve McQueen to dinner as the "new kid" in town to meet the Hollywood old guard. Peter said Steve had little in common with the older actors, so they went up to Peter's room, smoked a joint, and wrote a new song together. Another story I cherished was when Ronald Reagan called their house—this was when Reagan was the mean-spirited governor of California before he became the mean-spirited President. He called the Lewis home looking for Loretta. Even though Loretta was home, Peter picked up the kitchen phone first and said abruptly, "She's not here," then quickly hung up.

Back in St. Clair Shores, Peter and I put together an album of material and recorded it at Jef Reynolds's Detroit Sound Record label on the beautiful Lake St. Clair. After that recording, Peter wanted to do more shows in his hometown of Hollywood.

Peter and I played many live shows in Detroit, but we primarily performed in Los Angeles, Venice Beach, Berkeley, and San Francisco. We played at the Pig & Whistle on Hollywood Boulevard at Los Palmas several times and performed at Beyond Baroque in Venice a few times as well. The Pig & Whistle was the old bar where Peter's mother and her Hollywood friends used to hang out back in the day. We had many special guests join us in both LA and San Francisco. Our first show in LA featured a band with an all-star lineup, including Mark Tulin of The Electric Prunes on bass; At that time, Mark was playing bass with Billy Corgan. While I'm not a fan of The Smashing Pumpkins, I do appreciate Billy and the music he created and continues to produce. Plus, he was a Chicago kid, which is where I started what I call my "national" career. In addition to Mark, Alex Del Zoppo from Sweetwater, Jerry Miller of Moby Grape, Freddie Krc from Roky Erickson's Explosives, and Al Staehely of Spirit, George Wendt's son, Joe, once sat in on bass with us. I performed Slim Harpo's "King Bee," with Peter and Jerry trading some wicked lead guitar licks. When we wrapped up for the night, George Wendt, who was there to support his son, came up to me and said, "Wicked blues singing, my man, very, very good." I then recalled that he was a Second City alum, born in Chicago. High praise indeed! To complete the band, Peter brought in the legendary record producer Neil Young's PR guy and music business giant, Bill Bentley, to play drums. Another talented studio musician, Willie Aron, who co-produced with Leonard Cohen and is a great guitar player, joined the fun. Willie still plays with me to this day in what I call The LA Coyote Monk Band, which also features Dave Soyars on bass and music business impresario and Los Angeles record producer extraordinaire Pat Thomas on drums. It's a small world because Dave Soyars played in an LA Irish bar band with my long-gone old high school friend and singer-songwriter Brandon Curtis, who was formerly known in St. Clair Shores as Chuck Craven.

Peter and I gigged quite a bit in California, Detroit, and various places throughout the Midwest and Tennessee. We even performed at a prison and a college in South Dakota and northern Nebraska. In fact, we had a really cool and fun show at Northeast Community College in Johnny Carson's hometown of Norfolk.

Over the years, we hosted a benefit in Berkeley for former Detroiter Joyce Jenkin's Poetry Flash, featuring Jimmy Preston of The Sons of Champlin on drums, and we were joined by the legendary 1960s Serpent's Power poetry band leader, Beat poet, and exceptional performer David Meltzer. My old musical partner, Country Joe McDonald, who lived just around the corner from the venue, took part in the benefit for his hometown literary paper. The program was fantastic, and the audience was large. Peter and I had just released *The Coyote & The Monk* CD, which sold out quickly. Jef Reynolds even flew in from Detroit to play bass. Nowadays, when I need a copy of our album, I have to buy a used one online or on eBay. However, it is available on all streaming platforms.

I think I was starting to feel burned out from gigging with Peter, and I believe he was also growing tired of me. We amicably parted ways shortly after. Now, we remain good friends but with much less gigging.

Shortly after the West Coast shows in the fall of 2012, I began collaborating with deaf Detroit hip-hop star Sean Forbes. I met him by inviting him to participate in a literary series I was producing and hosting. He accepted, which opened a whole new chapter in my life that could not have been scripted. Sean was a huge hit with Wayne State students and Detroit's literary fans, prompting WSU to ask if he would open a larger show featuring the major hip-hop act Far East Movement. Sean agreed but insisted that I introduce him. I consented and arrived at the Majestic Theater during soundcheck. While standing there, a man approached me. He introduced himself as Steve King, Sean's technician. We shook hands, and I asked the question that everyone in Detroit seemed to ask: "Are you the Steve King of The Dittles (a well-known local bar band)?" He replied no and explained that he was an engineer at 54 Sound. I recognized 54 Sound as the famous studio where Eminem recorded his major early albums, including 8 Mile.

He seemed to recognize me too and mentioned that he had my books and some of my recordings, which I found interesting. I asked, "You don't play bass, do you?" He answered, "In fact, I do." He then mentioned he had a friend coming by shortly whom he would like me to meet. I asked, "He doesn't play drums, does he?" He confirmed that he indeed played drums, referring to his close friend, Cass Corridor musician and painter Leonard Johnson. This was the seed for a new idea planted that night in 2012, which eventually evolved into my Coyote Monk project. I already had an excellent guitarist ready to join a band, as I had promised Charlie Palazzola a spot in a good group. I later added a seasoned pianist, my Wayne State Labor Studies colleague Frankie Kocelski, and we were off and running. At each rehearsal, we wrote new pieces, reaching a point where we had too many to remember or perform in a single show. Some became instant classics for us, like "Mother's Day," "The Train Is Your Blood," "Deliver Me," "Assassination," and several new pieces for which I wrote the music and lyrics, such as "Green Moon" for Peter Green, "The King Tree," and others.

I had the band learn a new version of the great Bill Fay's "Life is People." This was the title of Bill's first album in over 40 years, and I later became good friends with Bill Fay from England. I still visit him on my many trips to the U.K. He is a master British songwriter whom I believe more people need to discover. His story is somewhat similar to Detroit's Rodriguez. He had a significant album that became a cult favorite in 1971, entitled *Time of the Last Persecution*, released on Deram Records. Nothing much happened with it, and after a while, he settled into a working-class life in the city outside of north London where he was raised and still lives. His Christian faith grew and sustained him through what must have been lonely, disappointing years. So, we had our faith in common. However, I wouldn't classify Bill as a "Christian singer/songwriter." About 40 years passed before Jeff Tweedy of Wilco was introduced to his music by a younger colleague whose father had been a fan and held an old copy of *Time of the Last Persecution*. Wilco recorded two Fay songs, including the popular "Jesus Etc." Bill joined Wilco on stage at Shepherd's Bush Empire Theater, one of my favorite places to see concerts in London, and this was captured in the documentary *I Am Trying to Break Your Heart*. Knowing Bill as a recluse who does not seek the limelight, I remarked, "You likely took the Tube to Shepherd's Bush, went in, did the song, and slipped back out to the Tube and home." He replied, "That's right, Mike," as if there were any other way.

He also mentioned that since the release of his new album, Jools Holland wanted him to appear on his popular BBC music show, but Bill wasn't interested. Jools conceded and arranged for Bill to come down during the day to film his segment for the show. At one point, I asked Bill if he would consider visiting me in Detroit to do a solo show. He told me he had never been to America and had no desire to come now, adding, "Besides, Mike, you're doing a great version of my song, so there's no need for me to come over." I find Bill to be an inspiration and a genuine guy. He writes and records his music (he's released several albums since 2012). He truly has no ego and is completely at peace with his life situation, and I admire him deeply for that.

In the summer of 2018, I decided to revive the glory days of The Monks by creating an updated version of The Coyote Monk Poetry Band for a major festival at Hart Plaza. It was a weekend filled with eclectic music and art. The art underground was curated by my friend Cary Loren, the owner of Book Beat and founder of Destroy All Monsters. Cary wanted me to create something, so I enlisted my trustworthy and talented drummer, Leonard Paul Johnston, and brought in key players from the past Cass Corridor music scene, George Kirby and Keith Buchanan. We rehearsed for about a month, and I must say, the show was a significant success, leaving us all feeling great. Thus began the final iteration of M.L. Liebler & The Coyote Monk Poetry Band.

We played numerous gigs until the COVID-19 pandemic struck in early March 2020. That upheaval has really slowed everything down. It has been quite a while since I have performed or read in public. I immediately began hosting an online Literary Series, which has provided readings and music for thousands. Still, COVID and the online format haven't given me any chance to perform with musicians.

My contributions to the literary arts in recent years include an anthology of poems titled *R=E=S=P=E=C=T: Poets on Detroit Music* from the Michigan State University Press, which I co-edited with the wonderful working-class poet Jim Daniels, and a collection of new and selected poems called *Underneath My American Face*, published in 2021 by a press in northern India.

Ah, showbiz! I thought I hated it, but I've missed it over these long COVID years. Maybe I'll be like Old Blue Eyes. I'll keep doing my last book, my last album, my last show, and teach my last class well into eternity!

Stevie Wonder
© Creative Commons

David Blair
© Creative Commons

M.L. with his security team in Jalalabad, Afghanistan
Photo © U.S. State Department

BLAIR CHANNELS STEVIE WONDER

Squeezing Out "Every Drop of Rain"

2012

As the plane took off from Kabul International Airport in a light rain, I put my earphones on, pushed back my seat, and pressed play on my iPod. I closed my eyes and thanked God for this important and exciting time and for returning me safely to Detroit and my family. At just that serendipitous moment, the voice of my good pal, a well-known and much-loved Detroit poet, folk singer, and singer of opera and Stevie Wonder, David Blair sweetly washed into my ears and over my soul:

And every raindrop falling from the sky
Is like a tribute to the blue skies following behind
And every raindrop falling to the sea
Is like a testament to a new life that will come to be.

Since 2000, I have built a significant reputation within the US State Department's Cultural Affairs Division for conducting cultural and educational programs abroad with students in middle school and high school, teachers, and students attending college and university. They saw something in the way I related to international audiences and students. It was more chance than skills at first. A State Department official forgot to apply for my funding in early summer 2004. The official followed me to several venues around Munich. I think she was impressed with the way I handled college students, schoolchildren and adults—making sure to be inclusive and to have fun. When she drove me back to the Munich airport, she mentioned her faux pas of forgetting to file for one of their artist's grants. I said "I don't care. I enjoyed this visit and the places we visited." She mentioned at the curb at the Munich airport that she had an idea to send me on a multicity tour of Germany in Fall 2004. If I'd accept. I accepted.

So, Germany is where my new job as cultural ambassador during the Bush years for the State Department started. Since then, I've gone to many unique and different places like Israel, the West Bank, Gaza, Russia, Germany, England, Macao and, now, Afghanistan. I usually spend a fair amount of time helping instructors, teachers, and professors with ideas for creatively teaching and engaging them with English, writing and literature classes on a user-friendly way. In addition to offering classes, workshops, and consultations, I am always requested to read and perform my poetry. That is not my prerogative for these journeys, but "give the people what they want," I say.

I am usually hosted by the US Embassy in the countries I visit. I am often one of only a few American poets or writers invited to many of these programs. For example, as far as I know, only one other poet—from Iowa—visited Afghanistan in recent months, or maybe even in recent years. Some of the places I go don't exactly top a "must visit" list for other writers I know. Many are leery of even visiting Israel or the West Bank, let alone Afghanistan.

Look, I am not brave; I am just a dedicated teacher-poet who keeps focused on the task I am assigned in any overseas assignment. For some reason, I am able to block out possible dangers.

More, the US State Department does not, in any way, censor my work, performances, lectures, or talks overseas when I work for them. Their Cultural Affairs Division is quite liberal and art-and-artist friendly. I am also always aware of how far I can push the envelope in certain locations and with certain audiences. I think the State Department is very comfortable, after 12 years, with the fact I am always very respectful of a country's traditions, religions, and customs. My international assignments are not for every artist, but they fit my work and who I am.

I want to write, I want to write about
My dreams which never come true,
My power that has always been ignored,

My voice which is never heard by this deaf universe,
My rights which have never been counted,
My life decisions which are always made by others.

Oh my destiny, give me the answer, what am I for in this universe?

—From "Read My Poems on the
Reddish Stream of My Blood" by Emaan

This is a poem by one of the brave young women I met upon my arrival in Kabul in early May 2012. I was asked to go to Afghanistan for 10 days by the US State Department's Cultural Programs Division. They called me two days before the Thanksgiving in 2011 and told me that I had been requested in Afghanistan by a Cultural Affairs officer with whom I had worked successfully in the West Bank a couple of years ago.

The gentleman on the phone asked if I'd "take this mission." I'd worked in dangerous places before for the State Department—such as the West Bank and Israel during the 2006 Lebanon War—so I said I'd do it. After a long trip, I started working early my second morning in Afghanistan.

For my first in-country assignment, I was driven to an undisclosed place in a quiet Kabul neighborhood. For the next three hours I visited with several strong, courageous young women involved in the Afghan Women's Writers' Project (AWWP). The project was started by American writer and novelist Masha Hamilton in 2009 after she viewed a disturbing underground video of Zarmeena, a mother of seven who, 10 years earlier, was executed by the Taliban in Kabul's Ghazi Stadium for allegedly killing her husband. A videotape of the execution was smuggled out by RAWA (Revolutionary Association of the Women of Afghanistan). Masha was determined to find out about this executed woman so she could honor her memory. She founded the WWP for that purpose and to offer the women of Afghanistan hope through their creative words, images, and art.

I arrived early by way of an armored SUV with tracking devices and "jammers" turned on to keep anyone from activating roadside bombs through cell phones (jammers stop all cell phone usage within the range of the passing SUV). I found the gathered women to be alive with creativity, with energy, and they were eager to meet an American poet and talk poetry as a way to express their personal and cultural struggles. We sat on pillows on the floor in traditional Afghan style. The host served cookies and plenty of traditional tea. The women were hungry to create new work, to read their new and older poems to me, and to share stories of their recent protests at local colleges on behalf of women's rights.

Some said their actions earned them coverage on BBC News and the cover of U.K. newspaper *The Guardian*. They told me they'd have to give their blood to make things better for the next generation of Afghan women. This sounded very brave and admirable, but these ladies were only in their 20s, and at times they spoke as though their lives were over for their cause to liberate the women of Afghanistan.

I was shocked to see students the age of my own students at Wayne State University talking this way, but Afghanistan is a different place with different problems, and I could tell that they felt they had to face their struggles using desperate methods. One of the poets told me that the Afghans' women's rights movement was at the point where the American suffragist movement was here in the early 1900s. They were determined to win or die trying.

The poems they created were based on Native American poetry and music exercises that I gave them. They wrote beautifully using music and short poems as their lyrical and musical inspiration, which was totally foreign to them (to read the good work these women are creating in anonymity, go to awwproject.org and support them by purchasing the brand-new anthology of their work titled *The Sky Is a Nest of Swallows: A Collection of Poems and Essays* by Afghan Women Writers [Bellville Books Press 2012]).

After the AWWP meeting, we headed via our trusty bulletproof SUV to the Afghanistan National Institute of Music in another part of town near Kabul University. The sidewalks were jammed with pedestrians, and the unlined main roads were bumper-to-bumper with small cars, each packed full of passengers driving through the dusty, hot hazy streets of the capital. People on bicycles and on foot wore scarves or surgical masks over their mouths and noses to keep the car and dust pollution from their lungs. If you think the bus system in Metro Detroit is bad, try jumping in a moving Toyota minivan with sliding doors wide-open and broken seats for bus service commute. I watched an older guy in a suit miss the jump to catch a quickly moving bus- van and literally get left in the Kabul street dust.

When we arrived at ANIM (The Afghanistan National Institute of Music—a public arts-based high school in city-center Kabul) and entered the building, I guessed this school was some sort of *Fame*-style high school, or Kabul's version of *Glee*. The students were a combination of working-class and middle-class students. The boys and girls, ages 12–18, wore school uniforms. This school is famous for graduating some of Afghanistan's most acclaimed musicians. The kids were very serious about their studies and their music. My plan was to introduce them to performance poems by showing them one of my pieces with tape loops that I created in various studios around Detroit with area musicians. This is a technique I picked up after seeing the Postal Service perform at the Hollywood Palladium in Los Angeles several years ago. The loops are created so musicians in other countries can play along or poeticize along. Sometimes, I plug my iPod into a sound system or amplifier for a fuller sound.

I performed a couple of my standards in a large ANIM High School classroom, including John Sinclair's "The Screamers," so they could see how I performed poems with music. Next, we discussed Langston Hughes's poem "Harlem." I asked the students to identify all the concrete and abstract language used in his poem.

After that, I had them write some poems using repetitious lines starting with "I Have a Dream."

With this prompt, I am bringing a little M.L. King into the program. Next, I wanted the students to put the pieces to hip-hop. We were doing everything from Hughes's "Harlem" (with its famous question: "What happens to a Dream Deferred?") to Notorious B.I.G.'s "Juicy" to M.L. King with hip-hop thrown in for good measure. They were all totally unfamiliar with these American cultural signposts, but I could tell they were interested and ready to dig in.

These were amazing kids who communicated at various levels of English, which these students were all learning as a required second language. In addition, the students are all music students. As they were writing their "Dream" poems, I got the idea to have them play their own live hip-hop Afghan-style versus using a tape loop. I asked who had their instruments handy. Several hands went up. A very hip drummer kid had his doumbe (a sort of Middle Eastern and Asian conga) handy; another kid grabbed his sitar; and I got a very shy, quiet, veiled girl to fetch her viola. I started the drummer with a cool, funky beat. Next, I had the girl bow repeating chords on her viola, and I told the sitar player to make like Jimi Hendrix and rip some lead. Many in the room seemed to know the name "Jimi Hendrix." I was surprised because they had never heard of Detroit, Eminem, or hip-hop, but "Jimi" they got. *Breakthrough!* I thought. Yes, we were making good progress in Kabul.

After they jammed a bit, I started bringing poets of all ages up to rap their poems. Some were shy and more reserved, so they came up in small groups of two or three, but others jumped up and started reading their poems to the beats and sounds. It was beyond cool. A couple of dudes even free-formed after their written poems ran out.

The room was rockin'. They were on fire, and, like true open mic poets, I couldn't get them to stop, so we jammed on for an hour or so. Their unique instruments jammed funky beats, and we were grooving, Detroit stylin', ancient Afghanistan. This class was seriously rocking out, and a lot of other students gathered outside the door to see "sup" with the goateed bald dude rockin' the ANIM poetry class. It ended a very cool and culturally rewarding first day in the 'Stan. This homie quickly realized that he wasn't in Kansas, or Motown, anymore, Dorothy.

The next day, I met with my first group of A.C.C.E.S.S. students in Kabul. A.C.C.E.S.S. is a U.S. government-sponsored English-language training program administered around the world to make the study of English more accessible to students and teachers. I have visited several of these programs not only here but in Israel, the West Bank, and Russia over the years. These students were very fluent in reading, writing, and speaking English. I brought a little Paterson, NJ, with me to the class. I turned the students onto pediatrician and major American writer and poet William Carlos Williams, who often wrote short poems on the back of prescription pads. The students had all been to the doctor as children, so they knew what a prescription was and what it looked like. They seemed to find it amazing that a children's doctor wrote poems and stuffed his white doctor's coat with poems. I shared "The Locust Tree in Flower" and his very famous "The Red Wheelbarrow." The students were very familiar with wheelbarrows (which they called "carts") because it is quite common for Afghan men to push them down the sidewalks, down the middle of the busy streets and the side streets of Kabul. We even saw a guy pushing a red wheelbarrow down the road as we were leaving the compound for the class.

Anyway, I had them create short, imagistic poems with no more than two-to-three words a line, just like Williams. They did nice work, and then I hit the hip-hop loops for the background. The kids were geeked and excited to stand up "in the name of Allah" (as is their tradition) and recite to music. I got them moving and jumping to the beats, and I could see many of the students, both male and female, coming out of their usual reserved and quiet selves.

The teacher and I were both amazed at their uninhibited participation, and it felt like a worthy break from the much more traditional and ordered Afghan classroom. I'd meet up with some of these students later at a debate and they were excited to see me again.

The next day would be a major adventure that involved wearing body armor, a U.S. Army issued helmet and flying in military-issued machine-gun manned helicopters to the city of Jalalabad just to the east of Kabul. For some reason—and with all of the fears of possibly getting mowed down by machine guns or blown up by an IED (improvised explosive device)—I was at peace with all of this. I knew this was all part of an adventure that I would never, ever forget. I also know that God is good. Just for good measure, I got my prayer on by attending Mass at the Italian Embassy down on Masood Road that Sunday night.

Tuesday morning, we boarded a helicopter to travel out to orange blossom country in beautiful Jalalabad in Nangarhar Province. Jalalabad is a stone's throw from the famous Kyber Pass, which is the gateway to Pakistan. We helicoptered in from Kabul, passing over the beautiful snowcapped peaks of the southern slopes of the Hindu Kush Mountains heading east to Nangarhar. We landed at a military base that was once a Soviet R&R spot and later (rumor has it) a Taliban retreat where Osama bin Laden and his posse once stayed. Nobody knows if this is 100-percent true, but it certainly looks like old-school Soviet housing to me, and I have stayed in my share of old Soviet-style hotels in my several visits to Mother Russia. We were, also, near the famous Tora Bora caves where bin Laden was allegedly hiding when "Dubya" famously, and stupidly, said, "I don't know where he is. Frankly, I don't spend a lot of time thinking 'bout him anymore." This wasn't long after 9/11.

My roommate, and host, at the old Soviet R&R spa was a Detroit native and Wayne State University urban studies and planning master's graduate and U.S. Agency for International Development worker from Plymouth, Michigan. His parents are still there, and he gets home every so often to catch a Tigers game and live in the Detroit life. When he attended WSU, he lived in a loft down on the river. He told me that out of all his degrees (from University of Michigan, etc.), it was his WSU MA that has been the most valuable in his work in Afghanistan. Go Wayne State Warriors!

Anyway, Mike D. (I have withheld his name for security purposes) showed me around the compound and pointed out the dusty, empty swimming pool where the "urban legend" (Hey now—Jalalabad's a big ass city in these here parts!) is that the Taliban executed people there. It now has a basketball hoop with a hand-painted three-point line around it. I think the Taliban executed in the deep end—win more ways than one.

I was given three assignments in Jalalabad over two working days there. First, I did a workshop with thirty English A.C.C.E.S.S. micro-scholarship students from the area and their teachers. I turned the workshop into a lesson and poetry-writing session based, again, on William Carlos Williams's short poems.

The students were all Pashto school kids who were very reserved and very polite. I knew I had to quickly change that scene. Five minutes into our two-hour session, as can be typical in Afghanistan, the electric generator went out and left us with no A/C or lights. We were in what they call a container without windows, and it was over 90 degrees and sunny outside. Oy! Oy! Oy!

I had the kids write their poems on big white sheets of paper that we hung all around the room. I then had them get up and rap the poems to the instrumental music of Eminem's "Lose Yourself." I heard one of the soldiers in the back of the room yell his approval for my musical taste. These youngsters had never heard of hip-hop music—ever, but they loved it. The look in their eyes must have been like my own when I first heard The Beatles on a car AM radio in 1963. They were excited. I told them to jump around and "free-form" words with the music. They did. They like! They like! This experience was one of the coolest overseas educational ones I have ever had. Young students enthusiastically reciting poetry to a beat while jumping and running in place. This was cross-cultural poetry heaven to me. This workshop is exactly why I do this in unusual places around this world.

The next day in Jalalabad, I was going to first meet with college students and professors from Nangarhar University. To get there, we had to suit up in full body armor and load into MRAPS, which are, essentially, Humvees on steroids and built to withstand roadside bombs, bullets, grenades, etc. It took four of these to get me to the location in downtown Jalalabad. Two led the way, I was in the third tank, and a fourth backed us up just in case any of those nasty insurgents lay in wait for a goateed Detroit poet passing by in a tank. Once we arrived, we had to exit and stand in the middle with our flak jackets while several heavily armed soldiers walked us to the lecture hall.

I'll say right here that all these soldiers are highly well-trained and are some of the most dedicated people I have ever met. Seeing them in action here makes me feel both proud and very safe. I know people say crap like this all the time, but I am telling you the truth. I have seen them work up close and personal, and they saved my life every minute of every day I was in Afghanistan.

Anyway, the students and professors wanted to talk contemporary American poetry, so I walked them through a little Dickinson, Whitman, Williams, Hughes, and some Ginsberg. The discussion was full and meaningful. I performed a couple of pieces for them, and they seemed to like the "M.L. music-and-poetry thing" quite a bit, too. We had a super great session followed by a traditional Afghan lunch (they serve some great pita over there, people).

After lunch, I met with a good-sized group of young poets, and we talked, and some of them read their poems in English and others in their native Pashto. We had decent translators at various programs who offered solid translations—according to what some of the bilingual poets in the audience told me. We talked about the importance of poetry in our lives, its importance in our respective communities in Jalalabad and Detroit.

On Thursday morning, we got back into our body armor and helicoptered down to Kabul for a meeting with Kabul artists and writers at the Afghan Cultural House. Upon arrival at this very contemporary cultural center, I met some very hip writers, filmmakers, painters, and musicians. I'd say this is Kabul's version of Detroit's own Museum of Contemporary Art.

I performed a few poems to start for them, to which they said, "We like! We like!" I did some "Blood in the Moon" (they seem very big on both "blood" and the "moon" over there). We talked

Afghan poetry, fiction, artwork, and music. I turned them on to some Whitman, Hughes, and Canada's Four Horsemen (long live bpNichol!!)

I encouraged all the artists there to think outside the box for collaborations between different types of artists. I told the established writers and artists in the audience that I sincerely believed there would be a market for their work in America where there is a conspicuous lack of literature and art from a country we have been so connected with for nearly 12 years. They seemed encouraged by my words. I gave them some of my CDs for themselves and the Cultural House's library.

As I was leaving for the armored SUV, a young Afghan woman artist stopped me to show me her paintings on her iPhone. They were very impressive and intriguing and quickly grabbed my attention. The paintings were colorful, and each included pieces of human hair inserted into the acrylic. She asked me, through our interpreter, to collaborate with her by putting some of my new poems to her paintings. She said that she was ready to "how you say 'think outside the box?'" I enthusiastically agreed to the project. She told me that she created all of her work as a statement on behalf of women's rights to help empower all the women of Afghanistan. This is very brave for her to do where women are treated as second-class (or less) citizens. I told her I was eager to collaborate with such a fine artist for such an important cause, and I thought we could get the book published over here in the US by some forward-thinking publisher.

Friday is their Sunday in Afghanistan. It was, also, my day off for a little R&R American style. The cultural affairs officer at the US Embassy (my crib when in-country), a very cool dude and major Rolling Stones fan, took me to the weekly Friday bazaar on the nearby NATO compound. I found some less-than-legit DVDs, bought several Pashto hats, cool Afghan scarves for my bride, and for my longtime bandmate and poetry partner Faruq Z. Bey, I picked up some genuine amber prayer beads and a cool new Muslim lid, which I am sure he'll sport the next time you see him playing in Motown. I watched a little of the embassy softball team play in a field on the other compound (the Tigers were on the

Armed Forces Network every morning there live from the West Coast—O Yea!), and I headed back to my hooch to relax because the next day we were heading to the wild, wild south in Kandahar.

We had to get up at 4 a.m. to allow time to drink my requisite pot of Starbucks before heading on the journey of a lifetime to the Taliban stronghold Kandahar. I have long traveled exclusively with Starbucks. I have to brew it in some pretty unusual places, such as a sleeping car on the Trans-Siberian Express, a broken-down Soviet hotel room, and a Hong Kong Nunnery Hotel, not to mention my embassy hooch in Kabul.

The travel plan to this gig consisted of a small State Department jet, a Chinook helicopter ride with machine guns that were tested—en route—into the side of a mountain, and a four tank/MRAP convoy to an undisclosed location to meet the 30-plus primo poets of the Kandahar poetry scene. We had a wonderful two-hour session reading our poems to each other and discussing the importance of poetry in Afghan and American societies. I told them all about the hip scene we have in Detroit. One poet dude even looked just like Smokey Robinson. He had never heard of Motown or Smokey, so I sang a chorus of "Being With You" and "Tears of a Clown." They liked that.

I can tell you all that poetry is important in Afghanistan and everywhere around the world I have traveled. It reminds me of a line by my close poet friend Antler from Milwaukee when he wrote about Americans and poetry. He wrote "Poetry is more important than even most poets realize."

I performed my spiritual piece "Deliver Me" with Coltrane's "Love Supreme" riff as a loop, and they went bonkers because religion is huge in Afghanistan along with poetry. They thought it was very cool that an American poet was willing to display his faith in God/Allah in a public setting, which is way normal and acceptable in Afghanistan.

I taught them to click their fingers after poems were read aloud and to say "dig that!" There was much "clicking" and "digging" later during the rest of the workshop. As we were offering concluding comments (there's a tradition here at public gatherings for the guest to make a small speech), the head of the educational-cultural organization that hosted us stood up and said in Pashto: "Your visit here today as an American poet is more important than 500,000 US soldiers in Afghanistan." I was moved very deeply when I heard the translation. I told them that we, as poets and as Afghans and an American, were all meant to meet in this location on that Saturday in Kandahar long before we were all born, and that day was allowing us all to fulfill our destinies.

After the gig, we were hustled out to the tanks by a team of professional Army staffers, heavily armed and ready for anything that might happen. They circled us, walked us into the tanks, and we drove back to the base. At the base, we had pizza for lunch, discussed the very positive experience and event, and suited back up with our body armor and helmets to head back to Kabul by Chinook, by plane, and by armored SUV. All in a day's work on the Afghan beat. Does stuff like this really happen to a working-class kid from Motown?

It is still very hard for me to believe it happened.

Now, with the Kandahar, Jalalabad, Kabul, and the other Afghanistan experiences behind me, and in hindsight—most of these visits had elements of danger for members of the audiences, for the military who assisted us at each location, and, dare I say, for me. But I was warmly welcomed in very loving ways by each of my hosts and my audiences and the high school and college students along the way. I found all of the Afghan people I met to be supportive and appreciative of Americans and American culture. I did not sense even a slight hint of hostility toward myself, the military escorts, the USAID staff members, or the Embassy staff members.

According to recent speeches at that time by their president and other politicians in Afghanistan, I do get a sense then that it is close to the time we need to turn over all security to their military and withdraw most of our troops. At that time, Kabul appeared to be a secure place, but I think your average citizen on the street is fairly happy that we helped them get rid of the Russians and, later, the Taliban. Most Afghan people want to live in freedom and safety, and I believe the majority respect us for helping them with that. The people here are strong, kind, and creative.

Hopefully, they will find their way home once again to an Afghanistan of peace, but that may just be this poet's hope for them. They have had peace before in their long, long history, so it is not impossible. I hope I made at least a small cultural and humanitarian contribution to them and to my country.

Maybe the dude was right in Kandahar? Maybe 500,000 poets would've solved this problem quicker than war, fighting, and death. I don't know—I am just a Detroit poet. However, I think America could still play a significant diplomatic role in Afghanistan as we do with other embassies worldwide. There will likely always be a need for cultural and educational exchanges between artists and educators between America and Afghanistan. Frankly, I see my job as a working-class artist and educator in the way Allen Ginsberg once wrote:

Well, while I'm here, I'll do the work—
and what's the work?
To ease the pain of living.
Everything else,
Drunken dumbshow. . . .

As I headed back to the U.S. via Dubai and Amsterdam to my beloved Motor City, I knew I was leaving a piece of my heart and soul in Afghanistan with the poets, students, and artists I encountered during my brief stay there. I promised them all that I would bring their poems, their many kind words, and their overwhelming love and goodwill back to America and Detroit. No Americans (or foreigners) remain in Afghanistan forever. Most of us are "short-timers," but what a week it was over there.

Like my fellow Detroit poet Em' said, "Look, if you had one shot / or one opportunity / To seize everything you ever wanted in one moment / Would you capture it / or just let it slip?"

I'm here to say that I "captured" and embraced every moment I was given in Afghanistan. I took a good, long ride on the Kabul beat. I think I brought something to the cultural and educational table that worked here and might last for at least some time to come.

As the best-selling novel *The Kite Runner* states, "We have a chance to be good again." We did have that chance, America, but it didn't quite work out that way after we departed.

We have a chance here in Detroit to rebuild and rise again! Keep the faith. One thing I noticed while in-country was that the people of Kabul, Kandahar, and Jalalabad loved their cities just as much as many of us love Detroit. To the outside world, both places seem broken and unfixable, but it's the people who can and will make the difference. They can't destroy hope, love, and faith. They have it there, and we have it here too. Let us all stand up for each other and continue to fight the good fight.

The Afghan people matter, and what happens to them symbolizes what happens to all of us, whether we recognize it or not. After 12 long years, their lives are now forever intertwined with ours, and we share the responsibility. The lessons of war and struggle can teach us in Detroit how to "rise from the ashes" once more. Hey, Detroit, we have "one opportunity" and another chance "to be good again." I intend to seize it and not let it slip away!

The plane took off from Kabul International Airport in a light mist. I looked at the rain on the windows, put on my earphones, pushed my seat back, and pressed play. Blair's sweet voice sang to me from beyond his too-early grave as I sat, a stranger in a strange land.

M.L., Shelby Liebler & Kenny Ensroth at Comerica | Jorma Kaukonen © Open Commons)

JORMA KAUKONEN

Jorma, Kenny, & Me (Bringing Kenny Home)

Just as long as I'm in this world, I am the light of this world.
—The Reverand Gary Davis
as channeled through Jorma Kaukonen

2012

It started with a fistfight on a gray, chilly spring day in 1962. I have to admit it was a bit embarrassing moving to a new neighborhood and living with two people who were nearly twice the age of everyone else's parents, and whose apparent father (who was really my grandfather) drove a rusted-out 1947 Dodge sedan down Lincoln Street, up to Gratiot, and south to Hamtramck. But I'm thankful it wasn't an Edsel. My uncle Andy and his son-in-law each owned one of those monsters. Talk about double embarrassment when they visited—we'd have two Edsels and a 1947 Dodge sedan parked out front on a Sunday. Nowadays, that would be seen as a "classic" car show, but back then it screamed "working-class schlub" to all our new neighbors and, especially, to my new friends.

I had just moved to Lincoln Street in St. Clair Shores, so I was the new kid on the block. One of my two new friends, Kenny Ensroth, wasted no time in punching me in the head during an impromptu backyard basketball game at my new house. "Son of a bitch," I yelled. "What the hell, man? What was that for?"

My feelings were hurt more than my head. I thought we were all equal. We were freaking kids for God's sake, but I believed back then, and I still think today, that it had more to do with our working-class status. The neighbors and their kids likely thought our family was some uppity factory worker family that decided to "move on up" to St. Clair Shores and live on a paved street, no less. The neighbors might have thought we were seeking equality. But we didn't. Grumps, Ma, and I knew exactly where we came from and who we were. We were working-class—end of story.

My grandfather worked on the assembly line for Dodge, and my grandma worked part-time in an ice cream shop, Alinosi's, in their old German neighbor's house on McNichols (6 Mile Road) and Gunston on Detroit's Eastside.

So, after Kenny punched me, I will admit that I started to cry, and I ran into the house. My grandma was sick with a bad cold. I ran into her bedroom crying. She asked what was wrong. I said, "These new kids hate me, Ma!"

Grandma pulled me close, wrapping my nine-year-old self in her loving, secure arms. I remember her saying words I have never forgotten: "Michael, you are no better than anyone, but no one is better than you. Remember that!" I did. I have carried that wisdom into adulthood. That was one of the most dramatic moments I can recall from my early elementary days. When you're a kid, you don't notice things like class or race for that matter, but to me, those kids were just snotty, "rich kids" from "white-collar" families. They were not!

As the days went by, I noticed that everyone else's fathers wore shirts and ties to work. But my Grumps left early each morning with his charcoal-colored lunch bucket and thermos, which he always packed himself. He carefully placed his sandwich and a thermos full of Eight O'Clock coffee with condensed milk and sugar inside. I imagine that on days when Grandma baked a cake or pie (which was often), he added a slice wrapped in wax paper. He walked out to his beat-up "work jalopy," as Grandma called it, in the early morning darkness and headed to Hamtramck to Dodge Main. There wasn't another old car like that anywhere on our street. It got him to Dodge Main for the next couple of years before he retired in 1965. Now that I think about it, if I were Kenny Ensroth back then, I would have boxed my ears too. But this little flare-up was the start of a lifelong friendship with two neighbor brothers whom I loved, and it all began in that backyard on Lincoln Street. Our friendship has lasted for more than 60 years. Eventually, we became family when I married their first cousin Pam Morrill. The three of us were a tight team until it all ended one early cold December morning in 2017.

The three of us had seen a lot over the years we spent together. We enjoyed the same stringy pizza from George's Market at the corner of Lincoln and Jefferson. We teased the neighbor kid who had to wear an eye patch; Kenny called him an "Eyerite." Another kid slurred his "s's" because of a speech impediment. If you say "suffering succotash" ten times fast, you'll understand what this kid sounded like to us. We weren't angels all the time.

We did everything together during those early years and throughout our lives. We lived just a few houses from Lake St. Clair, so we fished in the summer and hung out at what we called "The Green Dock." We spent a lot of time there in our youth. We ice skated there in the winter, smoked pot there in junior high, and tripped out on LSD while fishing overnight in high school. Once, we all caught the bus downtown by the Green Dock to see Jimi Hendrix at Cobo Hall in November of 1968.

Other rock 'n' roll adventures took place very close to home. We would sneak into the Crow's Nest-East, an unusual spot in the well-known Shores Shopping Center at Harper and 13 Mile Road. We went to see our favorite Detroit bands like Third Power (featuring the great Drew Abbott, who later became Bob Seger's main guitarist, and Jem Targal, may he rest in peace, on bass) and Dick Wagner's band, The Frost. "Baby, Once You Got It…You Got It." It's incredible that I ended up becoming good friends with Dick later in my life. Dick would visit my Detroit classes to talk about '60s rock 'n' roll, Alice Cooper, and the Lou Reed band years. I joined him on stage a few times, and he joined Coyote Monk on stage several times as well. Great memories until Dick passed away in July 2014.

Along with our deep love for music and the blues, we attended nearly every Detroit Tigers baseball game in 1984, including one playoff game and the three home games of the World Series during that unforgettable season. The Tigers won 104 games that year. We cared for each other when we were sick and even when we were sick of each other. It was a wonderful life and childhood, especially once my boxed ear stopped hurting. Damn you, Kenny!

One New Year's Eve when I was 14, I was sick over the holidays that Christmas. I had one of those awful colds with fever and the dreaded sinus infection. Kenny came over to be with me at my grandparents' house. We played the hell out of my new Jeff Beck Truth album. At that time, I wasn't familiar with the great Willie Dixon; I had only seen his name on Beck's and Led Zeppelin's first album. However, as life is stranger than fiction, I would meet and talk to Willie Dixon at a blues club in downtown Detroit. I would later meet him again and even take a photo wearing my dashiki while sporting a Detroit Tigers 1968 pork pie lid that my good neighbor and friend, Denny Chabot, gave me. We played "Ain't Superstitious" repeatedly until midnight, savoring the sound of the wah-wah pedal for hours. We ate Cheez-Its, Gino's cheap pizza rolls, drank gallons of Faygo Rock N Rye, and made the best of an otherwise shitty New Year's Eve. I am no longer attached to Cheez-Its, but I still love me some wah-wah and Willie Dixon's "Ain't Superstitious." This song remained a favorite of Kenny's for the next 50 years. He loved Jeff Beck, and he loved the Allman Brothers. The Allmans' "Southbound" was his jam

Once, we all went to see the Allmans play, and Kenny stood atop the hill at Pine Knob, screaming, "Play 'Southbound!' Play 'Southbound,' boys!" He waved his white T-shirt around and swilled cheap beer like it was fine wine. The Brothers usually came through and played his song. Whenever I hear it now, I know it's for Kenny. Kenny was the first among us to snag Gregg Allman's solo album from 1973, entitled Laid Back. I also bought that album and later the CD. It always reminded me, and still does to this day, of Kenny, especially Gregg's rendition of Jackson Browne's "These Days." Whenever I hear it, I picture old Ken standing on that hill, waving his white T-shirt toward eternity. That boy loved his blues.

Because of Kenny's love for the Allmans, I took him down to Toledo to see them. I had befriended Jorma Kaukonen in 1982 in his green room at Traxx Bar on Gratiot in Detroit. At the time, I was working with Frankie "Eddie Parker" Kerouac, who was heading off to Naropa to celebrate the 20th anniversary of *On the Road*. The Grateful Dead were set to be the house band for the week's festivities, and I knew Jorma was friends with Jerry. I asked him if he was going, and he said he'd like to, but he was doing more gigs to support his most recent record, *Barbeque King*. While I was there, I got him to sign a bar napkin for my good friend Greg Hallock, who had been a Hot Tuna fan for many years. I wanted to gift him his hero's signature.

As time went on, I grew closer to Jorma and his wonderful wife, Vanessa Lillian. The Kaukonens had moved to southern Ohio to build the Fur Peace Guitar Ranch. Over the years, I had the opportunity to visit them there, break bread, and talk about everything life had to offer. Our first significant meeting was in Columbus, Ohio, in 1995, when I took my son to hear his hero, Jorma.

Jorma often left tickets at Will Call for me for any show he was doing in and around Detroit. If I mentioned I would be in Chicago or New York, he typically left tickets waiting for me. Once, we even connected while I was working in State Department Cultural initiatives in Jerusalem. He again left two tickets in my name at the door in both Jerusalem and Tel Aviv. I was in a government vehicle near the Old City in Jerusalem when I noticed a poster featuring Jorma's name. Upon returning to the hotel, I emailed him, saying, "Jorma! Are you really in Israel?" He quickly replied that he was. So, there I was backstage in the Middle East with my old friend. It was incredible, and the show was, as usual, very good.

I knew Electric Hot Tuna was opening the Allman Brothers summer tour, so I told Kenny to get in the car, and we were off to Toledo. When we arrived, I remembered to walk up to the Will Call window, and sure enough, Jorma had left me two tickets with backstage passes. Kenny could hardly believe it. I said, "Let's go backstage and say hello." We walked in just as Hot Tuna was about to start. I took Kenny backstage to check it out and see the Allmans prepping for their set. We walked out into the Toledo Convention Hall. There weren't a huge crowd at that point, and Jorma spotted me walking in from the backstage area. He and Tuna guitarist Michael Falzarano started razzing me from the stage and having a bit of fun with us as we sat down.

Jorma yelled out, "Hey M.L.! How's the sound out there?" Kenny and I gave him four thumbs up. I know Kenny enjoyed that show and the backstage access, and I couldn't think of a better person to share something like that with.

Kenny, his brother Jeff, and I were as close as three guys could be without being related. When I married their cousin, we became family. We shared many nights taking care of each other during all sorts of situations in the 1960s and early 70s—too much to drink, LSD trips that started going sideways, and more. We often talked one another down from a bad trip, sticking together until morning when the acid wore off. Too much hash oil? Just stay calm and steady, boys. I'd say it was real love, and that's all we needed. We celebrated birthdays, Christmases, New Year's Eves, summer and winter nights, ball games, and music together. Kenny loved the blues, and we loved each other. This friendship has lasted since I got my ears boxed in while playing basketball in my backyard in 1962.

Once, during the 1984 playoff game against the Kansas City Royals at Tiger Stadium, we all got so drunk that we lost Kenny. We searched everywhere. Drunk and stoned, we stumbled back to our car, which we always parked on a back street away from the stadium. I opened the door, and there was old Kenny lying on his back, passed out, with a big piss stain on his blue jeans. We drove him home and put him to bed.

We took Kenny home one last time on December 4, 2017. He passed away in his sleep at 65 years old. It has been hard for me to picture a world where Kenny, Jeff, and Denny don't live just down the street on Fifth and Sixth Streets, respectively. But as Jorma sang the words of his early mentor, the Reverend Gary Davis, that night during his set in Toledo:

Death don't have no mercy in this land.
Death don't have no mercy in this land.
He'll come to your house, and he won't stay long
You'll look in the bed and somebody be gone.
Death don't have no mercy in this land.

To this day, I often think about those times when we all laughed, cried, and were terrified by the dreadful years of war, estrangement, hatred, civil rights, desire, revolution, drugs, and the trauma of growing up during those turbulent times. I understand better now what Yeats meant when he said, "a terrible beauty is born."

Walking through the old neighborhood in recent years, I reflect on those days and start to sing the words I first heard when Kenny played Gregg Allman's debut solo album, Laid Back, which he had bought at E. J. Korvette's on Gratiot and 12 Mile Road Roseville.

Well, I've been out walking.

> *I don't do that much talking these days*
> *These days--*
> *These days I seem to think a lot*
> *About the things that I forgot to do*
> *For you*
> *And all the times I had the chance to"* Jackson Brown

I was a lucky kid to have met this gang—"The Lincoln Street Gang," as we called ourselves. We were a group of special friends who formed a unique family. It hurts to think about all the good times now gone, but I wouldn't change a thing.

We lost two members of the old Lincoln Street Gang: Kenny in 2017 and Donnie "Duke" St. Germaine in 2023. The rest of us just "keep on choogling," as Creedence once sang on one of our favorite albums, *Born on the Bayou*.

Kenny, come on and wave your T-shirt flag now from Heaven for all the good times of rock, revolution, and the redemption we all sought! I can still hear the ghost notes of the Allman Brothers wafting through the air on the hill at Pine Knob one hot summer night when we were all together, and my son Shane was barely old enough to come with me and his uncle Cal.

> *Well I'm Southbound, Lord I'm comin' home to you.*
> *Well I'm Southbound, baby, Lord I'm comin' home to you.*
> *I got that old lonesome feelin' that's sometimes called the blues.*

—The Alman Brothers, "Southbound"

Steve King & M.L. perform with their Coyote Monk Poetry Band

EMINEM

Lose Yourself

You get one chance.

2013

I've never met Marshall Mathers, but somehow, I found myself welcomed into his inner circle. For a few invaluable years, I delved deep into an environment filled with friendship, love, and astonishing creativity. I was honored in the fall of 2011 when Wayne State's Dean of Students asked me to host a poetry slam event for their "Thursdays in the D" Series. This program was not just an event but a gateway to unique experiences for students and the broader community. Every Thursday, WSU presented opportunities to attend exhilarating Red Wings or Detroit Tigers games, enjoy captivating Broadway plays, witness major concerts, or even engage in an exciting night of rock 'n' bowling at the Garden Bowl, nestled within the Majestic Theater complex on Woodward, just steps from the Wayne State campus.

On a vibrant Thursday evening at the D Poetry Slam event, I found myself drawn to a local gem, a deaf rapper and hip-hop artist named Sean Forbes, whose talent had been whispered about in circles I frequented. Sean, the son of the renowned Scott Forbes from the beloved Detroit band, The Forbes Brothers, was set to make waves. While I hadn't crossed paths with the band personally, I clearly remembered their distinct alt-country sound and engaging performances from a benefit program several years back. Despite my usual aversion to country music, there was something evocative about their energy that left an impression on me. Inspired by the legacy of his father, I felt compelled to invite Sean to join the lineup for the upcoming Thursday in the D Poetry Slam at the Scarab Club, positioning him amidst a tapestry of both local talents and national slammers. I placed Sean strategically in the middle of the lineup, ensuring that he would perform for an eager and warmed-up audience, fully energized from previous acts. Though I hadn't experienced his performance in person before, something deep within me told me that his rhythmic words and beats would resonate with the students. Even if Sean didn't see himself as a poet—perhaps still not today—I recognized the poetic soul within him. To me, a skilled lyricist transcends traditional definitions of a poet; he was not just good, he was phenomenal.

The night of the poetry slam arrived, and with Sean came his father, Scott Forbes, and his manager, Scott Guy of D-Pan Productions, supporting the budding artist. I later discovered that Scott was worried the students might misinterpret Sean's performance, perhaps even laugh at him. At the time, I hadn't considered this possibility and dismissed his worries, attributing it to what I called the "stage father syndrome." When my moment came, I delivered a rousing introduction for Sean, who then took to the stage, launching our audience into his captivating universe of beats and lyrical depth. The atmosphere transformed as positivity radiated from his words; students were entranced, hanging onto every beat and lyric. With a performance that could only be described as electrifying, Sean brought the house down, leaving behind waves of thunderous applause. It was an exhilarating moment, and the joy on his father's and manager's faces reflected my own elation. That night, I forged new friendships with Sean and his team, unknowingly stepping into a world that would expand my horizons, my artistic endeavors, and my belief in humanity.

Little did I know that I was about to enter the monumental shadow of Slim Shady himself, at the legendary Detroit recording studio, 54 Sound—where Eminem had crafted hits spanning from *The Slim Shady LP* to *The 8 Mile Soundtrack* and beyond. For me, hip-hop is a contemporary form of poetry. I hold deep appreciation for it, just as I do for Slam Poetry, as both styles weave a rich tapestry of spoken word that invites everyone into the vast realm of poetic expression.

Since my college days, when I first began intertwining poetry and music, I have been fully invested in any spoken word movement that beckons others to explore the beautiful art of poetry. Marshall Mathers, from Detroit's east side along the now-famous 8 Mile Road, had a way with words and a special delivery that is undeniably among the best in his craft. I appreciate his phrasing, word choices, and his smooth, easy blend and delivery. Marshall had one constant engineer and occasional collaborator throughout all these recordings, and that constant would become my best and closest friend, as well as one of my most important musical collaborators. I could never have imagined where I was heading on that late September night at the Scarab Club when I introduced a young Sean Forbes to a full house of cheering college students. To quote Chuck Berry, "The joint was rockin', goin' round and round."

That night, I gave Sean's dad, Scott Forbes, a copy of my newest CD titled *The Coyote & The Monk*. This CD was a new collaboration with Moby Grape guitarist and songwriter Peter Lewis. I admired the Grape, but I was an even bigger fan of his mother, the Academy Award-winning actress Loretta Young. Being a first-generation TV baby, I loved all those classic shows in black and white, and I really cherished "Old Hollywood." Peter was my link to that era through his famous film star mother and later, a major television icon.

It turned out that Scott loved our CD, especially the tone of my "blues" singing—or rather, my "blues shouting" style as he called it, which he compared to his producer brother's, Dennis Forbes, renowned client, Bob Seger. Sean and his production team felt they needed a singer with a bluesy sound for one song on Sean's upcoming debut album. This song was essentially set to be the CD's thematic centerpiece, titled "Don't Let Anything Hold You Back!" When Scott listened to our *The Coyote & The Monk* album, he discovered the sound he was searching for.

A few days after the electrifying Poetry Slam, WSU was so taken by the event that they approached me with an exciting proposition: could I persuade Sean to open for the renowned hip-hop group, Far East Movement, at the next big Thursday in the D event at the Majestic Theater? I conveyed this opportunity to Dr. David Strauss, the Dean of Students, letting him know that hosting a concert would demand a higher budget than a poetry event. To my delight, he was all in for it, and I jumped at the chance to organize the gig. Sean was on board but insisted that I bring the same lively energy from my poetry slam to his introduction. Despite his inability to hear, he could still sense the vibrant buzz from my words. I happily accepted and made my way to the venue early that night for soundcheck. As Sean was collaborating with Jake Bass—son of one of the legendary Bass Brothers who first discovered Eminem and Sean's primary musical partner—I noticed someone darting around, fine-tuning the sound at the board, adding to the charged atmosphere.

I played at the 54 Sound Christmas Party that year. They asked me to come over and perform a couple of blues songs on a Sunday early in the 2011 holiday season. I brought my friend and trusty teaching assistant, Eddie Baranak, of the famed local alt-rock band The Sights. What started as two songs turned into two-and-a-half straight hours of jamming that left my clothes soaked with sweat and my voice shot from the long performance, including an even longer 30-minute version of "Who Do You Love" alongside members of the Forbes Brothers' band.

However, it was my performance with Grammy winner Steve King and the exceptional drummer Leonard Johnson that solidified the backbeat; together, they became the backbone of what would later become M.L. Liebler & The Coyote Monk Poetry Band in 2012.

I added my friend and excellent guitarist Charlie Palazzola to the mix, along with my WSU Labor Studies colleague Frankie the K (Kocelski) on keyboards, and together, the five of us created something I had never achieved in my nearly 30 years of doing "performance poetry" or my poetry with music. People could hear the next level of what I'd been doing all these years.

Audiences started clamoring for more shows and often asked when our "next gig" was. We had created what the young hipster rockers now call a "fanbase." Who knew? With this incredible group of musicians, we never worried about building an audience; people came just as they did in Dyersville, Iowa, to "The Field of Dreams." We built it (a solid performance poetry band), and people came. *Wow!* I thought. "That only took 35 years, but the audiences got it." I guessed the wait was worth it. I finally had the musicians I'd been looking for after years of searching, and there was a real sense of love, friendship, and camaraderie among the Monks. I not only found the best musicians, but I also found my best friends. It was the weirdest combination of personalities imaginable, but it worked. Leonard was the surly one, Frankie disliked everything in a loving way, Charlie was easily intimidated by the others for no reason, as he was a first-rate guitarist, and Steve was the smooth bond that kept everyone together and on an even keel. Steve knew exactly what he was doing with the music, in the studio and in production. We made 54 Sound Studios our home base for recording. 54 Sound in Ferndale is where Eminem recorded all his super-hit records, where The Romantics did the same in the late '70s and '80s, and where George Clinton got the funk and "maggots" out of his "brain." The owner, Joel Martin, let us have the run of the place. He respected and loved Steve, so whatever Steve wanted was more than okay with him. That was how we all felt, especially me. Steve was the friend and collaborator I had been searching for my entire life to work with professionally. We started our Monk collaboration in earnest, creating several new pieces of music to accompany my poems, with four to six pieces at every rehearsal. Soon we had a catalog approaching The Grateful Dead's length, and we struggled to remember all the pieces. When we went into the studio to record in early January of 2013, we had so many pieces that our CD lineup kept changing every half hour. We nailed as many pieces as possible over the next few months. Some pieces I created the music and poems for on the spot in the studio. Probably my best-known pieces created while the tape was rolling were "Green Moon" for Peter Green and "Assassination." We then began creating medleys that were creatively insane and wonderful. One of my personal favorites was what we called "The Water Suite," stringing together Blake's "London," Al Green's "Take Me to the River," The Standels' "Dirty Water," and ending with Neil Young's "Down by the River." Just that piece could fill an entire set. It was crazy. It was wicked! It was a wonderful time. I felt so alive and reconnected to this process that I had started in the mid-'70s while in college. I was finally hearing my music and poetry the way I had always imagined it could be. The bad memories, the ups and downs over nearly 40 years of working in this form and genre, became distant memories with these guys, my Coyote Monks—my heroes!

    Eventually, everything fell apart over the next two years due to personality conflicts, alcohol use, and a narrow range of musical tastes (which didn't even seem possible at the beginning), culminating in Steve's sudden and completely unexpected death on June 3, 2014. Wow! What a tough break. The dream was over. It dies both slowly and quickly at the same time it is born. For the first time in my entire life and career, I had come within inches of my long-held dream of making poetry accessible to the general public. I always felt that if I ever got the chance to record this material with great musicians in a major studio, I could convince people that poetry was genuinely good and not half bad. It almost worked. It nearly, actually, worked. Charlie quit first due to Leonard's drinking and constant badgering, which stripped our music of major songwriting talent and expert guitar skills. We struggled along with new guitarists, John "Sunflower" Bardy and one from my old Magic Poetry Band, but it just wasn't really clicking like it had been.

    Then, the unthinkable happened. Steve was rushed to the hospital at 1 a.m. on Tuesday, June 3, and by 4:10 p.m. that same day, he was gone. Just like that! I received a text message that morning when I woke up from Steve's wife, Roberta, saying they had to rush Steve from White Lake Township to Harper Hospital Downtown for "emergency surgery." I thought, What the hell? I finally heard from Roberta around 7:30 a.m. that Steve had passed out, and blood was pouring out of his mouth. They needed to stop the bleeding, and Harper was the closest place with those capabilities. By 6 a.m., the bleeding had stopped. Me, Joel, and the 54 Sound guys had just returned from Israel and Palestine two days before. Steve was supposed to have joined me, Sean Forbes and his band, and Joel Martin's family on the trip of a lifetime. We had a great time. One day while showing Joel, Deneen and their son Benny (whom we nicknamed Hummus) the Upper Galilee region of northern Israel. We went to the Jordan River, and then I took everyone on a ride around the "Sea of Galilee." We were driving and driving, and it dawned on me that this was an unfamiliar road to me. I knew we were driving north. Just then, we passed some barbed wire and fencing and an Israeli makeshift memorial for a murdered soldier. It was then I noticed that we had driven into Syria. Yikes! I turned the car around quickly and nervously and beat it back to Capernaum.

 The doctors had prohibited Steve from traveling with us outside the US. He was totally bummed out, but I kept in regular contact with him while I was in The Holy Land. I prayed the rosary everywhere in the Old City for Steve. I sat on Mt. Calvary praying, outside Christ's tomb praying, in the Upper Room, and on Mt. Zion praying. I took photos and texted them to him from the Jordan River, promising him we'd get there together one day. He was eager for the experience, and I truly think he was yearning for God. One time, several years before 2014, while talking with Steve alone in the studio, I blurted out, "You know, Steve, I didn't just walk into your life by accident."

 He responded in a reassuring way, "I know."

 I thought, *You know? What do you mean, "you know?"* I didn't even know why I said such a thing. After June 3, it started to become a little clearer to me. I needed him in my life for support and comfort, and he needed me to help ease him into his death, which he sensed would occur in a short time.

 We lost him right after we all returned from Israel. Steve and I had a long talk Sunday night. That morning, he had gone to a Pentecostal church with one of his old friends. That was a bit odd, but not unbelievable. The Monks had rehearsed that Friday, and everyone was very pleased with the session. I heard from everyone, including Steve, about the success and positive vibe of the rehearsal. Steve and I planned to visit my daughter's middle school where she taught in Southwest Detroit. We intended to do a little poetry and music for the kids, as we had recently done in Paterson, New Jersey. Steve loved joining me on these occasions. I woke up on June 3, ready to go to 54 Sound and pick up Steve. I saw a text on his phone saying, "This is Roberta on Steve's cell. Steve was rushed to Harper Hospital for emergency surgery." The text was from 12:30 a.m. I thought, *What???* I started trying to track Roberta down. I called Joel to check in with him, and he became very distraught. What none of us knew or could imagine was about to happen. If someone had told any of us the day before that this could occur, we would have called them a liar

For a minute, everything was fine. Joel called to say he had just spoken to Steve in his hospital room. That felt reassuring. Roberta had gone home to teach her class before returning to Harper. I was preparing to do the middle school gig solo, planning to stop by and see Steve afterwards.

Just as I pulled up in front of my daughter's school, my cell phone rang. It was Joel. In a sad and shocked voice, he said, "Get over to Harper, M.L., things are really bad." I told my daughter what was happening, and I raced through the streets of Detroit to get to Harper Hospital as quickly as I could. I parked and walked into the wrong building. A very kind receptionist found out Steve's whereabouts, and a security guard rushed me up to ICU. I ran into the room to find Roberta, Joel, and Steve's son, Nick, in various states of distress. Joel was in shock, Roberta was weeping uncontrollably, and Nick was in an anguished state of trauma.

We all walked into Steve's room. His hospital clothes were stained in his own blood. He had been losing units by the minutes. In fact, they had already restarted his heart three times at that point. He kept stabilizing and fading. He twisted his body, arms, and legs in what looked to me like serious agony and pain. His eyes were opened just a crack. I could see his yellowed whites through the openings. I prayed for his healing. I made the sign of the cross on his head and held his hand. I said, "Steve! You're going to make it through this and come back to us." He grabbed my hand, turned his head directly toward me, and I saw him slightly shake his head. It crossed my mind that he knew more than we did about death, and our Steve was crossing over. I never mentioned this exchange to anyone that day, and I have told very few people about it since. As they wheeled Steve to surgery, I couldn't shake the thought of his negative response from my mind. He wasn't coming back. He knew it, and worst of all, I knew it, too. The guy who saved my life and I his would fade over to the other side. I prayed and prayed for a miracle, but I realized that this was God's plan for Steve. I couldn't make sense of it, yet it made all the sense in the world.

You know, Steve, I didn't just walk into your life by accident! kept echoing in my mind. With his familiar, ever-pleasant head shake, he replied, "I know." Then the conversation shifted, and I heard Steve whisper, "You know, M.L., I didn't just walk into your life by accident either." Stunned and broken, I tried to make sense of it all then, but I was confused and worn out from the day's events.

Then, out of the corner of my teary eyes, I saw the doctor appear out of nowhere, and he walked into the surgery waiting room shaking his head no. It reminded me of when I had seen Steve whisper on his deathbed when I told him, "Someday, we will laugh about this weird scene." However, this was not to be. I thought all of this was very surreal. It felt like I was watching a movie about a movie where the star dies on the operating table.

"Folks! It's not good. He's bleeding again, and we can't perform the surgery while he's bleeding," the doctor told us.

Roberta nearly collapsed and shouted, "Please don't let my Steve die. Please, doctors. Please!" Roberta went into the operating room, and the staff pastor took us into a special room with phones, tissues, and water. We all sat staring at the floor.

I texted Steve's longtime collaborator and good friend, Luis Resto, former keyboardist of Was Not Was and Academy Award-winning co-writer of "Lose Yourself." I texted, "Luis, if you're anywhere near Harper Hospital, please come. Steve is dying." Luis arrived and joined us in the surgery waiting room within minutes.

When the Marshall Mathers train arrived at 54 Sound, Joel, Steve, and Luis were among the first passengers on that long journey. Joel remarked that the train had taken a toll on everyone aboard. When the ride concluded in the late 2000s, everyone tried to regroup and carry on as if none of it had happened. It was tough for Steve, and I believe it was for Joel as well. It was never about money for either of them; it felt like a huge void had opened in their lives that could never be filled.

When we all returned upstairs to the ICU, the head surgeon came in to deliver the painful update. "I'm so sorry, folks, but he's gone." Damn! He left me, Joel, his son Nick King, Sean Forbes, Jake Bass, and many others to mourn and never forget his generous spirit. I think of Steve often. I play our old rehearsal tapes and the solo album of poetry and music we were working on with his electronic nighttime creations. In the end, I never met Marshall, but I believe all our bones are forever connected through words, poetry, beats, and Steve King.

EPILOGUE

In the attics of my life
Full of cloudy dreams; unreal
Full of tastes no tongue can know
And lights no eye can see
When there was no ear to hear
You sang to me
—The Grateful Dead

And in the end, the love you take is equal to the love you make.
—The Beatles

If you don't know, now you know.
—Notorious B.I.G.

As I wander through the tapestry of my life, I am transported to a time when the very essence of America shimmered with hope before the shadows of Vietnam loomed large. I recall the somber grayness of the 1950s, an era painted in stark contrasts, much like the black-and-white television shows that filled our screens before 1965. I entered this world just as the echoes of the Korean War were fading away, heralding a moment of renewal—a rebirth of America marked by the election of our youngest president ever. Yet, amid this heartbeat of progress, we were plunged into sorrow with the tragic assassination of our beloved leader, the firstborn of the 20th century.

We forged through the craziness of high school politics, and we carried our convictions on our sleeves into the halls of high school and onto the universities. As our generation witnessed major shifts during the mid to late 1960s and early 1970s, we felt the winds of change. Yet, we couldn't help but recognize that the battles against racism, women's rights, and more were, and still are, far from over. Today, it seems like we're slipping backwards into the shadows of our past—a stark reminder of the work still ahead of us.

After the assassination of J.F.K., the civil rights movement surged, only to be overshadowed by the Vietnam War and the tragic assassination of Martin Luther King Jr. in April of 1968. Just two months later, Robert F. Kennedy was also murdered in early June of 1968 in Los Angeles, deepening our sadness and mounting despair. The Pentagon Papers unveiled the deceit behind the Vietnam War, igniting public outrage, followed by the infamous Watergate Break-In that unraveled the nation's trust, culminating in the Fall of Saigon in 1975. With each event, my disappointment in America deepened; the ideals I once held dear in the late 50s and early 60s felt to be slipping away.

Since the sixth grade, I have refused to recite the Pledge of Allegiance, nor have I ever sung the National Anthem at my beloved baseball games. In fact, I even walked away from baseball, a passion that once filled my heart, especially in '68 when the Tigers went to the World Series. I adored that game almost as much as my music! But as I witnessed others, the so-called "children of the revolution," continued to cheer for our team and revel in the World Series, a pang of regret surfaced within me. Perhaps it wasn't the first time my stubborn dedication clouded my judgment and led me astray. Damn it!

Once upon a time, my life mirrored a scene from *Leave It to Beaver*. My grandma, a steadfast figure in the household, donned her house dress as she bustled about tidying up. After school, I was greeted by the sweet comfort of cookies and milk—Pecan Sandies or Windmill Cookies were my favorites. I sported a quirky Daniel Boone-style coonskin cap, prancing around the second-grade lunchroom like my Disney movie hero, Fess Parker.

I found joy in playing marbles, relishing the shiny Steelies and Pearlies while feeling the sting of the no "hunchies" rule. This carefree youth nurtured my budding passion for films, particularly the thrilling horror flicks and vibrant rock 'n' roll films of the late fifties and early sixties. I grooved to the rhythm of on-screen heroes like James Brown, sang along with Jackie Wilson (who, unbeknownst to me at the time, hailed from Detroit), and reveled in the flamboyant stylings of Wayne Cochran, his blonde hair puffed high. And, of course, there was my one true love—Elvis Himselvis.

Each weekend was an adventure, my grandparents would drop me off at the local Roseville Theater, where a 25-cent ticket opened the door to infinite worlds. Popcorn costs only three cents, and a box of candy, Hot Tamales? Just six cents! After the show, I'd wander across Utica Road to a dumpy hamburger joint with its wooden floors that creaked beneath my seven-year-old self and a jukebox that played my all-time favorites—Elvis and Dion, each note sparking my youthful spirit.

Those Saturdays, spent amidst the magic of cinema and lively tunes, were golden moments of a life well spent. Looking back, I marvel at my grandparents' trust, allowing a seven-year-old to wander freely for hours in the dim glow of a movie theater, alone or with a friend from the neighborhood. Back then, such adventures were commonplace, wrapped in the reassuring embrace of innocence and safety.

As our weeks came to a close back then, Saturdays became a ritual filled with much comfort. After my weekly bath, we'd head to the bustling intersection of 10 Mile and Gratiot, where the smell of pizza from Cloverleaf Bar called us in. It was a family-friendly spot, with laughter and joy filling the room until 9 p.m. I can still picture my grandparents enjoying their solitary shells of draft beer, the warm glow of our little tradition wrapping around us. That was indeed a lovely slice of life in more ways than one.

My childhood was filled with vibrant events woven with the warmth of my grandma and grandpa, the timeless tunes of Elvis, Ricky Nelson, and Dion echoing in the background, and the delightful aroma of pizza filling the air. What child could imagine such a joyful existence in the late '50s and '60s? Back then, my life felt carefree and blissful. I truly believed everyone enjoyed the charm of a tidy home, savored Cloverleaf pizza and Coney Island hot dogs, and relished Kresge's ice cream sandwiches alongside their scrumptious subs. My taste buds danced at the thought of Sanders' Bumpy Cake, Awrey's Coconut and Lemon Layered Cake, and delicious cream puffs from Sanders. To top it all off, I was showered with many presents during Christmas and birthdays, making each occasion an incredible celebration. When I first ventured into my friends' homes, I was shocked to discover that their lives were strikingly different from mine. I had naively thought my life was the standard for all Americans. Though I might have felt a flicker of empathy for my playmates, I reveled in the joy of my own exciting upbringing. It was nothing short of extraordinary! While countless tales of hardship echo through the quiet suburbs, mine isn't one of those.

Soon The Beatles would appear in black and white during our Sunday evening ritual of watching *The Ed Sullivan Show*. The war in Vietnam would grow harsher, cities would erupt in anger and burn, and I wrote my first poems in solitude until Jim Morrison set me free.

As we moved into the late 60s, my reality became a bittersweet relationship with the America I had known. Still, we pushed on to find ourselves in the 21st century, regressing to the old dark ages of America filled with hate, anger, and sadness, all while sleepwalking into authoritarianism. As the darkness settles in, I recall the lyrics to "This Is Not America'" by David Bowie:

A little piece of you,
a little piece of me,
will die.
This is not America.

GLOSSARY

Musical and Cultural Figures

Dion DiMucci

Hailing from the Bronx, New York, Dion DiMucci rose to fame in the late 1950s and early 1960s, blending doo-wop, rock and roll, and rhythm and blues. As the frontman of Dion and the Belmonts and later a solo artist, he captured the voice of urban youth with a streetwise swagger and heartfelt vocals. A great introduction to his style is the 1961 hit "Runaround Sue," which showcases his knack for catchy melodies and emotionally charged storytelling.

Pearl Bailey

Born in Newport News, Virginia, Pearl Bailey was a celebrated jazz and Broadway singer whose career spanned from the 1930s through the 1980s. Known for her warm, witty stage presence and sultry contralto voice, she broke racial barriers in entertainment and was awarded the Presidential Medal of Freedom in 1988. Her rendition of "Takes Two to Tango" (1952) is a lively example of her charm and vocal finesse.

The Ink Spots

Formed in Indianapolis, Indiana, The Ink Spots were active from the 1930s through the 1950s and are credited as pioneers of the rhythm and blues genre that would later evolve into rock and roll and soul. Their smooth vocal harmonies, featuring a distinctive "talking bass" technique, influenced countless vocal groups, including the doo-wop acts of the 1950s. Their 1940 hit "If I Didn't Care" remains a quintessential track that captures their romantic, melancholic style.

Sophie Tucker

Born in Russia and raised in Hartford, Connecticut, Sophie Tucker was a vaudeville star and singer active from the early 1900s through the 1960s. Known as "The Last of the Red Hot Mamas," she performed bold, bawdy songs with a jazz and ragtime flair, often challenging gender norms and expectations. A defining track is "Some of These Days," which she recorded in 1926 and performed throughout her career.

Elvis Presley

Hailing from Tupelo, Mississippi, and later Memphis, Tennessee, Elvis Presley was active from the mid-1950s until his death in 1977. Dubbed the "King of Rock and Roll," he fused rhythm and blues, gospel, and country to create a style that electrified youth culture and transformed American music. "Heartbreak Hotel" (1956) offers a haunting and iconic introduction to his early sound.

The Beatles

Formed in Liverpool, England, The Beatles were active from 1960 to 1970 and became one of the most influential bands in history. With a sound that evolved from Merseybeat pop to experimental rock, they reshaped global music and youth identity during the 1960s. Their album *Sgt. Pepper's Lonely Hearts Club Band* (1967) exemplifies their creative peak and cultural impact.

Bob Dylan

Born in Duluth, Minnesota, and raised in Hibbing, Bob Dylan emerged in the early 1960s as a folk singer-songwriter and quickly became the poetic voice of a generation. Known for his cryptic lyrics and social commentary, his work spans folk, rock, blues, and gospel. "Like a Rolling Stone" (1965) marks a pivotal shift in both his sound and popular music at large.

Country Joe McDonald

A native of Washington, D.C., and raised in California, Country Joe McDonald fronted the psychedelic rock band Country Joe and the Fish in the 1960s. Known for his anti-war activism and satirical protest songs, he became a fixture of the counterculture movement. His most famous work is the "I-Feel-Like-I'm-Fixin'-to-Die Rag" (1967), a biting critique of the Vietnam War.

Jimi Hendrix

Born in Seattle, Washington, Jimi Hendrix was a revolutionary guitarist and singer active from the mid-1960s until his untimely death in 1970. Blending blues, rock, and psychedelia, he redefined electric guitar playing with feedback, distortion, and dazzling improvisation. "Purple Haze" (1967) is a landmark track that captures his innovative sound.

The MC5

The MC5 (Motor City Five) were a proto-punk band formed in Detroit, Michigan, active mainly in the late 1960s and early 1970s. Known for their raw energy and radical political stance, they helped lay the groundwork for punk and hard rock. "Kick Out the Jams" (1969), with its famous live introduction, is a defining document of their incendiary style.

Al Kooper

From Brooklyn, New York, Al Kooper is a keyboardist, songwriter, and producer known for his work in the 1960s and beyond. He played with Bob Dylan, co-founded Blood, Sweat & Tears, and discovered Lynyrd Skynyrd, showcasing a wide range across rock, blues, and soul. His swirling organ on "Like a Rolling Stone" is one of his most iconic performances.

Paul McCartney

Born in Liverpool, England, Paul McCartney rose to fame as bassist and songwriter for The Beatles and later led the band Wings before becoming a prolific solo artist. His melodic genius spans rock, pop, and classical influences, with themes often centered on love, peace, and storytelling. A classic McCartney showcase is "Maybe I'm Amazed" (1970), written after The Beatles disbanded.

Neil Young

Originally from Toronto, Canada, Neil Young has been active since the 1960s, both as a solo artist and with groups like Buffalo Springfield and Crosby, Stills, Nash & Young. His distinctive high-tenor voice, poetic lyrics, and raw guitar playing explore folk, rock, and country with themes of loss, rebellion, and environmentalism. His 1972 album *Harvest* includes "Heart of Gold," a defining track in his career.

Tom Waits

Born in Pomona, California, Tom Waits is a genre-defying singer-songwriter and actor known for his gravelly voice and eccentric persona. Active since the early 1970s, his work blends jazz, blues, vaudeville, and experimental sounds into gritty, surreal storytelling. "Rain Dogs" (1985) offers an excellent introduction to his offbeat yet emotionally resonant world.

Edie Parker Kerouac

A socialite and writer from Detroit, Michigan, Edie Parker was best known as the first wife of Jack Kerouac and a member of the early Beat Generation circle. Though not a public artist herself, she played a significant role in supporting and preserving the writings and ethos of the Beats. Her memoir, "You'll Be Okay," provides rare insight into the personal side of this literary movement.

GLOSSARY • 235

Sun Ra

Born in Birmingham, Alabama, and later based in Chicago and Philadelphia, Sun Ra was a visionary jazz composer and bandleader active from the 1940s until his death in 1993. Known for his cosmic philosophy and theatrical performances, he fused swing, bebop, avant-garde jazz, and Afro-futurism into a singular sound. "Space Is the Place" (1973) exemplifies his unique musical and philosophical universe.

George Harrison

The lead guitarist of The Beatles, George Harrison was born in Liverpool and pursued a solo career that combined spiritual themes with thoughtful songwriting. Influenced by Indian classical music and meditation, he helped introduce the sitar and Eastern philosophy into Western pop. "My Sweet Lord" (1970) is a spiritual anthem that reflects his solo voice and beliefs.

Maharishi Mahesh Yogi

An Indian spiritual teacher born in the early 20th century, Maharishi Mahesh Yogi introduced Transcendental Meditation to the West and gained global attention in the 1960s. He became widely known after The Beatles studied with him in India, helping popularize meditation among artists and the counterculture. Though not a musician himself, his teachings profoundly influenced the era's music and consciousness.

John Lennon

A founding member of The Beatles, John Lennon was born in Liverpool and later became an outspoken solo artist and peace activist. His music ranged from introspective ballads to avant-garde experiments, often reflecting personal struggles and global concerns. "Imagine" (1971) remains his most enduring solo work, promoting a vision of peace and unity.

Hüsker Dü

Formed in Minnesota in 1979, Hüsker Dü were a hardcore punk band that evolved into melodic alternative rock pioneers. Known for their emotional intensity, distortion-heavy sound, and introspective lyrics, they influenced countless indie and grunge bands. The album "Zen Arcade" (1984) is a landmark concept record that blends punk aggression with ambitious storytelling.

Robbie Robertson

Born in Toronto, Canada, Robbie Robertson was the lead guitarist and principal songwriter for The Band, active primarily in the 1960s and '70s. Known for weaving Americana, rock, and folk into vivid tales of mythic American life, his songs helped shape the roots rock movement. "The Weight" (1968) is one of his most iconic compositions.

The Doors

Formed in Los Angeles in 1965, The Doors blended rock, blues, and psychedelia with a dark, poetic edge, led by charismatic frontman Jim Morrison. Their music often explored themes of rebellion, mysticism, and consciousness. "Light My Fire" (1967) is their breakthrough hit, known for its hypnotic organ riff and dramatic delivery.

Blair (Detroit poet)

Blair is a poet and spoken word artist based in Detroit whose work often centers on urban life, racial identity, and emotional resilience. Though lesser-known nationally, he has been a respected voice in local literary and performance scenes, contributing to Detroit's cultural landscape. His work bridges the gap between poetry, music, and social commentary.

Jorma Kaukonen

A virtuoso guitarist born in Washington, D.C., Jorma Kaukonen is best known for his work with Jefferson Airplane and Hot Tuna. His fingerpicking style combines blues, folk, and psychedelic rock,

GLOSSARY • 237

contributing to the sound of the San Francisco scene in the 1960s and beyond. His performance on "Embryonic Journey" (1967) showcases his intricate acoustic guitar work.

Captain Beefheart

Born Don Van Vliet in Glendale, California, Captain Beefheart was an avant-garde musician and artist known for his genre-defying blend of blues, rock, free jazz, and surrealist poetry. Active primarily from the mid-1960s to the early 1980s, he led his group The Magic Band through a series of groundbreaking and often challenging recordings that earned him a cult following. His 1969 album *Trout Mask Replica*—produced by Frank Zappa—is a seminal work that captures his experimental spirit and remains one of the most influential records in underground rock.

M.L. Liebler & The Magic Poetry Band

Based in Detroit, Michigan, the Magic Poetry Band is an innovative spoken word and jazz fusion project led by poet M.L. Liebler. Active since the early 1980s, the group blends live poetry with improvisational jazz, rock, and funk, creating performances that are both musically rich and lyrically provocative. Their album, Paper Ghost Rain Dance, captures the spirit of the city's literary and musical legacy. Original Members in the mid-1980s: Faruq Z. Bey, Alan Franklin, Ralph Franklin, Mel Rosas, Gerard Smith. Late 20th and 21st century members: Ted Nagy, Brigitte Knudson, LouDLou and Jim Carey.

M.L. Liebler & The Coyote Monk Poetry Band

Coyote Monk is a rootsy, meditative music and poetry collaboration led by Detroit poet M.L. Liebler. Drawing influence from Americana, folk, rock, and funk, the project offers reflective, sometimes surreal storytelling through poetic narratives backed by some of Detroit's finest musicians: Steve King, Leonard Paul Johnson, Charles Palazzola, and Frankie Koscielski The band attracted a large following until its conclusion in 2014 following the passing of Steve King. Coyote highlights its blend of poetic narrative and sonic atmosphere. Many videos of them are available on YouTube.

Eminem

Raised in Detroit, Michigan, Eminem (Marshall Mathers) emerged in the late 1990s as one of hip-hop's most technically skilled and controversial voices. Known for his rapid-fire delivery, introspective lyrics, and alter ego "Slim Shady," he brought Midwest grit and emotional complexity to mainstream rap. "Lose Yourself" (2002) is a Grammy-winning anthem of ambition and self-doubt.

Steve King (producer)

A Detroit-based engineer and producer, Steve King was known for his work with Eminem and other artists in the hip-hop and rock scenes. His engineering on tracks like "Lose Yourself" helped define the polished, cinematic sound of early-2000s rap. He was instrumental in shaping the sonic identity of Detroit's modern music scene before his untimely passing in 2009.

Joel Martin (producer)

Joel Martin is a Detroit music producer and co-owner of 54 Sound Studio, a key location for the recording of Eminem's early work. A behind-the-scenes figure in hip-hop and pop, he helped connect major talent with local production resources. His partnership with the Bass Brothers and Eminem played a crucial role in bringing Detroit hip-hop to the global stage.

Pete Brown

Pete Brown is a British poet and lyricist best known for writing lyrics for the rock band Cream. He co-wrote several of their most famous songs, including "Sunshine of Your Love" and "White Room." Brown helped bring a literary, poetic sensibility into late-1960s rock music.

Timothy Leary

Timothy Leary was an American psychologist and writer who became a leading voice in the 1960s counterculture. He promoted the use of psychedelic drugs as tools for expanding consciousness and personal freedom. His ideas strongly influenced artists, musicians, and youth culture of the era.

William S. Burroughs

William S. Burroughs was an American writer associated with the Beat Generation. His work explored themes of addiction, control, and rebellion against authority, most famously in *Naked Lunch*. Burroughs had a lasting influence on writers, musicians, and experimental artists.

Allen Ginsberg

Allen Ginsberg was an American poet and a central figure of the Beat Generation. His poem "Howl" became a defining work of postwar American literature and challenged censorship laws. Ginsberg was closely connected to musicians, writers, and political movements of the 1960s.

Stevie Wonder

Stevie Wonder is an American singer, songwriter, and musician who began his career as a child artist at Motown Records. He became one of the most influential figures in popular music through his innovative songwriting and use of new musical technology. Wonder's work combined social awareness with wide commercial appeal.

ACKNOWLEDGMENTS

Thanks to Maria Mazziotti Gillan, who pushed me for more than 15 years to write this memoir. To Joel Martin for his years of kind support and friendship. To Kenny Ensroth for sharing these many adventures with me. Jeff Ensroth without whom. To my many Rock'n'roll friends: Al Kooper, Peter Lewis, Country Joe McDonald, Jorma Kaukonen, Mike Watt, Ed Sanders, Ray Manzarek, John Desmore, Frank Pahl, Pete Brown, Bill Fay, Pat Thomas, Ted Nagy, Brigitte Knudson, and Lou D Lou and many others. I am grateful for Diane DeCillis, the fine editors I have worked with through the years: Annie Martin (who first believed in this manuscript), Herb Scott, Mark Donovan, Gary Metras, Rebecca Emanuelsen, John Klages, and Brandon Wade. Special thanks to the excellent staff at Cornerstone Press: editor Brett Hill, Allison Lange (fantastic cover design), Sophie McPherson and Sam Bjork with (sales/media), and Dr. Ross K. Tangedal, Director & Publisher. Thanks, especially, to Tanya Whiton, who extensively and lovingly guided me from the start of this book. To my supportive WSU English Department Chairs, Caroline Maun and Jaime Goodrich, and College of Liberal Arts and Sciences Dean Steffi Hartwell. Also, to my family and Lincoln Street Posse, Denny Chabot, Maureen Chabot, Uncle Earl, Aunt Jim, Aunt Bren, Ron DiBartolomeo, the late Bobby Rusch, and especially my grandparents, who raised me on Lincoln Street, Mabel and Vern Liebler. I am especially grateful to my wife Pam for putting up with all my travels and literary organizing for more than 50 years. Also, much love to my children and their spouses, Shelby (Dan Kukuk) and Shane (Jennifer), and my grandchildren, Kass, Harrison, and Olivia, whom I live for every day. I love and appreciate you all "more than you'll ever know," as my friend Al Kooper once sang.

M.L. LIEBLER is an internationally recognized and widely published poet from Detroit, a university professor, a literary arts activist, and an arts organizer. In 1974, he co-founded, and still directs, The Ridgeway Press. Liebler is the author or editor of fifteen books and chapbooks, including the award-winning *Wide Awake in Someone Else's Dream* (2008), *Working Words: Punching the Clock & Kicking Out the Jams* (2010), *I Want to Be Once* (2011), *Heaven Was Detroit: From Jazz to Hip-Hop and Beyond* (2016), *Bob Seger's House and Other Stories* (with Michael Delp) (2016), and *RESPECT: Poets on Detroit Music* (with Jim Daniels) (2018). Several of his books have earned the prestigious Library of Michigan Notable Book Award.

Liebler was awarded the 2017–2018 Murray E. Jackson Scholar in the Arts Award at Wayne State University, where he has taught English, creative writing, American studies, labor studies, and world literature since 1980. He currently directs the WSU Humanities Commons and the Detroit Writers' Guild.

www.ingramcontent.com/pod-product-compliance
Lightning Source LLC
LaVergne TN
LVHW040044080526
838202LV00045B/3479